Professor of Film at Brooklyn College of the City University of New York, Foster Hirsch has written twelve books including studies of the Actors Studio, Laurence Olivier, Woody Allen, Film Noir, and Tennessee Williams. His history of film acting will be published next year, and he is now at work on two theatre books, a biography of the Shuberts and a chronicle of American theatre in the twenties.

DIRECTORS IN PERSPECTIVE

General editor: Christopher Innes

Harold Prince

What characterizes modern theater above all is continual stylistic innovation, in which theory and presentation have combined to create a wealth of new forms – naturalism, expressionism, epic theater, and so forth – in a way that has made directors the leading figures rather than dramatists. To a greater extent than is perhaps generally realized, it has been directors who have provided dramatic models for playwrights, though of course there are many different variations in this relationship. In some cases a dramatist's themes challenge a director to create new performance conditions (Stanislavski and Chekhov), or a dramatist turns director to formulate an appropriate style for his work (Brecht); alternatively a director writes plays to correspond with his theory (Artaud), or creates communal scripts out of exploratory work with actors (Chaikin, Grotowski). Some directors are identified with a single theory (Craig), others gave definitive shape to a range of styles (Reinhardt); the work of some has an ideological basis (Stein), while others work more pragmatically (Bergman).

Generally speaking, those directors who have contributed to what is distinctly "modern" in today's theater stand in much the same relationship to the dramatic texts they work with, as composers do to librettists in opera. However, since theatrical performance is the most ephemeral of the arts and the only easily reproducible element is the text, critical attention has tended to focus on the playwright. This series is designed to redress the balance by providing an overview of selected directors' stage work: those who helped to formulate modern theories of drama. Their key productions have been reconstructed from promptbooks, reviews, scene-designs, photographs, diaries, correspondence and – where these productions are contemporary – documented by first hand description, interviews with the director, and so forth. Apart from its intrinsic interest, this record allows a critical perspective, testing ideas against practical problems and achievements. In each case, too, the director's work is set in context by indicating the source of his ideas and their influence, the organization of his acting company, and his relationship to the theatrical or political establishment, so as to bring out wider issues: the way theater both reflects and influences assumptions about the nature of man and his social role.

Christopher Innes

TITLES IN THIS SERIES

Adolphe Appia: Richard Beacham
Ingmar Bergman: Lise-Lone and Frederick J. Marker
Roger Blin: Odette Aslan, translated by Ruby Cohn
Bertolt Brecht: John Fuegi
Joseph Chaikin: Eileen Blumenthal
Jacques Copeau: John Rudlin
E. Gordon Craig: Christopher Innes
Vsevolod Meyerhold: Robert Leach
Harold Prince: Foster Hirsch
Max Reinhardt: John Styan
Peter Stein: Michael Patterson
Andrzej Wajda: Maciej Karpinski

FUTURE TITLES

André Antoine: Jean Chothia
Peter Brook: Albert Hunt and Geoffrey Reeves
Tyrone Guthrie: Ronald Bryden
Ariane Mnouchkine: Robert Leach
Constantin Stanislavski: Peter Holland and Vera Gottlieb
Giorgio Strehler: David Hirst
Robert Wilson: Arthur Holmberg

Hal Prince, 1987 (photo courtesy of Martha Swope)

Harold Prince

and the American musical theatre

FOSTER HIRSCH

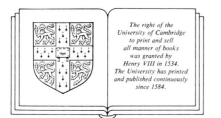

The right of the
University of Cambridge
to print and sell
all manner of books
was granted by
Henry VIII in 1534.
The University has printed
and published continuously
since 1584.

CAMBRIDGE UNIVERSITY PRESS

CAMBRIDGE

NEW YORK   NEW ROCHELLE

MELBOURNE   SYDNEY

Published by the Press Syndicate of the University of Cambridge
The Pitt Building, Trumpington Street, Cambridge CB2 1RP
40 West 20th Street, New York, NY 10011, USA
10 Stamford Road, Oakleigh, Melbourne 3166, Australia

First published 1989
Reprinted 1989

Printed in Great Britain at the
University Press, Cambridge

British Library cataloguing in publication data

Hirsch, Foster
Harold Prince and the American musical
theatre. – (Directors in perspective).
1. American musical shows. Directing.
Prince, Harold, *1928–*
I. Title   II. Series
782.81'092'4

Library of Congress cataloguing in publication data

Hirsch, Foster.
Harold Prince and the American musical theatre / Foster Hirsch.
        p.   cm. – (Directors in perspective).
Bibliography.
Includes index.
ISBN 0 521 33314 8   ISBN 0 521 33609 0 (pbk.)
1. Prince, Harold, 1928–   – Criticism and interpretation.
2. Musical revue, comedy, etc. – United States.   I. Title.
II. Series
ML429.P78H6   1989
792'.023'0924 – dc 19   88–29941   CIP

ISBN 0 521 33314 8 hard covers
ISBN 0 521 33609 0 paperback

Contents

List of illustrations		*page* viii
Foreword I, by Harold Prince		x
Foreword II, by Stephen Sondheim		xv
Acknowledgments		xvii
1	Overture	1
2	The Abbott touch	22
3	On the job	40
4	Musical metaphors	59
5	A little Sondheim music (I)	71
6	A little Sondheim music (II)	85
7	A little Sondheim music (III)	106
8	A few follies	131
9	Nights at the opera	141
10	The British connection	157
	Theatrical chronology	174
	Notes	176
	Select bibliography	181
	Index	183

Illustrations

Hal Prince, 1987   *frontispiece*

1   A play within the play: on the stage of the "Cotton
    Blossom" in Hammerstein and Kern's *Show Boat* (1927)   *page* 11
2   Playing with politics: the Gershwins' *Of Thee I Sing* (1931)   12
3 and 4   Brecht on Broadway: *The Threepenny Opera* in 1933   16
5   George Abbott's peppy finale for *The Pajama Game* (1954)   28
6   Brecht? No, *Fiorello!* (1959)   30
7   "Mister Abbott" at work on *Flora, the Red Menace* (New
    Haven, 1965)   31
8   Turning *Anna Christie* into a song-and-dance frolic, *New
    Girl in Town* (1957)   33
9   Elevation in an early Prince musical, *She Loves Me* (1963)   34
10 Shades of *Bye Bye Birdie* mixed with Meyerhold in *It's a
    Bird . . . It's a Plane . . . It's Superman* (1966)   36
11 Hal Prince at work on *Pacific Overtures* (1975)   41
12 "Framing" the audience in *Cabaret* (1966)   42
13 Alexander Okun's "Escher" set for *Roza* (1987)   52
14 and 15   Al Jolson meets Brecht: *Cabaret* (1966)   62–63
16 German Expressionism by way of Orson Welles: *Cabaret*·   65
17 Stephen Sondheim and Hal Prince, opening night of
    Merrily We Roll Along (1981)   73
18 Beginning at the top: *West Side Story* (1957)   77
19 Witty lyrics for a low comedy: *A Funny Thing Happened
    On the Way to the Forum* (1962)   81
20 Breaking the musical-comedy song form: *Anyone Can
    Whistle* (1964)   82
21 "I'm Not Getting Married Today": *Company* (1970)   92
22 The past and the present intersect at the Follies reunion   94
23 and 24   "A Proustian fracturing of time": *Follies* (1971)   96–97
25 "Loveland": *Follies*   99
26 Ben's "turn": *Follies*   100
27 Reconciliation at dawn in the demolished theatre: *Follies*   102
28 "The show never stopped moving": *Follies*   104
29 The quintet in *A Little Night Music*   107

30 The night waltz that opens and closes the romantic
    rondelay in *A Little Night Music* (1973)   108
31 Prince, Gemignani, and Sondheim at a rehearsal for
    Pacific Overtures (1975)   112
32 The Kabuki reciter in *Pacific Overtures*   114
33 Broadway Kabuki: *Pacific Overtures*   116
34 To approximate Japanese staging, Prince designed
    "everything in *Pacific Overtures* to be horizontal"   117
35 Japan in the modern age: *Pacific Overtures*   119
36 "What do they make in this factory? – A show called
    Sweeney Todd" (1979)   121
37 Prince's scenic abstraction: *Sweeney Todd*   122
38 The recognition scene in *Sweeney Todd*   126
39 Rehearsal clothes in a Broadway musical: *Merrily We
    Roll Along* (1981)   134
40 Prince's love of elevation, deep focus, and simultaneous
    action: *A Doll's Life* (1982)   137
41 Backstage at Harry Earle's burlesque house in *Grind*
    (1985)   139
42 Hunger trails a new millionaire in Weill's *Silverlake*
    (1980)   146
43 Opera as circus: *Ashmedai* (1976)   148
44 *On the Town* (1944) had "a new look and sound and
    style of movement" that beckoned Hal Prince   150
45 and 46   Prince's environmental staging of *Candide* (1974)   152–153
47 *Candide* (1982): a street-theatre performance presented
    on pageant wagons by Dr. Voltaire's band of traveling
    actors   155
48 and 49   Life in the public arena: *Evita* (1979)   160–161
50 The real Peróns hover over their theatrical counterparts
    as Che looks on: *Evita*   164
51 "The parody military are like wind-up killing machines":
    Evita   167
52 "Paraphrasing" Sequieros murals to create an illusion of
    crowds: *Evita*   168
53 and 54   Drama and spectacle in *The Phantom of the Opera*
    (1988)   170

Foreword I
BY HAROLD PRINCE

A couple of years ago I received a letter from a stranger, Foster Hirsch, saying that he had been commissioned by Cambridge University Press to write a book on my life in musical theatre. He had begun working on it and would appreciate an interview. Subsequently, in the way of such things, I began to read his byline on stories in diverse publications as well as a book on the Actors Studio. Our meetings, though infrequent, continued.

In the meantime, I did catch sight of him unobtrusively in London during the *Phantom* previews and on opening night; in Baltimore, Los Angeles, Washington, D.C., where musicals were shaking down; Cleveland at a week-long George Abbott seminar; the Palace Theatre for Abbott's hundredth birthday party, and so on.

Once, in Wilmington, I know I surprised him by inviting him to my rooms with the *Cabaret* principals for a drink and what the opposite of a postmortem is (the first performance had gone marvelously).

The next week I phoned him to say that everything said in that session was on the record. What did I mean? I meant especially the business about my nervous breakdown at age fourteen. "But that's personal, not professional," he replied, and he had respected my privacy. No, I'd gone into the business about the breakdown – for the first time – because it was definitely professional, or rather responsible for so much of my professional behavior and, more significantly, my productions and the drive behind them.

My wife, Judy, and I have a running gag – I believe it's a gag – though it seems to drive her crazy. On the opening nights of everything from *The Visit* to *Sweeney Todd* to *Phantom of the Opera*, as people approach eagerly to express how moved they were, I interrupt asking, "Did you really have a GOOD TIME?"

There's a connection between my putting these experiences down and the tone of so much that I say in interviews, that I've read quoted in Foster's book. All that goes back some forty-five years. When I broke down.

It lasted nearly six months – black despair alternating with a deadening lethargy. And no one to share it with. I came out of it slowly, each day a little less cloudy. After three months, I slept at night. And slowly I began to create a person, quite a friendly, extroverted, hyper person – a sponge as far as information was concerned. Not just the stuff of Broadway, where I wanted to work, but as much literature, history, philosophy, travel, as I could cram. I believed then (I was applying to universities) and continued to believe until I was twenty-five that if I failed at making a life in New York in the theatre, then there was no point in a life at all.

It took years to kick the fear of it returning. I still experience recurring melancholy.

The point is, I don't believe I would be the subject of this book had I not paid for it traumatically that summer.

After *The Pajama Game* happened, I used to tease myself imagining what if it hadn't happened – drive myself nutty with that, too. There was a hell of a price to pay for such obsessiveness. Some of that was shared by my wife. We married, we had a son and a daughter. It took years, and her determination, to bring me into the family way. I loved them, but I didn't tend to them. It was only after I reached my middle forties and the kids were approaching teenage that I began to enjoy tending. And each year I get better at it.

And where does all this fit into the category of information affecting my professional life? Quite simply it explains why, though I experienced six redundantly unsuccessful years on Broadway, they made little impact on me.

When Foster Hirsch sent me this book, he included a note: "I am well aware that you have not asked to see the manuscript pre-publication" and then he asked whether I would contribute to it. I held off until I had read it. And now, of course, I accept the offer. For one thing, I want to make the earlier point that I don't really want to know whether you've "had a good time." That's a cover, as is so much of the way I minimize the process of what I do. I used to defend this proudly as a kind of no-shit, pragmatic rejection of the pomposity and histrionics of people who make art. I don't really believe it – not for a minute. I would like to be as publicly pompous as I know I am in work sessions, but it's too late.

You create a person. And he sticks.

Recently I auditioned a team of composers recommended enthusiastically by Steve Sondheim. After listening to a dozen songs written for two specific projects, I asked them how long they had been writing together. "Five years." And where had they seen their work performed. "Nowhere." Never? "Never." This is a phenomenon of our times. Two extremely talented writers meeting daily turn out scores for shows circulated in the theatre community, where the word is definitely that they are the ones to watch. But where?

There is a game which people play: in what period would you choose to be born? The answers invariably take flight – the Victorian age, Elizabethan times (no newspapers), ancient Greece. Were I to play that game, I would have chosen to be born twenty years earlier. I hope that Foster's book has documented clearly how fortunate I was to have been born when I was, but twenty years earlier would have been even better. There was company then:

thirty first-rate composers, lyricists, librettists, playwrights, directors. There were a couple of dozen producers presenting at least one play every season. There existed a community, interacting and supportive, confident that its work would be seen. I don't doubt there is as much talent today, but where's the activity? We have lost the nurturing process.

Time is short. There are Young Turk producers; people are meeting; people have ideas, are making plans, searching out new ways and more places to work. I hope that by the time this is published, some of this activity has borne fruit. It's going to take uncharacteristic cooperation among unions, the guilds, the media, the City of New York. It can happen.

Foster Hirsch doesn't use a tape recorder; he takes few notes. He is rightfully proud of his ability to remember 99 percent of what he's told and quote it later verbatim. It's the missing 1 percent that I'd like to correct. Also, I would like to disagree with him, though not as far as his opinions of my shows are concerned. They are his. Also, his negative opinions of the work of some of my collaborators are his as well. Not mine. His. So, in chronological order:

1. Page 19: I do not think *Company* is a "dark" musical (Judy Prince emphatically agrees with Foster).

2. Throughout: I'm not really into directing hits. I submit that no one who was would undertake a production of *Pacific Overtures*. Or *Follies*. Or countless other prestigious flops. (I insist there are hits and flops. And there are successes and failures.) I am definitely into successes. Both *Pacific Overtures* and *Follies* I consider successes.

3. Page 34: George Abbott was not responsible for Anna Christie dancing in *New Girl in Town*. As for Thelma Ritter's "vulgar comic songs," I disagree. I think they were in character. So it's unfair to label the failure of the show "[Abbott's] travesty." We were all to blame for thinking it was an intelligent project. However, its strongest moments – for example the scene in which Verdon encountered Ritter for the first time in a barroom – were pure O'Neill and directed sensitively.

4. Throughout: Foster accuses me (paranoia!) of compromising to achieve success. I believe he's wrong. I think my taste dictates these compromises.

5. Page 67: I think it's unintentionally unfair to Alyson Reed [Sally Bowles in the 1987 revival] to imply that *Cabaret* "doesn't want a singer who sings well." It's a dilemma built into the casting for that role. Sally shouldn't sing well, but *Cabaret* is a musical. And the second time around we settled on a singer who sings well indeed. It becomes instead a matter of performance – acting: can you believe, despite her excellent voice, that she's a dilettante pretending to be a nightclub diseuse? For my taste, good as Liza Minnelli was in the film, her singing was too contemporary, too Las Vegas presentational.

6. Page 68: By inference Foster credits me with Boris's tilted mirror in *Cabaret*. Incorrect. It was Boris's idea and a surprise "gift" to me in the design.

7. Page 106: Much as I would have liked the Liebeslieder Waltzers to have been my idea, they were definitely Steve's. My original image (and perhaps one of the attractions of working on *Smiles*) was that I wanted a musical whose pace would accommodate a lady striding wearily across a room, pulling aside a corner of the drapes, blinding herself with the glorious moonlight, and sighing deeply. Kind of Chekhov. I'd never seen such a musical.

8. Page 129: In the analysis of *Sweeney Todd* the number "God, That's Good!" is mentioned. There's one incident which comes to mind and illustrates the Sondheim/Prince work process. Steve wrote that number to open the second act. In keeping with his decision to give the director staging options, he envisioned tables set across the stage in an arc, surrounding Mrs. Lovett's pie shop. The customers (our chorus) were to devour meat pies, swilling them down with beer and beating the tables for "more hot pies." Meanwhile, Sweeney, above in the barber shop, was awaiting delivery of his new lethal barber's chair. Mrs. Lovett, torn between the demands of her customers and Sweeney's heightened euphoria, becomes crazed. For all of this Steve created twenty separate dramas, each uniquely consistent with one of the chorus members eating and drinking. These stories were to be sung contrapuntally. Obviously an impossible task for the audience to understand what they were hearing. Brilliant in the living-room − impossible on the stage.

I had no idea how to do it and it was scheduled for the next morning's rehearsal. I went to sleep on it. I have come to rely on what happens in your head when you're sleeping. The next morning I woke up with the problem solved. Instead of ten tables, there would be one long table and seated at it the entire chorus eating, swilling and pounding tankards for more. It worked because your focus was divided equally among Lovett, Sweeney, and a third character − the chorus. Of course you couldn't understand the brilliant lyrics, but you got the point.

9. Page 141: A further word should be said about my view of the star system, whether it applies to opera or the theatre. It would be incorrect to say that I don't like stars. I haven't used a great many for the reasons stated in this book, but if they are the appropriate people for the assignment, I'd be a fool not to want to work with them. Angela Lansbury is a star, and so are those opera ladies and gentlemen.

10. Page 166: Apropos *Evita*, I think Foster Hirsch hasn't emphasized what it really is about for me − which isn't politics. Media manipulation, that's what it's about. And the fact that we have next to no idea who really lives in the White House, for whom we're voting, what's going on. We've learned too

well how to package things and, now, people. I tend to shy away from technology (despite what Foster thinks!), but in this instance the film, the slides, the mirror, the flashbulbs, were appropriate.

11. Throughout: I don't think this book covers sufficiently the desperate need for creative producers in the theatre. I consider that I was one of the best producers in the business. Long before I began to direct I was full of ideas about the material and the production values of the show I was producing or co-producing. But I was sensitive enough to know *when* to offer suggestions and *how* to offer them. Further, I didn't indulge every notion that came to mind. I remember making a long list of what I thought was wrong with a show once it began previewing and watching while most of that list was taken care of by the director and choreographer. If there was something outstanding that still bothered me, then I'd speak up. Today, producers never shut up. They attend rehearsals (or expect to). They're frequently accompanied by members of the family with pads and pencils. And everyone spews out everything, no matter how obvious or negligible it may be. And all of this is because they have money.

And that does it for corrections and emendations.

Fifteen years ago I wrote my own book and called it *Contradictions*. On rereading Hal Prince in Foster Hirsch's book, I'm aware I come out glaringly inconsistent. In defense I quote twice from Oscar Wilde: "A truth in art is that whose contradictory is also true." And if that doesn't get me off the hook, perhaps this will: "Early in life you try to resolve your contradictions in the name of weakness. Later you come to see them as a source of strength ... The object of life is not to simplify it."

Foreword II

BY STEPHEN SONDHEIM

To write a Foreword to a book about someone still alive, especially Hal, strikes me as peculiarly inappropriate. Even the book itself is a contradiction in terms. Hal embodies life; a book necessarily freezes its subject. His career is all about forward motion. In fact, Hal doesn't think of what he does as a "career" because he's always in the middle of it: he's too busy to be interested in an overview. This is not to denigrate Foster Hirsch's valuable and accurate study but, like all commentaries, it deals with history. Hal is still making that history.

What I envy most in him is not his talent: I have no desire to direct or produce, and Hal's wild visual imagination is something I would rather collaborate with than possess, requiring as it does so much time with so many people in order to realize it. No, what I envy is his energy, that continual forward motion, unflagging even (perhaps especially) in the face of humiliation and dismay. He never whines, he works. He doesn't complain about unjust treatment, he rages. He won't waste time in post-mortems or profuse apologies; when he feels he's been wrong or done bad work, he either acknowledges it briefly or not at all. He forgets – and forgives – his own injustices as quickly as those of others. Once a show has opened, whether a success or failure, whether a source of pride or disappointment, for Hal it's over and done with. Most of us are lingerers; Hal, as the song says, moves on.

He is also a very funny fellow, sharp and quick and explosive and literate, and never more intensely so than when theatrical disaster strikes, when the scenery is jamming, the costumes unfinished, the lighting miscalculated, the sound inaudible or screeching with feedback. This is not a coincidence. It's humor born of impatience, black with that selfsame energy, hilarious and cathartic for everyone around him as well as himself. A good director has a responsibility that his collaborators do not: he is in charge. He has to bring about the best possible realization of his own vision while making sure that others bring about theirs. He has to conceal discouragement, or defuse it. Hal conceals through humor and defuses through enthusiasm. Sometimes he bullies. Sometimes it works.

Hal worries about posterity, though why anyone should care about what people think of your work when you're no longer around to glow or groan is beyond me. Certainly, a theatre director's art is more ephemeral than a writer's, although not as much as it used to be, not in this photographic century. Hal often chooses to ignore his influence, however. I've sat with him through musicals and pop operas (and in one notable instance, a long and highly acclaimed play) far more commercially successful than any of our collaborations, and observed with bewilderment his equanimity, indeed his lack of recognition, as he sees the director pilfer moment after moment from him. He's more aware of it these days, though; so much "homage" is becoming transparent, even to him. Well, imitation can be an irritating form of immortality, but if immortality is what he wants, he's got it.

I hope this book will make him feel he's improved his chances, even though it will almost certainly be outdated by the time it reaches print: Hal will have imagined or coordinated or directed another musical or opera or two or three or founded a theatre company or invented a new way of producing shows or merely opened our eyes to theatrical possibilities and, in his favorite phrase of Diaghilev's, astonished us. This book can be only Volume I of a series. And a good thing, too.

Acknowledgments

George Abbott; Kristofer Batho; Michael Bavar; Barbara Baxley; Pat Birch; Maureen Brennan; Mary Bryant; Len Cariou; Arlene Caruso; Dorothy Collins; Gregg Edelman; Larry Fuller; the late Hermione Gingold; Larry Grossman; June Havoc; Betsy Joslyn; Judy Kaye; Florence Klotz; Patti LuPone; Nora Mae Lyng; Joe Masteroff; Joanna Merlin; Ruth Mitchell; Grace Mizrahi; Julian More; Ann Morrison; Robert Nassif; Bill O'Connell; Alexander Okun; Mandy Patinkin; Lonny Price; Harold Prince; Alyson Reed; Philip Rinaldi; Mary-Lou Rosato; Richard Ryan; Tana Sibilio; Patricia Sinnott; Stephen Sondheim; David Staller; Dorothy Swerdlove and the staff of the Theatre Collection, New York Public Library at Lincoln Center; Martha Swope; Fran Weissler; the late Hugh Wheeler; Van Williams.

Figures 1–6, 8, 18, 20, and 44 are reproduced by permission of The Billy Rose Theatre Collection, Music Division, The New York Public Library at Lincoln Center, The Astor, Lenox and Tilden Foundations. Figures 42 and 43 are reproduced by permission of the Music Division, The New York Public Library at Lincoln Center, The Astor, Lenox and Tilden Foundations. Costumes by Florence Klotz in figures 22, 23, 24, 29, 33, and 40.

Lyrics from "Being Alive" and "Another Hundred People," © 1970 – Range Road Music Inc., Quartet Music Inc., and Rilting Music, Inc. Used by permission. All rights reserved.

Lyrics from "Loveland," "Could I Leave You," "Live, Laugh, Love," and "I'm Still Here," © 1971 – Range Road Music Inc., Quartet Music Inc., Rilting Music, Inc. and Burthen Music Company, Inc. Used by permission. All rights reserved.

Lyrics from "The Advantages of Floating in the Middle of the Sea," "Next," "Poems," and "Pretty Lady," © 1975 and 1977 Rilting Music, Inc. and Revelation Music Publishing Corp. (ASCAP), a Tommy Valando Publication. Used with permission. All rights reserved.

Lyrics from "By the Sea," "Epiphany," "A Little Priest," and "My Friends," © 1981 Revelation Music Publishing Corp. and Rilting Music, Inc., a Tommy Valando Publication. Used with permission. All rights reserved.

Lyrics from "We All George" (lyrics by Ellen Fitzhugh; music by Larry Grossman), © 1985 by Fiddleback Music Publishing Co., Inc., and New Start Music, Inc., a Tommy Valando Publication. Used with permission. All rights reserved.

xvii

1 Overture

"It's more than a musical!" a woman exclaimed on leaving the opening-night performance of *Cabaret* in Wilmington, Delaware. The original production of *Cabaret* in 1966 had been Harold Prince's first major directorial success. Now, in February 1987, on the first stop of an extensive national tour, the show generated the same kind of excitement as it had twenty-one years earlier; and that spectator's comment can be seen as a capsule summary of Prince's forty-year career in the American musical theatre. As producer and director, cautiously at first and then with increasing audacity, Prince has been presenting shows that are not "just" musicals. Working at the center of the American theatrical marketplace, in a form riddled with convention, Prince and his carefully chosen collaborators have altered the popular idea of what a musical can be.

"This is the best kind of show," Prince announced to his *Cabaret* company on the first day of rehearsals. "It makes an important statement, to be received by those who want to get the message, and it provides entertainment."[1] In *Cabaret* song and dance comment on a fatally contaminated society, Berlin before the start of the Third Reich, and it is exactly this symbolic edge which makes the show "more than a musical."

Giving a cultural lift to a popular show-business staple, Prince has worked a risky terrain. For fans of traditional light-hearted musical comedy, he is the architect of the "dark" or "anti-" musical. On the other hand, Prince has sometimes offended serious theatregoers by treating powerful subjects (like the rise of Fascism in *Cabaret*) within what they regard as the trivializing and philistine framework of the Broadway musical. But to audiences for whom the "Broadway musical" need not be an inevitable prescription for good-natured fluff, Prince is a true pioneer, the *auteur* of the modernist concept musical who has expanded a genre's thematic and theatrical possibilities.

Who directed the annual editions of the Ziegfeld *Follies*? Who directed the Gershwins' *Lady, Be Good!*? or George White's *Scandals*? Or Jerome Kern and Oscar Hammerstein II's *Show Boat*? In the early history of musical theatre, producers like Florenz Ziegfeld and John Murray Anderson presented revues which expressed their own tastes while leaving the actual job of directing to hired hands like Julian Mitchell, Ziegfeld's in-house stage manager. Musical plays, as opposed to revues and extravaganzas, were tailored as vehicles for stars: Jerome Kern wrote *Sally* for Marilyn Miller, the Gershwins composed *Oh, Kay!* for Gertrude Lawrence and *Lady, Be Good!* and *Funny Face* for Fred and Adele Astaire. The director did no more than arrange a frame for the music and the stars; production was merely a question of packaging, and imposing a visual concept or a unifying theme would have been redundant.

That a director like Hal Prince has exerted so forceful an influence on a collaborative form like the musical reverses historical precedent. But over the last thirty years the director (and except for Prince that means the director-choreographer) has emerged from the anonymity of the chorus line to claim a long-delayed celebrity status. Jerome Robbins, Gower Champion, Bob Fosse, Tommy Tune, Michael Bennett, and Prince have orchestrated the work of composers, lyricists, librettists, performers, and designers into musicals stamped by their own individual styles. A Hal Prince or a Bob Fosse musical became an identifiable product that attracted loyal audiences who in earlier periods would have supported the latest show by Ziegfeld or Cole Porter, or the latest Ethel Merman or Eddie Cantor vehicle.

Before the 1950s few directors sustained entire careers in the field; few understood the demands of the genre or could work within its byzantine collaborative structure. According to Prince, "Joshua Logan led the way to the modern style in 1949, when he directed *South Pacific* without any breaks between scenes. He was the innovator of *continuous action.* Any alternative after that was unacceptable."[2] Hassard Short and Rouben Mamoulian also helped (pre-1949) to give texture and pace to the musical play, while George Balanchine and Agnes de Mille turned dance into choreography, transforming movement from its earliest assembly-line choruses kicking in unison to expressionist dream ballets and production numbers with stylized comments on a show's characters and situations. As a result today it is generally recognized that, as Prince says, "A musical has an arc, which only the director is in charge of: I learned about that arc from George Abbott and Jerome Robbins."

Unlike most of the major directors of musical theatre (George Abbott brought his fabled "touch" to musical comedy while continuing to write and direct farces, light comedies, and melodramas; Rouben Mamoulian divided his career between theatre and films; Joshua Logan spent as much time on plays as on musicals; and Jerome Robbins abandoned Broadway in order to co-direct and choreograph for the New York City Ballet), Prince has remained primarily dedicated to the form, helping to assemble musicals on a continuous basis for four decades, and thrives on the collaborative process of making a musical. "Who is the Prince of Broadway?" is a question stitched onto a pillow placed prominently in his office. As the winner of more Tony Awards than anyone else (sixteen up to now), who has maintained his loyalty to the Main Stem even during rough times, Prince might truthfully claim that he is.

After six years working for George Abbott, as assistant stage manager and occasional casting director, Prince, at twenty-six, co-produced a hit musical, *The Pajama Game*, in 1954. Defying the odds he and his partner Robert Griffith presented three further hits in quick succession: *Damn Yankees* (1955), *New Girl in Town* (1957), and *West Side Story* (1957). Continuing to produce mostly winners (*Fiorello!* in 1959, *A Funny Thing Happened On the Way to the Forum* in 1962, *Fiddler on the Roof* in 1964), he also began to direct. His first Broadway assignment was *A Family Affair* (1962), a small musical about a Jewish wedding inherited from another director. Then came *She Loves Me* (1963), which he also produced ("No one else would hire me, so I had to hire myself"), *Baker Street* (1965) for another management, and *It's a Bird . . . It's a Plane . . . It's Superman* (1966), his own production. None made money, and before *Cabaret* opened in November 1966, Prince told his wife that if the show didn't work out he would have to quit.

After *Cabaret* confirmed his ability Prince directed (and often, until the early eighties, produced) a series of unusual yet in general commercially successful musicals: *Zorbá* (1968); six collaborations with Stephen Sondheim – *Company* (1970), *Follies* (1971), *A Little Night Music* (1973), *Pacific Overtures* (1976), *Sweeney Todd* (1979), and *Merrily We Roll Along* (1981); a revival of *Candide* (1973); *On the Twentieth Century* (1978); *Evita* (1978); *A Doll's Life* (1982); *Grind* (1985); *Roza* (1986); *The Phantom of the Opera* (1986); and the 1987 revival of *Cabaret*. As if in answer to his own question, "Why not think of opera as a form of musical theatre with different conventions?", since 1976 Prince has regularly staged operas. For the New York City Opera he has directed *Ashmedai* (1976) and *Silverlake* (1980) as well as two works originally conceived for Broadway, *Candide* (1982) and *Sweeney Todd* (1984). For the Chicago Lyric Opera he has staged a *Girl of the Golden West* (1978) and a *Madame Butterfly* (1982). He directed *Turandot* (1983) for the Vienna State Opera and *Willie Stark* (1981) for the Houston Grand Opera.

Germany as Hitler comes to power; Perónism in Argentina; what happens to Nora after she slams the door in *A Doll House*; the Westernization of Japan; a mass-murderer at the beginning of the Industrial Age – these are among the unlikely subjects that give a Hal Prince musical its distinctive slant. Even his pieces set in a more conventional musical-theatre terrain, stories about show business and musicals in which the characters are preoccupied by love and marriage, resist formula. Prince sets musical performance – cabaret turns, the Follies, burlesque, the musical-comedy tradition itself – in a social and political context. Like show business, romance in a Prince musical also undergoes unexpected variations: boy meets/loses/often doesn't get girl in the end, or if he does get her we don't quite believe it. And always, whether they're lovers or clowns or performers or dictators, characters in a Prince musical sing and dance with thematic import.

Pumping serious meaning into a form that has traditionally thrived on fizz, Prince approaches the musical not with airy academic notions but as a practical theatre man who received his training on the job, from the pragmatic George Abbott, whose basic principles of giving the customers good value while protecting his backers' investment he shares. Yet Prince also "made the kind of musicals I wanted to see myself. My shows were created from a personal need for a change of diet." That his instincts are not "dangerously avant-garde" certainly eased his way, for despite its deviations from the norm a Prince show has the verve and the delight in spectacle which have always been part of the musical-theatre idiom.

At bottom all musicals are about themselves, a celebration of their own energy and skill. And for all his love of metaphor and concept, Prince has continued to honor the performance impulse – selling it to the audience – from which all musical theatre is derived. The best of his work – *Cabaret, Follies, Pacific Overtures, Sweeney Todd, Candide, Evita, The Phantom of the Opera* – has a cunning theatricality that places him in a Broadway tradition which includes such artisans of the American popular theatre as David Belasco, Florenz Ziegfeld, George S. Kaufman, as well as his one-time mentor, George Abbott. Indeed, Prince is proud of being a Broadway showman. "I don't feel at all defensive or apologetic about making a career in the commercial theatre," he says. Although its reputation has been seriously tarnished because of escalating costs and what he calls the resulting "five-million-dollar mentality," Prince feels that historically Broadway has represented the best the American theatre has had to offer:

I've seen many productions of *A Streetcar Named Desire* but by far the best was the original Broadway production directed by Elia Kazan and starring Marlon Brando. I've seen many productions of *Guys and Dolls*, though none can compare with the Broadway original. Before economics killed it, Broadway was a magnet for all the best talents; it was a true theatrical elite.

Despite its European origins the musical has become a specifically American artifact. No other country has surpassed America in either the quality or the quantity of its musical productions. The musical has become America's world-wide theatrical ambassador, a synonym for the brashness and energy of distinctive American showmanship. Even in America the musical is often the only kind of theatre that audiences outside New York either choose or have the chance to see. At a time when "the road" has diminished, most national touring companies perform big hit musicals.

Because of their popularity, and because inherent in the genre is a desire to please a wide audience, musicals have been critical stepchildren, often looked at as a plebeian, ephemeral, unliterary kind of performance theatre that defies serious analysis. Prince's career, however, seems to have been designed to entice intellectual skeptics. "Musicals don't have to be superficial," he says;

Now, because of economics, you can't really deal with issues in a musical, but when I got started in the fifties you could. In fact you could do more in musicals about politics, social issues, dealing with a sense of impotence, because music is a placebo, a way of sugar-coating your statement but not erasing it. By the mid-fifties straight theatre seemed to be losing its serious voice, and our shows took up the challenge.

Critics who keep their distance from musicals are right about them in one sense: musicals *are* a form of performance art whose impact can be gauged only in the theatre. A musical's spirit as well as its "meaning" can never be released in a study of its text alone. Designed to provoke applause, musicals depend on interaction (the livelier the better!) between performers and an audience. "In any realistic terms the musical is hilarious," Stephen Sondheim says; and as an artificial medium the musical requires consistent stylization, the creation of an unreal space in which characters can move easily between speech and song, between normal movement and dance. To protect the fact that its characters express themselves in ways that in life might get them arrested for disturbing the peace, a musical production has to be detached from any semblance of being "merely" natural.

Because they depend on theatrical conventions, musicals are as out of place on film as in the library, though good film musicals have cleverly managed to disguise this. Film's need for – or at least the general movie audience's expectations of – verisimilitude contradicts the musical's essential playacting spirit, its artifice and contrivance. The abstraction of theatrical design is a more comfortable frame for musical performance than films which suspend song and dance in a stylized milieu, or place numbers in real locations. That performers on film can't feed on audience response cancels the mutual release of energy which is part of what makes the musical a specifically theatrical event. "The theatre is the musical's natural home," Prince says. "To me, movies and musicals seem a contradiction in terms."[3]

While acknowledging, indeed celebrating, the musical's inherent artifice, Prince and his collaborators have at the same time explored ways of extending its theatrical signature. Their ideas about narrative, musical structure, movement, set design, and lighting have presented new ways of connecting a show's score to its book, of enfolding lyrics within dialogue and action. A brief glance at some of the conventions they inherited will help to appreciate the magnitude of their achievement.

The Broadway musical has a mixed ancestry which includes various traditions of European operetta and music-hall – the British comic opera of Gilbert and Sullivan, the Viennese light opera of Lehár and Strauss, the French *opéra bouffe* of Offenbach, British and French styles of burlesque, revue and extravaganza – laced with homegrown musical forms like minstrelsy, ragtime, jazz, and Tin Pan Alley. Although from the beginnings of the American musical theatre the "high" operetta style frequently intersected with the "low" revue, then as now shows fell into two general categories: the musical play that developed from operetta models, and the musical comedy that was first or second cousin to vaudeville. Both kinds of musicals rested on firmly set conventions in plotting, characterization, and musical development.

Until World War I, when their Austrian fragrance began to seem unpatriotic, operetta styles dominated American lyric theatre. Before the Jazz Age the biggest hits on the American musical stage had been Gilbert and Sullivan's *H.M.S. Pinafore* (1878) and Lehár's *The Merry Widow* (1905). With its delight in absurdities of setting and situation, the astringent and staccato Gilbert and Sullivan style mocked the lush Viennese operettas in which comic characters played second fiddle to royal romance and tales of well-born adventurers. However, Viennese strudel proved a more popular item on the menu than British irony, and the three leading composers whose work established the style of American operetta – Victor Herbert, Sigmund Romberg, and Rudolf Friml – were closely tied to the Viennese tradition.

As in the European models, themes of misalliance (*The Student Prince* in love with a commoner), masquerade (in *The Desert Song* a seeming lack-wit is really the fearless Red Shadow), and heroic endeavor (in *The New Moon* a renegade French nobleman founds a democratic Utopia) course through the American operetta canon. Also following the European plan, secondary characters often provided low comic relief, as in *The Red Mill* in which a typical misalliance in a foreign setting is cross-cut with the antics of two crafty American adventurers, roles created for well-known vaudevillians David Montgomery and Fred Stone.

Designed as a popular alternative to grand opera, with dialogue between numbers, plenty of action, and lush melodies, sweeping waltzes and brisk military marches, the European operetta style retained its hold on the American stage through the twenties. Nonetheless, after the war operettas began to be displaced by musical comedies which featured homespun characters, contemporary settings and themes, and a musical palette that included jazz, dance rhythms, and pop tunes. But virtually any show that is not clearly a musical comedy is still indebted to the operetta tradition. Though billed under the protective labels of "musical play" or "musical drama" or simply, to avoid confusion or bias, "musical," shows of mixed moods and musical idioms like *Carousel*, *The King and I*, *Fiddler on the Roof*, and *A Little Night Music* are operetta's legitimate heirs.

In contrast to operetta's continental manner, musical comedy evolved from various kinds of revue in which both the music and the performance style were distinctly native. Although vaudeville certainly had non-American origins and early revue performers like Harrigan and Hart and Weber and Fields exploited foreign accents and humor while revue composers were often indebted to musical patterns based on African rhythms or the modal tonalities of Jewish folk music, the style which emerged was decidedly American. From Tony Pastor's "high-class" vaudeville established in 1879 to Ziegfeld's *Follies*, *The Passing Shows*, George White's *Scandals*, *The Music Box Revues*, *The Grand Street* and *Greenwich Village Follies*, *Shuffle Along* and the *Blackbirds*, the revue tradition mixed song, dance, satire, and spectacle in a style that was brash, topical, and star-oriented and that offered a clear-cut entertainment alternative to European operetta. Unlike operettas, in which music was usually integrated with dramatic action, the early musical comedies had the fragmented structure of the motley vaudeville program. With their multistranded and often illogical plots, their frequent scenic changes, and their interpolated songs, the shows were closer in form and spirit to revue than to the narrative demands of the legitimate stage. As in variety of whatever type, what counted was the spot, the gag, the routine, the specialty – for any of which story and character development could always be sacrificed. Shows were fabricated for stars. An Eddie Cantor musical, *Whoopee!* (1928), for example, with the star cast as a hypochondriac adrift in the Wild West, grew like Topsy, as it added song and comic skits to showcase Cantor's beloved vaudeville persona. Typical of the show's absent-minded storytelling, Ruth Etting appeared in front of the curtain without preparation or motive to sing "Love Me or Leave Me," the ballad that became her signature song; performed "in one," the number was merely a way of filling time to cover a change of scenery.

The librettos for the typical musicals of the twenties that starred Fred and Adele Astaire were flimsy pretexts for song and dance. In his autobiography Fred Astaire offers a comment on *Lady, Be Good!*, one of his most successful vehicles, which might well serve as the epitaph for all pre-literate formulaic musical comedy: "What the plot of *Lady, Be Good!* was I really can't remember, but I do know that it was pretty stupid . . . It didn't matter, that weak plot. Somehow there was an indefinable magic about the show."[4]

Like the title of a Cole Porter show, the rule of thumb in assembling the book and the score for old-fashioned musical comedy seemed to be "anything goes." Interpolation was the byword as songs were imported to service stars and comic skits were interjected to accommodate the top bananas. Except for the notably integrated *Kiss Me, Kate*, Cole Porter's shows were display cases for his list songs, his risqué lyrics, his sly references to the beau monde, his intricate rhymes. Though it appeared first in *Anything Goes*, a Porter standard like "You're the Top" could be squeezed into almost any Porter musical. Indeed, in his will Porter permits numbers to be transposed from show to show, in effect sanctioning a musical movable feast which acknowledges that the song, rather than the play, is the thing.

Although a manufactured, disposable commodity, the typical musical-comedy book of the twenties took up more time, and had more dialogue and a more complicated story than modern audiences would be likely to tolerate. Farce elements usually served as narrative underpinning: mistaken identity, outrageous coincidence, mistiming, and masquerade were rampant. Rather than characters from show business, the usual cast was made up of contemporary types like bootleggers, gangsters, and shopgirls. *No, No, Nanette* (1925), about a flapper who wants to have some fun before she settles down to "Tea for Two," was the most popular musical comedy of the postwar decade. Imported from England, a series of Gaiety Theatre shows produced by George Edwardes (the first, *A Gaiety Girl*, opened in 1894, and was followed by such titles as *The Runaway Girl, The Quaker Girl, The Sunshine Girl*) introduced a Cinderella motif popular in the money-conscious Roaring Twenties: poor girls like *Irene* and *Sally* strike it rich through marriage or career.

"Those old musical-comedy books were terrible, simply terrible," George Abbott says. "When I revived *On Your Toes* [first produced in 1936] – and that was one of the better books – I had to change it considerably to make it tolerable to a contemporary audience. Yet my farces of about the same period, *Room Service* and *Three Men On a Horse*, could be revived today without changing a word." If the Gershwins and the Astaires, the Porters and the Mermans are the heroes of musical theatre, the Henry Blossoms and Harry B. Smiths and Guy Boltons, who among them wrote hundreds of librettos, are the victims. Always blamed when a musical fails and rarely praised when a show succeeds, the librettist, then as now, has a difficult and thankless job, one in which he can afford little ego as he concocts a concise framework of words and actions that must service the needs of the performers, the composer, the designers, the choreographer, and the director. "It's a job no sensible grown-up would ever want," said the late Michael Stewart, who nonetheless had a successful career as a musical book writer.

Designed as ephemeral entertainment rather than art, the old-fashioned non-integrated musical comedies are fragile artifacts, "antiques," as Hal Prince says, "that are revivable only as curios." But when performed in the proper spirit (their books trimmed and adjusted), they have an appealing energy and insouciance. A brisk 1987 New York revival (with an updated book by Timothy Crouse and John Weidman) of *Anything Goes* demonstrated the theatrical viability of the format that creators like Prince and Sondheim have helped to put out of business. Presented in a light style that happily avoided the condescensions of camp, the show was a delightful resurrection of antiquated formulas: loosely integrated songs and production numbers, busy plotting (mistaken identity, misalliance, disguise, contrasted romantic couples), and topical thirties satire (when gangsters are treated like celebrities . . . anything goes!).

Early in their development the narrative stencils, character types, and musical portfolios of romantic operetta and dizzy musical comedy were locked into provably popular patterns. But like any enduring genre the musical has been periodically regenerated; the reforms conducted by Prince and Sondheim were built on a long-standing tradition of internal experiment that notably enhanced the musical's resources. Artists who in their own time opposed the restrictions of formula prepared the way for the exploratory Hal Prince musicals, as Prince's shows have in turn suggested ideas for productions with new shapes and textures, new musical and dramatic statements.

Histories of musical theatre routinely inform us that *The Black Crook*, presented in New York in 1866, was the first "musical comedy," yet contemporary audiences would not discern even a remote musical-theatre ancestor in this curious five-and-a-half-hour amalgamation of ballet, spectacle, transformation scenes, romantic melodrama, and the supernatural which in fact was made up of two separate shows spliced together. When the sets for a visiting French ballet troupe were accidentally burned, the dance company was inserted into a ready-made melodrama short on cash. The real forerunner of what came to be the standard-make musical comedy was to be found in the work of George M. Cohan, who wrote book shows to display the persona he had developed in vaudeville. Unlike operettas, Cohan's aggressively American musical plays had characters and settings that would have seemed familiar to his audiences. His colloquial dialogue tried for a naturalism that would have been misplaced in the fanciful kingdoms of operetta, and his simple, bouncy melodies were distinctly less rich than the usual light-opera pastry. In his archetypal *Little Johnny Jones* (1903), Cohan played an American jockey in England, a true-blue patriot duped by shady foreigners.

Like Cohan's tailor-made vehicles, the famed Princess Theatre shows such as *Nobody Home* (1915), *Very Good Eddie* (1915), *Oh Boy!* (1917), *Oh Lady,*

Lady (1918) and *Leave It to Jane* (produced in 1917 at the Longacre Theatre), with music by Jerome Kern and book and lyrics usually by Guy Bolton and P. G. Wodehouse, continued to set the musical on strictly home territory. Presented at the intimate Princess Theatre, the shows were created to oppose operettas "tainted" with foreign settings and characters as well as the urge toward spectacle which had been part of musical-theatre packaging since the oversized *Black Crook*. With only two sets for each show and a small ensemble, the light comedies concocted by Bolton and Wodehouse celebrated the antics of homespun characters like college students and working-class honeymooners. Moving away from the operettas for which he had composed interpolated songs, Jerome Kern wrote a string of infectious melodies for ballads, comic and patter songs, novelty numbers, and dance routines, in effect setting the patterns for the musical staples of musical comedy. With their uninsistent shrewd social satire, Wodehouse's wry lyrics also established a traditional musical-comedy mold, while the heroine of *Leave It to Jane*, cleverly solving problems of romance and intermural athletics, was to become a musical-comedy archetype, the young woman whose energy is naturally released through singing and dancing.

The charm, innocence, modestly cozy manner, and catalogue of hummable tunes with a plausible if relaxed link to what was happening on stage, which characterized the Princess shows, set a standard throughout the postwar decade, until the arrival in 1927 of *Show Boat*. "Before *Show Boat*," Stephen Sondheim says, "musicals were either operettas or frivolous comedies with a thin topical overlay. Oscar Hammerstein II changed that, combining the two in *Show Boat* and, really for the first time, using the musical form to create a real sense of character, which does not gainsay the show's naiveté. The Rodgers and Hammerstein collaboration that began with *Oklahoma!* had its start with what Oscar was trying to do with *Show Boat*." Adapted from Edna Ferber's sprawling novel about show folk on the Mississippi, *Show Boat* was genuine American operetta, a new genre. Rather than topical light comedy, with its regulation flappers, playboys, bootleggers, and assorted comic con artists, *Show Boat* was romantic melodrama (a misalliance between a gambler and a lady contrasted with a miscegenation subplot) set against the symbolic backdrop of the great river.

Ferber's episodic story is inherently novelistic and in adapting it for the musical theatre, where pace and concision are essential, Oscar Hammerstein had few guidelines. Telescoping events that occurred over a period of many years, Act II presented structural problems never entirely solved. Different versions of *Show Boat*, on stage and film, have been variously revised and trimmed, eliminating characters and scenes, cutting the time sequence and changing the order and number of songs. But even in cut-rate versions the show has proved to be as enduring as its ol' man river. Kern's score, in effect a history of American popular music from minstrelsy to Broadway, transfigures a dated libretto.

The first musical to be published in book form was also the first to win the Pulitzer Prize. Like *Show Boat, Of Thee I Sing*, a 1931 political satire by George S. Kaufman and Morrie Ryskind, with music and lyrics by George and Ira Gershwin, pushed the musical into new thematic territory. Presidential candidate John Wintergreen campaigns and wins on a platform that promotes Love; a bathing beauty contest is held to determine who will be the new First Lady; the victor, a French descendant named Diana Devereaux, files suit against the government when Wintergreen rejects her in favor of a secretary, Mary Turner, who bakes good corn muffins; the offended French government wants revenge; the Supreme Court threatens impeachment. But

1 A play within the play: on the stage of the "Cotton Blossom" in Hammerstein and Kern's *Show Boat* (1927), the landmark musical that combined elements of operetta with musical comedy

2 Playing with politics: the Gershwins' *Of Thee I Sing* (1931), with a libretto by George S. Kaufman and Morrie Ryskind, the first musical to win the Pulitzer Prize and to be published in book form (William Gaxton and Lois Moran as John and Mary)

by announcing she is pregnant, Mary Turner prevents the fall of her husband's Presidency, and Diana Devereaux is placated when the Vice-President, Alexander Throttlebottom, ever on the look-out for something – anything – to do, offers to marry her. Sending up politics as a popularity contest, mocking political rhetoric and manipulation and the gullibility of the public, and taking pokes at the Vice-presidency and the Supreme Court, *Of Thee I Sing* has the structural neatness and rapid-fire wisecracks which were Kaufman's trademarks. For all its coyness it remains a libretto with a satiric sting.

The show's premise inspired George and Ira Gershwin to shed the style they had perfected in such twenties shows as *Funny Face* and *Lady, Be Good!*, in which songs like "Fascinating Rhythm" and "Do-Do-Do" expressed generalized feelings and were easily detachable from theatrical context. For *Of Thee I Sing* the Gershwins composed a light-opera score with echoes of Gilbert and Sullivan that for the most part bypassed the standard thirty-two-bar song form for longer and more complex musical sequences, ensembles and extended finales. Their music is often used satirically, as ironic choral comment: *Of Thee I Sing* is America's first Brechtian musical, a harbinger of the Prince-Sondheim shows of the seventies.

In 1933 the collaborators presented *Let 'Em Eat Cake*, a much darker political satire, with pointed references to the contemporary Depression. In this sequel the buoyant spirit of the original curdles into an anti-populist fable in which the defeated President Wintergreen establishes a dictatorship after leading a blue-shirt revolution against the new President, John Tweedledee. The show examines the human cost of unemployment and the potential consequences of economic dispossession – and its failure, with its abrasive book and unconventional score, almost certainly inhibited the development of the American political musical.

To meet the demands of this acrid satire which democratically upends every subject it touches, from motherhood to the Supreme Court, from anarchists to a fickle electorate swayed by demagogues, the Gershwins composed their most ambitious score to date. In continuing to replace separable songs with recitative, choral counterpoint, and fully developed musical scenes, many of the harmonies and musical structures anticipated *Porgy and Bess*, which Stephen Sondheim calls "the only musical that will last – that will still seem great – one hundred years from now." Which branch of the lyric theatre can claim Dubose Heyward and Gershwin's masterwork – whether *Porgy and Bess* belongs on Broadway or the opera stage – is a matter of continuing debate, and as such a testimony to its revolutionary composition. Through the musical languages of melody, harmony, and rhythm Gershwin transforms racial stereotype (blacks as superstitious and sexually rapacious) into a love story between the crippled beggar Porgy and the man-hungry self-defeating Bess that takes on the illumination of an archetypal myth. For this fable of characters driven by passion Gershwin has composed a musical fabric in which jazz and symphonic elements, soaring melody and recitative, are uniquely interwoven.

Moving restlessly from musical comedy to satiric operetta to opera, and from Broadway to the concert hall, Gershwin did more than any earlier composer to unify elitist and popular, classical and vernacular, musical styles. Aside from Leonard Bernstein, the only other composer who attempted the same agenda on the same scale was Kurt Weill, a classically trained German expatriate excited by the possibilities of the Broadway musical. From 1936 to 1949, with socially astute works which anticipate many of Prince's ideas, Weill and his collaborators significantly deepened the American musical. Weill's *Johnny Johnson* (1936), with book and lyrics by Paul Green; *Knickerbocker Holiday* (1938), with book and lyrics by Maxwell Anderson; *Lady in the Dark* (1940), with a book by Moss Hart and lyrics by Ira Gershwin; *Street Scene* (1947), with book and lyrics by Langston Hughes based on the play by Elmer Rice; *Love Life* (1948), with book and lyrics by Alan Jay Lerner; and *Lost in the Stars* (1949), with book and lyrics by Maxwell Anderson, based on Alan Paton's novel, *Cry the Beloved Country*, chart a series of experiments in musical texture and dramatic form. Though they are often seen as a betrayal of his European heritage, a concession to the demands of a popular American style, each of these shows added new notes to the Broadway musical's scale.

When he arrived in America in 1935, to collaborate with Franz Werfel on a religious pageant, *The Eternal Road*, Weill had of course already evolved a radical musical-theatre technique in often embattled partnership with Bertolt Brecht. Their three best-known works, two caustic comedies, *The Threepenny Opera* (1928) and *Happy End* (1929), and a folk opera, *The Rise and Fall of the City of Mahagonny* (1929), were Marxist musicals set in mythical foreign realms, fanciful versions of Victorian London and America which served as metaphors for a rotting contemporary Germany. Telling stories of thieves, beggars, whores, capitalist sharks, criminals who act like businessmen and businessmen who act like criminals, and unholy alliances between religious and criminal "gangs" and between the law and the underworld, Brecht and Weill used music and lyrics to support their satiric themes. Rather than expressing romantic uplift and a surge of energy, songs carry the authors' cynicism about bourgeois proprieties and the capitalist creed. Their abrasive pop operas inform us that love doesn't last, that not being able to pay a bar bill is a capital offense in a capitalist society, that it's better to rob a bank than to own one, that the way of the capitalist world is betrayal provoked by greed. Theatrical as well as political radicals, Brecht and Weill overturn the forms as well as the shibboleths of popular entertainment: the ironic happy endings in *The Threepenny Opera* (the Queen not only pardons Mackie the Knife but rewards him with a castle) and *Happy End* (the mob boss is reunited with her long-lost husband, a member of the Salvation Army) satirize narrative conventions and the audience's desire for sentimental finales.

Adhering to ballad opera tradition, in *The Threepenny Opera* and *Happy End* songs literally stop the show. Moving into a spotlight at the front of the stage, actors step out of their roles to become performers who sing songs that comment on the action. In *The Threepenny Opera* the "Solomon Song" tells us of the vanity and the evanescence of being "top dog," the "Barbara Song" illustrates the belief that women fall for brutes rather than gentlemen. Bristling with paradox and provocation, songs interrupt the action and break the psychic bond between the actor and his role: Brecht wanted the singing actor to think of his character in the third person, just as he intended songs as a form of *Lehrstück* to point a moral or underline a contradiction. In Brecht's epic theatre music was thus one of the methods of frustrating an audience's natural desire for wanting to be carried away.

With their sly parodies of popular and classical styles Weill's scores complement Brecht's multiple ironies, his jeering, raucous wit. Commenting on his sources, Weill often achieved the alienation effect that Brecht wanted. But like Brecht's complex characters, Weill's bewitching melodies sometimes aroused audience identification rather than detachment.

Evolving organically out of a Marxist viewpoint, the Brecht–Weill idea of musical theatre will always be temperamentally as well as politically at odds with the Broadway musical. Nonetheless their work supplies an enticing model whose influence has filtered into the American mainstream primarily through the collaboration between Prince and Sondheim, even though neither the director nor his composer will admit any specific impact. "I have not remotely been consciously influenced by Brecht," Prince claims:

Unlike Brecht, my purpose is not to eliminate emotional response – it isn't by design that a show of mine is cold. Brecht flooded his stage with white light; I like shadows. I was flattered when the widow of [Brecht's teacher] Erwin Piscator said *Evita* was close in spirit to her husband's work, but in fact Russian theatre has influenced me far more than Brecht's tradition: Joshua Logan told me my work resembled Meyerhold's. Furthermore, I've been bored to death by Brecht-inspired productions.

"Brecht and Weill worked in a tradition of *Lehrstück*; my background is Broadway, and the two are very different," Sondheim says. "I like *Threepenny Opera* but not really anything else. Basically, I hate Brecht. Jerome Robbins and Leonard Bernstein asked me to collaborate on a Brecht project, adapting *The Exception and the Rule* into a musical. I tried, but I had to drop out. Actually, I prefer Weill's American to his European work."

Critics can sometimes see artists' work in a different way than the artists

3 and 4 Brecht on Broadway: *The Threepenny Opera* in 1933, with settings by Cleon Throckmorton based on original designs by Caspar Neher. Premonitions of dark Hal Prince musicals

themselves, however, and it is my belief that both Prince and Sondheim have instincts in their approach to the musical theatre that echo Brecht and Weill. Pure Brechtians, Marxist propagandists, they certainly are not; but in the kinds of statements they want the musical to make, and in the tone in which they have expressed their themes they have incorporated elements of the epic theatre into a form that would seem to be its opposite number, the Broadway musical.

Often called a musical chameleon, a composer who never looked back as he acquired a French patina when he was in Paris and "went Broadway" once he arrived in America, Weill in fact never entirely disowned the original musical idiom he had created in his work with Brecht, nor did he forsake the idea of using music to make social and political statements. If his American work is not as harsh or cutting or "difficult" as his German pieces neither is it ever bland or self-effacing. Working in a commercial forum Weill remained both an idealist and a theorist.

Collaborating with the left-leaning Group Theatre Weill composed *Johnny Johnson* as a picaresque comedy about the experiences during the Great War of a holy simpleton whose attitudes provide pointed contrasts to those of the war-machine bureaucrats. With an operatic ballad, a tango, a French music-hall song, a Civil War song, a cowboy ditty, musical irony (using the same melody for both an anti-war and a military song) and musical surrealism (guns and the Statue of Liberty sing to a group of soldiers), Weill's score is an astonishing pastiche, unlike anything that had yet been written for the American musical. Set in early New York, *Knickerbocker Holiday* is about a tyrannical governor, Peter Stuyvesant, challenged by an egalitarian upstart. In both these shows with overtly political subjects Weill was recalling his own circumstances as a refugee from Fascism.

With the exception of the ill-fated *Firebrand of Florence* (1945), for his later shows Weill chose subjects closer to the American present, though in both form and subject matter his choices were unusual for the musical stage: psychiatry in *Lady in the Dark*; life in a tenement, culminating in a crime of passion, in *Street Scene*; a revue-like survey of the institution of marriage in America from 1776 to 1947 in *Love Life*; race relations in South Africa in *Lost in the Stars*. Although the treatment of psychoanalysis in Moss Hart's libretto for *Lady in the Dark* now seems quaint, and certainly oversimplified, Weill and his lyricist Ira Gershwin experimented with a mini-operetta format. Except for one key song at the end, the music appears only within a dream framework, as the patient recounts traumatic incidents to her therapist. Songs are linked into expressionistic musical sequences which reflect the character's anxieties. With its variations-on-a-theme format, *Love Life* (which deserves a major revival) is a progenitor of the modernist concept musical. "It was a useful influence on my own work," Sondheim says, "but it failed because it started out with an idea rather than a character."

In *Street Scene*, Weill consciously tried to close the gap between the Broadway musical and the operatic stage, a goal Hal Prince has continued to pursue. With arias that demand operatically trained voices, together with street songs and Broadway ballads, Weill's score offers a surprising conjunction of subject and treatment: *Street Scene* is a Bowery opera. In *Lost in the Stars* Weill again avoids musical stencils as he distils African idioms into a more universal texture, nearly operatic at times. His use of a chorus as a communal voice, at times a witness to the unfolding tragedy, at times a participant, prefigures a trademark of Hal Prince musicals.

Only once in his Broadway career did Weill fully camouflage his *Lehrstück* origins. *One Touch of Venus* (1941) is a standard musical comedy designed as a star-vehicle for Marlene Dietrich which evolved into a showcase for Mary Martin. The premise – a statue brought to life dispenses romantic instructions to wayward mortals – is a prescription for formula Broadway fun. Weill's score matches the clipped wit of Ogden Nash's lyrics and provides the inspiration for two renowned Agnes de Mille dances, "Broadway Rhythm" and "Venus in Ozone Heights." On this occasion – and this occasion only – Weill submerged his European roots to function as a hired hand fabricating sophisticated Broadway entertainment.

With a career of more than fifty years, Richard Rodgers was the most prolific Broadway composer, and although not a musical-theatre rebel like Weill or Gershwin, in his two historic collaborations he established the dominant patterns that the Broadway musical has continued to follow. Working with Lorenz Hart from 1920 to 1943 Rodgers set the pattern for musical comedy; during his shorter partnership with Oscar Hammerstein, from 1943 to 1959, he created a model for the musical play. Rodgers's flexibility is apparent in the way he adapted to the different qualities of his two co-workers, Hart's wit and Hammerstein's oratory, Hart's sting and Hammerstein's uplift. With the exception of *A Connecticut Yankee in King Arthur's Court* (1927), the Rodgers and Hart shows of the twenties are mostly unknown today. While their scores and librettos await restoration their subject matter suggests surprising variety. Alternating with conventional fare like *Poor Little Ritz Girl* (1920), a show about show people, and *Betsy* (1926), a Jewish family comedy built as a vehicle for vaudeville star Belle Baker, is a musical about the American Revolution (*Dearest Enemy*, 1925), a dream musical with Freudian motifs (*Peggy-Ann*, 1926), and a jazz musical about eunuchs in an Oriental court (*Chee-Chee*, 1928).

After leaving the theatre in the early thirties to spend several frustrating years in Hollywood (though during this time they wrote the score for *Love*

Me Tonight, a landmark film musical), Rodgers and Hart returned to Broadway in 1935. From their circus musical, *Jumbo* (1935), to *Babes in Arms* (1935), about kids putting on a show, to *I Married An Angel* (1937), *The Boys from Syracuse* (1938), *Too Many Girls* (1939), *Higher and Higher* (1941), and *By Jupiter* (1942), they contributed sprightly musical comedies to eight successive seasons. During this period a Rodgers and Hart show became a synonym for expert Broadway entertainment: light melodies and pungent lyrics. A Rodgers and Hart musical comedy had a kind of innocence that is probably no longer recoverable. Like most popular theatre, their shows were created to satisfy the tastes of a contemporary audience; as tastes change, the work inevitably dates. But if it no longer speaks out of a current sensibility a well-performed Rodgers and Hart musical can still entertain, as in a recent off-Broadway production of *Too Many Girls*, a modest college musical with a tuneful score. The frothy book has the courage of its *unimportance* and the peppy, straightforward production accomplished what musical comedy is always supposed to, sending the audience home in a jubilant mood.

Only two Rodgers and Hart shows of this period were consciously experimental. With choreography by George Balanchine, *On Your Toes* was the first Broadway musical to incorporate ballet. Balanchine's classically based "Scheherazade" in Act I and his jazz ballet, "Slaughter on Tenth Avenue," in Act II, led the way to the more thematic, symbolic use of dance in the dream ballets that, beginning with Agnes de Mille's choreography for *Oklahoma!* in 1943, became a Broadway staple for nearly two decades. *Pal Joey* (1940) introduced new hues into the musical-comedy palette. In its original form, a series of letters by a roué, petty hustler and night-club crooner, author John O'Hara's concern is with character and ambience; through his own slangy, semi-literate style Joey unknowingly exposes his mediocrity. Faced with transforming Joey's letters into a libretto, O'Hara with the help of George Abbott weakened his material, softening Joey's lingo and imposing an artificial blackmail plot. Nonetheless its seedy title character, low-life settings, sly sexual realism (when her fling with Joey is over, the heroine informs us that she is no longer "bewitched, bothered, and bewildered"), and its downbeat ending with Joey romantically stranded, anticipate dark musicals of the seventies like *Company* and *Chicago*.

Rodgers in partnership with Hammerstein produced a body of work that is the most popular and frequently revived in the American musical-theatre canon. Although they have the mostly non-contemporary or exotic settings and mixed moods typical of operetta, shows like *Oklahoma!*, *Carousel* (1945), *South Pacific* (1949), *The King and I* (1951), and *The Sound of Music* (1959) also presented conflicts that are more realistic and characters who are more plainspoken than the royalty and swashbucklers of the outmoded Romberg—

Friml pattern. The familiar Rodgers and Hammerstein catalogue may itself now seem to be reactionary ("their work appeals mostly to those over fifty, which doesn't bode well for posterity," says Sondheim) but at the time they were first produced each of the major pieces introduced dramatic, musical, and technical innovations. The fresh Rodgers and Hammerstein dramatic formula was to oppose two well-developed, strong-willed characters (Anna and the King, Nellie and Emile, Laurey and Curly, Billy Bigelow and Julie Jordan, Maria and Captain von Trapp) in an off-beat romance. The emotionally defective hero, often stubborn and tyrannical, needs the perky heroine who is his cultural, moral, or emotional antithesis, and who must tame him or learn to accept him. On the Rodgers and Hammerstein canvas, comedy is tinted with tragedy; entertainment is mixed with populist moral philosophy. No musicals before theirs had ever been quite so high-minded, so clever in issuing sunny liberal pieties ("The farmer and the cowman should be friends," "You've got to be carefully taught" to develop prejudice, "Climb every mountain," "With love in your heart you never walk alone").

Musically they often made their own rules: Curly singing "Oh What a Beautiful Morning" from offstage at the beginning of *Oklahoma!* ("it was an opening Puccini might have used," says Hal Prince); the expressionist dream ballet at the end of the first act of *Oklahoma!*; a musical soliloquy, extended musical scenes, and another dream ballet in *Carousel*; the "Uncle Tom's Cabin" ballet, a symbolic play within the play, in *The King and I.*

Although he is often described as having overturned the tradition of the Rodgers and Hammerstein musical play, Prince says that he is "idolatrous" of the form; "many people have imitated Rodgers and Hammerstein badly, but that takes nothing away from their accomplishment." Prince in fact received his first impetus toward musical theatre on the opening night of *South Pacific* ("that was a book!" he says enthusiastically), when he first met Stephen Sondheim. "It was right after *South Pacific* opened that we began meeting to talk about how we would like to contribute to the musical theatre."

While Sondheim prefers *Oklahoma!* and *Carousel* to *South Pacific* and finds *Allegro* most "useful" of all, he cites "Oscar's attempt to use lyrics to develop character" as of greatest significance for his own development. "Oscar taught me how to construct a song like a one-act play, which is what he always did, in essence, and how to use songs to strengthen character and theme rather than to provide easy breaks for the audience." Matching lyrics to the characters who sing them – his lyrics are rhythmic inflections of his colloquial dialogue – Hammerstein achieved an unprecedented level of integration between a show's libretto and its score. As Sondheim says, "You can transpose songs from *Lady, Be Good!* to *Funny Face* but you can't move songs from *Oklahoma!* to *Carousel*."

Prince particularly admires *Allegro* because it represents an alternative to the realistic musical-play tradition, and Sondheim observes that

shows like *South Pacific* and *The King and I* were becoming realistic plays with music. The only poetic convention in them was characters breaking into song when the pressure in a scene had built to a certain level. But in *Allegro* Oscar used theatre convention frankly as theatre convention: the chorus that oversees the action, the abstract scenic design. These techniques have had a large influence on Hal's work and on mine.[5]

Rodgers and Hammerstein understood the Broadway musical's dramatic potential as well as anyone ever has. Their narrative recipe of sparring romantic characters in colorful settings, Rodgers's sweeping melodies and Hammerstein's homespun lyric poetry, were the basis of a vibrant American folk art. Instead of providing a closed-form model, however, the end of a musical line, the Rodgers and Hammerstein musical plays invited variation and further experiment, as the careers of their ambitious inheritors Hal Prince and Stephen Sondheim have happily demonstrated.

2   The Abbott touch

"So many directors, actors, and writers have come out of the 'school of Abbott' because George Abbott is a very generous man," Hal Prince says. "He has always known how good he is and so he never resented when we went off on our own." Of all the "youngsters" to whom Abbott has given a chance, Hal Prince has remained the closest to him. As Abbott himself notes, with wry amusement, "Hal used to work out of my office; now I work out of his." When asked why he had hired Prince, Abbott said, "You know why: he's a live wire! He worked on a television project my then wife was running, and I could see he was a bright boy: it was self-evident." For Prince the attraction was equally basic: "Abbott was quite simply the most successful director on Broadway, which is where I wanted to be."

In 1948 when Prince began working in Abbott's office Abbott's position on Broadway as producer, writer, director, and play doctor had been secure since 1926, when he had directed and (with Philip Dunning) co-written *Broadway*, his first hit. In the twenty-two years since, not a season had passed without at least one Abbott show on the boards. Representative pre-1948 Abbott hits include *Coquette, Twentieth Century, Three Men on a Horse, Room Service, On Your Toes, The Boys From Syracuse, Pal Joey, Kiss and Tell*, and *On the Town*. Except for *Coquette*, a moralistic twenties melodrama with a tragic ending, the typical Abbott show was a farce or a musical comedy; fast-paced light entertainment was his specialty. "It would never have occurred to him to do a classic drama or comedy," Prince says, while Abbott, who enjoys Shakespeare ("he was a smart theatre man who was just writing shows which should be played for their guts rather than for fancy verse") admits he was never tempted by "wordy" writers like Ibsen or Strindberg or Pirandello. Abbott's one brush with the classics was adapting *The Comedy of Errors* into *The Boys From Syracuse*, the director's particular favorite among his more than 120 productions, which retains only one passage from the original.

"When I entered the theatre I had no thoughts of reforming it," Abbott says. "I was just struggling to get New York hits, to be successful on Broadway." His tastes were at least partially formed by studies in 1912 and 1913 with the legendary George Pierce Baker, whose "English 47" at Harvard was the first playwriting course in America. Admiring the nineteenth-century popular theatre exemplified by the well-made plays of Arthur Wing Pinero and Henry Arthur Jones, "Baker gave you a good sense of construction," Abbott recalls.

You've got to get your plot straight, and plots have to have a beginning, middle, and end. I don't understand plots like *Waiting for Godot*, which has no real construction . . . Baker taught me that the farce is as good as the drama. I also learned from him how to get the greatest good out of the scene. But being long-winded didn't bother him; he didn't know about cutting to the bone so the play travels.

While Baker's conservative tastes – his playmaking rules and his antipathy to modernism – made sense to Abbott, they caused another student to drop out of class. To Eugene O'Neill, Baker's fussy prescriptions about character and structure, and his recipes for achieving popular success, were worse than useless, they were crippling. Significantly, then, the student who wanted hits on Broadway profited from Baker's course while the one who became America's first great playwright, and who in effect made up his own rules, did not.

Absorbing Baker's formulas helped to sharpen Abbott's fabled instincts about construction, his skill in tightening and clarifying the plots of melodramas, farces, and musical comedies so that they "traveled." "I helped bring plot and common sense into the musical," he says. As co-author (like George S. Kaufman, Abbott seldom worked on his own), Abbott would take "what other people had written, and go off and rewrite, to cut and rearrange and make sure the plot was clear. In my librettos I always suggested places for songs; Frank Loesser told me that every song he wrote for *Where's Charley?* was where I had suggested." In the tradition of the well-made play that Abbott inherited, the story is a machine whose parts must interlock smoothly: if the machine doesn't work, it has to be fixed, tinkered with, until it moves as it is supposed to. "Fixing" a story for logic, clarity, drive and pace are Abbott trademarks, elements of his famed "touch," which Prince defines as "who Abbott is internally. Like the man, his work has great physical vitality; it's peppy, a favorite Abbott word; it is clear, logical, swift, and realistic. I learned from Abbott about establishing the emotional reality for whatever world you create on stage; he insisted on honesty and reality within the parameters of farce and musical comedy."

Abbott quarrels with the way his "touch" is often perceived:

It isn't speed for its own sake, rather it is taste and judgment about the scene, about where the emphasis should be. Pacing is only one factor, which has sometimes been misunderstood. You also have to know when to pause; I never want to do a show in which an actor says one line, and then the other actor says his – there's no spontaneity in that. Revivals of some of my farces have been misdirected; the actors mug and the frantic pace destroys the reality that farce must have.

In talking about his technique Abbott uses words like "reality" and "truth" that would seem to apply to a different kind of theatre than the manufactured farce and musical comedy in which he has achieved his greatest success. Abbott's "truth" is theatrical rather than psychological ("he's not particularly probing about people and what motivates them," Prince says); his primary concern is with establishing the truth and reality of the stage picture. Where characters are placed on the stage, how they speak and what they do must be logical and consistent – real – within the world that the play sets up. Abbott remembers with approval watching David Belasco ("personally he was a complete phony, but he was a great director") telling a group of actors that "in a particular scene he would rather hear the sound of the seltzer bottles than the dialogue. He wanted the scene to be real."

The clarity that Abbott particularly admires in directing is the quality that impressed Prince about Abbott. "He has a very logical mind; he's precise about every action on stage. The motivations in his shows are always so clear and honest, and *everything* is motivated," Prince says. "In an Abbott farce, a door opens and closes for a reason, as part of the situation and never simply for a laugh. ["I don't want a telephone on stage unless it gets used," Abbott says.] The people in *Three Men On a Horse* are behaving *truthfully*. Once Abbott postulates the premise, he does it with complete truthfulness."

One of the popular claims about Abbott is that he directs a farce as if it were *Hamlet*. Although the emphasis may be misleading – Abbott is never concerned with language and subtext and the psychology of characters at a level at which a director of *Hamlet* needs to be – the statement does reflect a respectful approach to popular theatre. Abbott directs light entertainment seriously, with attention to the truthful values of character and situation. "It's much funnier to see an actor believe his farce problems rather than think he's funny," Abbott says. "When I directed a recent revival of *Damn Yankees* [in the fall of 1986] I told Orson Bean, who was playing the devil, that I wanted the character to be serious about his problems: when his toe hurt, I wanted it to hurt. Actors in revivals of some of my shows try to be low comics; they make faces and think that's funny."

"Phony," the opposite of being "true," is another favorite Abbott word: "he can recognize mendacity at once," Prince reports. "With actors he knows when they are performing rather than being. He never analyzes; he can just look at an actor and say 'phony.'" Indeed for Abbott this emotional reality is the traditional basis of theatre: "When I first started out in the theatre they wanted you to have 'style,' which meant they wanted you to be artificial; but Shakespeare wanted you to be true." Although Abbott's approach to acting is quite different from the Method, he feels both his external techniques and the inner work that is the core of Method training share a common goal of believability. "I think a lot of the Method is phony ... They're learning how to be a tree when they need to be told how to pronounce their words. But the Method is really about feeling the part, it's as old as that, a way of getting the actor to understand his part."

"I never said your motivation is your salary," Abbott says, disowning a statement that has become part of the legend of his "touch." Nonetheless, discussion of the actor's motives and of his emotional connection to his role have no place at an Abbott rehearsal. "I hate prying into the actors' private lives," Abbott says, "and I never walk off into a corner with an actor. I tell things in front of the whole cast because what one actor does affects others on the stage. Belasco directed only the star, but today if the butler isn't good, the director isn't good: every director must have a picture in his mind of everything that happens on the stage."

"Abbott tells you where to move and how to say your lines, and you don't dare quarrel with him," recalls June Havoc, directed by Abbott in *Pal Joey* in 1940. "I hear the lines as I want them, so I give readings," Abbott admits. "The actors don't object, at least not out loud. Besides," he adds slyly, "there is only one *best* way to read a line."

Despite autocratic methods which would seem to limit actors' freedom and will − line readings, his belief in type-casting ("an old man is better at playing an old man than a young man in make-up, a pretty girl is better as the ingenue than an old actress made up") − his actors typically pay warm tribute to the director who told them just to say their lines, to pick up their cues and pronounce their final syllables. Ultimately Abbott's popularity with actors can be accounted for by his air of calm authority, the strong sense of self that has sustained the longest-running career in the history of the American theatre and that enforces respect. Yet Prince remembers him asking with genuine puzzlement,

"Why does everyone call me 'Mister Abbott'? . . ." I laughed. How could he not know? His persona is awesome. I was twenty when I went to work in his office, and I spent years trying to justify my own responses when I didn't agree with him: who was I to say it could be done in a different way? He had the kind of presence you didn't argue with, even when his opinions weren't your own. I'm now one of the few people who can tell him he's wrong, but it took me many years to be able to do it.

A tall trim man, and still remarkably commanding as he enters his second century, Abbott has a wonderfully resonant voice and a stern face that makes him seem like a New England farmer. Communicating absolute self-possession, he has an oracular presence − the law-giver standing at the helm of what Stephen Sondheim calls "totalitarian theatre." Abbott remembers watching George Kelly, a playwright who meticulously directed his own work, "tell an actor how to put out a cigarette and turn left. I thought then how wonderful it was to be a director: you can have such control, you can tell somebody what to do completely."[1]

But if Abbott is the undisputed boss, he is also a benevolent one. Indeed, the fact that he has had the most long-lived career in the theatre suggests he has extraordinary gifts for working with his colleagues. "He respects the artistry of anyone he works with," scenic designer Oliver Smith recalls.[2] Abbott's current collaborator, composer Robert Nassif (who is working on a musical version of *Broadway*), says that Abbott is "open and honest and never talks down. He makes you feel important and equal. He is tough yet kind; he is strong with a humorous touch." To be sure, Abbott's bone-dry wit, his spontaneous one-liners, continually soften the apparent severity of his deadpan expression.

For years Prince has ritualistically shown each of his productions to Abbott, to elicit a few words from the Master before the show is presented to the public. "Abbott is the only one in the audience," Prince says. "We do the show just for him. When he told us *West Side Story* was good and not to do anything to it, we were relieved. After seeing *Cabaret*, he said, 'Do it in two acts instead of three; I can't figure out where the curtain falls.' That's all he said. I couldn't figure it out either, then Ruth Mitchell [Prince's executive producer] suggested we combine the first two acts, and that's what we did. Abbott was right: the show played better in two acts."

Like Prince, many of Abbott's colleagues perceive gnomic insights in his characteristically terse pronouncements. "One of his words is worth five hundred of anybody else's," says Robert Nassif. Notoriously thrifty (with money and the outward expression of emotion, as well as with words) Abbott speaks in swift, sturdy sentences that are part of his time-saving pragmatism, what Prince calls the "Abbott shorthand." The Abbott sentence is a model of concision, the distillation of a career that virtually spans the history of the American theatre in the twentieth century, and it is precisely his power over language that helps to account for his legendary influence on his co-workers.

His laconic style leaves no room for qualification and nuance, for "discourse" or theory. "Ideas are either good or bad ideas and there are no grays, only blacks and whites," notes Robert Nassif:

Whenever there was some talk about theme Abbott would sink lower in his chair, with his arms folded, and he'd have an enigmatic smile. Early on in our work on *Tropicana* [a musical Abbott wrote and directed in 1985, with a score by Nassif] I mentioned how a song would thematically unify the show. "Oh, that's amateur night," he snapped, "just tell me who's on stage and what they're doing."

Oliver Smith recalls that the only advice Abbott gave him about scenic design was that "he wanted me to get his actors on the stage and off."[3]

Like George S. Kaufman, another founding father of the American popular theatre, Abbott has been surprised and secretly amused by scholarly interest in his work. When asked how he thought his work would hold up he replied (without missing a beat), "What was it Shakespeare said about sound and fury signifying nothing? I do it for now; I don't think anything much we're doing is going to last." And indeed, when Abbott was persuaded that his centenary justified transferring *Broadway*, which he directed for a "Classic Broadway" Symposium in Cleveland, to New York (where it opened on his one-hundredth birthday – June 25, 1987), the revival received a blast of negative reviews and closed after four performances. The consensus was that Abbott himself was more durable than his play, which was felt to be of historical interest as an early gangster story but no longer stageworthy.

"Abbott doesn't care about posterity," Prince says, "and neither for that matter does Steve Sondheim. *I do* . . . I want to leave a mark, to do something of artistic value. I suppose that's why Abbott has lived to be one hundred and I won't: he's stress-free and I'm not." As if confirming Prince's prognosis, Abbott says, "Hal would suffer so when a show failed while I would shrug it off and go on to the next one."

Despite Abbott's detachment, his air of almost imperial indifference, Prince told me that he called his 1974 memoir *Contradictions* "in honor of Abbott." "He's one of the most contradictory men I've ever met," Prince says, and indeed, for all his famous intolerance of complication, Abbott offers a number of tantalizing ones. He is a man without any apparent theatrical temperament who is the dean of Broadway showmen; a shrewd business man with acute artistic instincts; a director of breezy entertainment who demands realism from his actors; a writer with no patience for poetry who has created a vernacular poetry in some of his best work; a comic writer whose conversation has more gags and one-liners than his plays, in which comedy grows out of character and situation; a celebrated womanizer with a Puritan facade.

Despite their differences in temperament and artistic tastes, Prince has modeled his career on Abbott's example. "I learned discipline from Abbott, the lesson that there is no time in theatre for nonsense or self-indulgence. His own absolute professionalism taught me that the theatre is a place to work, to get the job done, and to respect one's colleagues." Prince's professional integrity, his own fabled discipline, his sense of pace and structure, his concept of the director as the gruff but fair master-assembler, his frank desire to have hits on Broadway, his enjoyment of discovering fresh talent rather than manufacturing vehicles for stars, his brisk, terse delivery, his well-chosen words issuing implicit commands – these qualities learned from Abbott have been the foundation of Prince's assault on the commercial theatre. Sondheim says that "both Abbott and Prince believe firmly in the director taking complete charge. And in a massive collaboration like the Broadway musical that's exactly as it should be: one man in command of the ship."

When he applied for a job with George Abbott, Prince offered to work for no salary. "I wrote a canny letter saying if anybody could tell I was not being paid they could fire me after four weeks," Prince recalls. His first assignment was in the television department, working with Abbott on the Hugh Martin variety show starring Butterfly McQueen. "Abbott wrote and directed the first show; I wrote and directed the second, after Abbott realized how unrewarding the work was." Prince's first theatre job was as assistant stage manager for a revue, *Touch and Go*; the stage manager and casting director was Robert Griffith, who was to become Prince's co-producer. Prince's job as assistant stage manager for *Call Me Madam* was interrupted by the Korean War; Abbott assured him of a position after his service had been completed, and "was as good as his word; I went back to work as assistant stage manager on *Wonderful Town*." Though from the beginning of his career Prince was interested in the job of the director, who shapes a show on the stage, the first step was to become a producer – responsible for raising the financing – a step which Prince and Griffith took in 1953 when they came across Richard Bissell's book $7\frac{1}{2}\xi$. Again it was Abbott who made it possible, not only co-authoring the adaptation, but arranging a backers' audition –

something he didn't need to do, to help us raise the money. He got up and said, "This is about a strike in a pajama factory," and you could see the money leaving on wings. I began then to run the backers' auditions and since I don't have the measure of his honesty I said, "The show is *Romeo and Juliet* in the Midwest." We raised all but ten percent of our budget; Abbott wrote out a check for the rest, twenty-six thousand dollars, because he said he loved the show: we were producers, and *The Pajama Game* was a hit.[4]

Over the next decade Prince produced eight shows directed by Abbott; all but one, a comedy called *Take Her, She's Mine*, were musicals. After *The Pajama Game*, *Damn Yankees*, and *New Girl in Town*, "Abbott gave us his blessing when we went off to do *West Side Story* in 1957," Prince recalls. But

5 George Abbott's peppy finale for *The Pajama Game* (1954)

Prince and Griffith returned to the Abbott fold for *Fiorello!* and *Tenderloin* (1960). After Griffith's death Prince produced *A Funny Thing Happened On the Way to the Forum* and *Flora, the Red Menace* (1965), both directed by Abbott. Aside from *West Side Story* and *Forum* (which Sondheim calls "an anti-Rodgers and Hammerstein show in which the music does not develop the plot"), the shows for the most part were in the mold of sleek musical comedy that Abbott had developed in the thirties working with Rodgers and Hart. While also indebted to the Rodgers and Hammerstein tradition each show flirts with characters and settings that anticipate Prince's later break from formula. Factory workers (*The Pajama Game*); baseball players (*Damn Yankees*); prostitutes and blue noses (*New Girl in Town* and *Tenderloin*); politicians (*Fiorello!*); communists (*Flora*); and slaves in ancient Rome (*Forum*) comprise an unusual cast of characters for a musical repertoire. While a few of the shows have political overtones – a clash between management and workers in *The Pajama Game*; politicking itself in *Fiorello!*; the infiltration of communism among the working class during the Depression in *Flora* – a reviewer's comment about *The Pajama Game* is applicable to them all: "Whose side is the show on in the battle between capital and labor? The audience's!"[5]

Abbott molded each action into variations on the formula of boy meets–loses–wins girl. In *The Pajama Game* the romance between the foreman and the shop steward overrides economic issues, and who but a humorless ideologue would complain? The strike is settled by plot contrivance rather than politics: the boss, discovered to have secretly added to his books the $7\frac{1}{2}$¢ wage hike the workers are demanding, quickly and agreeably capitulates. It isn't the system that's bad, the show cozily tells us, it's people like a greedy but reformable boss who need to be kept in line. *Fiorello!* has more sting. Two songs, "Politics and Poker" and "The Little Tin Box," take a waggish look at the machinations and masquerades, the playacting, of the political game. But the tantalizing possibilities that Fiorello might have been something of an actor himself, a wily strategist and as much of a manipulator as his opponents, are carefully avoided. Stubbornness, a quick temper, and imperviousness to an adoring secretary are the limits of his "sins." While stopping short of outright hagiography the show presents Fiorello as an American dynamo, a populist whiz kid whose political and romantic fortunes follow a regulation arc of early win, defeat at the end of Act I, climactic Act II victory.

As in *Fiorello!* politics in *Flora, the Red Menace* is merely a pretext for celebrating a character who has star quality. The message of both musicals is that charisma and drive can rout the enemy; Flora defeats communists as Fiorello triumphs over political corruption. Having been momentarily distracted by alien ideas Flora, enterprising capitalist, whisks communists from her boarding house as her tenants jubilantly serenade her. "You are you," they sing; "I am me," Flora agrees, lyrics loaded with extracurricular references to the fact that Flora was played by Liza Minnelli in her first starring role on Broadway: if Flora/Liza was herself, she was *not* Judy Garland, though in phrasing and sentiment her big second-act ballad, "Sing Happy," exploited the family connection in echoing Garland's "Get Happy" number from *Summer Stock*.

The shows rely on musical-comedy formulas to subvert their unusual and potentially inflammatory subjects – communists in *Flora*, politicos in *Fiorello!*, and capitalists in *The Pajama Game* are like the kids in *Babes in Arms*, eager to please as they pull together to put on a good show. To construct a tougher, more socially alert musical theatre Prince had to break away from Abbott's genial showshops. "Abbott has political convictions, but he won't commit his work to reflect them," Prince says. "He doesn't bring a need for issues; he doesn't want his shows to make a statement."

The Pajama Game offers a good example of the way conventional music is used to sanitize the libretto in Abbott's shows. Brimming with melody and high spirits the Richard Adler–Jerry Ross score consists of two kinds of songs, those that are dramatically integrated and the specialty and production numbers presented more or less for the fun of it. "Racing with the Clock,"

6 Brecht? No, *Fiorello!* (1959)

a rousing number that establishes factory routine, the timekeeper's comic creed "Think of the Time I Save," the climactic "$7\frac{1}{2}¢$," in which the workers celebrate their raise, and the title song characterize the play's setting while subliminally celebrating the capitalist status quo: if you don't ask for too much (only a $7\frac{1}{2}¢$ raise, after all), and you know how and when to compromise, you can get what you want (while being kept in your place). The other book numbers are carefully distributed between ballads for the romantic leads and comic songs for the secondary characters. The hero introduces himself in "A New Town is a Blue Town," a traditional "this is me" song that appears near the top of the show. The leads are given one song each — "I'm Not At All in Love" for her, "Hey There" for him — in which, in contrasting ways, they deny or express the obvious, that they have fallen for each other. Two songs chart the progress of their romance: "Small Talk" (he chastises her for evading her feelings) and "There Once was a Man (I Love You More)," a challenge song performed in a spirit of boastful competitiveness.

7 "Mister Abbott" at work on *Flora, the Red Menace* (New Haven, 1965): watching Liza Minnelli from the wings (photo courtesy of Van Williams)

"We auditioned several new teams for the show," Abbott recalls. "When Adler and Ross brought in 'Steam Heat,' they got the job, and we liked the song so much we wrote it into the show." Like the musical's other novelty number, "Hernando's Hideaway," "Steam Heat" does indeed feel "written in"; both spots provide a showcase of early Bob Fosse choreographic patterns: angular, sinuous movements in which hands and necks join legs, feet, and arms in kinetic explosions that have nothing to do with character or story development. A picnic in Act I provides the occasion for a polka, "Once A Year Day," which amplifies the show's folksy blue-collar ambience. (The "'Once-a-Year-Day' spot" has become Prince's term for "an obligatory Act I production number that the audience would feel cheated not to have.")

Whatever their level of integration the songs all function within a realistic framework. Unlike *The Pajama Game*, Prince's later musicals experiment with the ability of song and dance to enlarge and stylize a show's theme and to offer symbolic comment on character and situation, procedures likely to seem "phony" to Abbott. Clearly speaking in his author's voice, Hines the timekeeper announces to the audience at the beginning of *The Pajama Game*: "This is a very serious drama. It's kind of a problem play. It's about Capital and Labor. I wouldn't bother to make such a point of all this except later on if you happen to see a lot of naked women being chased through the woods, I don't want you to get the wrong impression. This play is full of SYMBOLISM."[6]

Abbott remembers that "the boys" had to talk him into doing *The Pajama Game* ("I didn't think a factory was a very glamorous setting") and *Fiorello!*, but *Damn Yankees*, a quintessential Abbott show, was his idea. A musical about the great American pastime, a pop variation on *Faust* in which a fan sells his soul to become the ace hitter his losing team needs but realizes in the end there's no place like home, *Damn Yankees* is as all-American as its director and co-author, himself a lifelong athlete and sports fan. Abbott's *Faust* reassures the audience that being yourself is better than being a star – if you really look you can find Oz in your own back yard – and that to win the game all you need is "Heart," the title of the show's oft-repeated hit song. The game metaphors that drive Abbott's musicals – "the pajama game is the game I'm in," announces the gung-ho timekeeper, while in *Fiorello!* politics is enshrined as a game ("Politics and Poker") that Americans are especially good at – complement Abbott's persona of the director as head coach, the captain of a team assembling shows for fun and profit.

Damn Yankees, The Pajama Game, Fiorello! are peppy shows, unpretentious popular entertainments that achieve their aims. But the kind of compromise and sentimentality that helped to make them hits is likely to be fatal if applied

8 Turning *Anna Christie* into a song-and-dance frolic, *New Girl in Town* (1957), with Gwen Verdon as the high-stepping "sunshine girl"

to material with a serious purpose. Although he usually avoided "literature," Abbott uncharacteristically turned to Eugene O'Neill's turbulent *Anna Christie* for the basis of a libretto, *New Girl in Town*, a show Hal Prince now calls "a real dumbbell musical."

"I got rid of all of O'Neill's symbolism and, rightly or wrongly, concentrated on the character," Abbott says. But is it possible to have the character without the symbolism? Abbott prunes the play's essential symbols of the "ol' devil sea" that is Chris Christopherson's antagonist, and of the obscuring fog that rolls off it, as if they were excrescences on the plot. The theme of the sea as Fate, the mystical, primordial, unknowable Force that bedevils O'Neill's characters, has been replaced in Abbott's "well-made" dramaturgy by characters in thrall to a contrived plot. The struggle in O'Neill between the characters' assertion of free will and the deterministic Fate that stalks them is reduced to the level of narrative necessity, with Marthy Owens spilling the beans about Anna's prostitute past at the Check-Apron Ball. Moving the production from 1920 to the turn of the century to "allow for more colorful costumes" and transforming Anna's private drama into a public comedy with a singing and dancing ensemble of waterfront pack rats, Abbott disemboweled his source.

Prince recalls that Bob Merrill, composer of such hit tunes as "How Much

9 Elevation in an early Prince musical, *She Loves Me* (1963) (photo courtesy of Van Williams)

is That Doggie in the Window?", "brought us a project – a movie score that he had written for an updated fifties version of *Anna Christie* to star Doris Day and Thelma Ritter. We were taken with the music and lyrics, but rejected the notion of a sympathetic prostitute on the waterfront in the fifties. Those numbers were the basis for the rest of the score which was written to a new libretto." Merrill's lyrics – "There ain't no flies on me," "Flings is wonderful things," "Roll yer socks up, fling 'em in the gear box," "The sunshine girl has raindrops in her eyes" – and the bouncy melodies that accompany them are appropriate to the hillbilly jamboree that Abbott made of *Anna Christie*.

If Abbott's anti-literary bias is characteristic, his turning a show into a double star-turn was not. Providing Gwen Verdon with irrelevant dances and Thelma Ritter with vulgar comic songs completed his travesty.[7]

West Side Story and *Fiddler On the Roof*, two non-Abbott shows Prince produced during this period, had a greater impact on the direction his own creative work would take than any of the Abbott musical comedies: both point toward the "concept" musical by which Prince was to earn his reputation. With its ghetto setting, its turbulent characters who dance their feelings, its thrusting symphonic score, "the integration and flow between song and book" (as Sondheim says) and its tragic ending, West Side Story was unmistakably a landmark musical, but the more modest-seeming Fiddler On the Roof with its family story of Tevye the milkman and his five unmarried daughters had a more pronounced influence on Prince's work. Hovering over the musical-comedy imbroglios, the romantic and familial conflicts, and ultimately tempering them, is the threat of a pogrom. The love stories as well as the rituals that bind the shtetl community are thus projected against a historical panorama that gives them special poignancy; for many of his later shows Prince has adopted Fiddler's shrewd double focus, with a sombre underlying theme boosting a conventional musical-theatre foreground.

Significantly, both West Side Story and Fiddler on the Roof were directed by Jerome Robbins, who had choreographed Abbott shows since the 1944 On the Town. Robbins introduced new kinds of subject matter, movement, production concepts, and acting styles into the musical-theatre tradition he inherited from Abbott; and in turn inspired Hal Prince, who worked on nine musicals with Robbins, to further exploration:

From Jerry I learned to look at musical-theatre form in a different way, and to allow myself to invent something I hadn't seen. Since I'm not a choreographer I haven't been as dependent on dance as Jerry (I want to shape what I do and the more I use dance the less am I in control), but from Jerry I learned that musical theatre is open to any influence, that it can borrow devices from non-musical theatre. Jerry taught me a new way of integrating music as well as the possibility of attempting serious subject matter.

Abbott admires Jerome Robbins's "objectivity" – "he threw out a ballet he worked on for Call Me Madam when he realized it didn't work, and overnight he created a new ballet; he was flexible" – and Prince says that "Jerry knew from Abbott how important discipline is." But apart from his objectivity and discipline Robbins's approach and sensibility are quite unlike those of his mentor. Where Abbott is clear and decisive, Robbins is ambivalent; where Abbott is secure, Robbins is sometimes painfully uncertain. Prince notes that "Abbott can go out of town with a show with the book unfinished and the score half done." He stages scenes quickly, and once an action is set actors are expected to follow the pattern that has been worked out without adding personal nuances. As Joanna Merlin, Prince's long-time casting director who played Tzeitl in Fiddler On the Roof, says, "Robbins is never certain until he's explored a scene every possible way and then he's still not satisfied. I auditioned at least eight times for Fiddler; we rehearsed the table-setting scene twenty-two different ways." Oliver Smith remembers that he would submit "endless numbers of sketches from which Robbins selects. Unlike George Abbott, Robbins isn't articulate; it's a question of intuition with him."[8]

Perhaps because Robbins's approach is emotional rather than intellectual he imported Method techniques of improvisation and sense memory to musical-theatre rehearsals. "The first two days of rehearsal for *Fiddler* he conducted a series of improvisations on being in a concentration camp," Prince recalls. "He created an exercise of what it would be like being black in a bookstore in the South, pre-Civil Rights. On *West Side Story*, when he felt the lovers were playing too nervously, he had them throw a rubber ball, which focused their attention on catching the ball and away from their self-awareness."

"I never absolutely believed any of the Method stuff," Prince says. "I wouldn't begin to know how to use it myself, though I have respect for anything that would solve your problems: an Abbott point of view. I found some of Jerry's exercises obfuscated, and I remember the first run-through of

10 Shades of *Bye Bye Birdie* mixed with Meyerhold in this production number ("It's Superman") from *It's a Bird . . . It's a Plane . . . It's Superman* (1966) (photo courtesy of Van Williams)

West Side Story was turgid with all this Method work. Then Jerry turned it
into a musical." Prince feels

the biggest value of the Method was to dignify the actors. Jerry got the chorus to identify
with the milieu of the Jets and the Sharks; he took a bunch of inexperienced gypsies and
gave them a sense of higher purpose. He gave them exercises which made them feel good
about themselves and connected to the play's situation. Following his example, when I
was directing *Cabaret* in 1966 I had the entire company delve into newspapers about the
surge of Fascism in the South to substantiate my claim that it *can* happen here.

Robbins's integration of the ensemble has had a lasting impact on Prince:

You try to find a unifying motivation, to get them to identify with a situation the way
Robbins did. I told the chorus in *Sweeney Todd* that this is a play about revenge and about
the inroads the Industrial Age made on the human spirit: living in a world without sun, in
polluted air, slowly but surely they are being diminished. This gave the entire company a
perspective which dignified their assignment, and they began to perform without my
having to go through a lot.

While Abbott is an easy character to draw, an American archetype,
Robbins remains enigmatic; except for Abbott, no one says Robbins is an
equable co-worker. Abrasion, conflict, temperamental eruptions seem to feed
his creativity; colleagues regularly describe him as "difficult" and "demanding." Nonetheless many Broadway veterans credit Robbins with the same
kind of theatrical inspiration they attribute to Abbott and, like the Master,
Robbins has often been called in to fix an ailing show. Both Abbott and
Stephen Sondheim credit Robbins with "saving" *A Funny Thing Happened On
the Way to the Forum* when he staged a new opening number. Robbins asked
Sondheim to write a new song to replace "Love is in the Air," which he felt
misled the audience into expecting a frivolous romantic comedy instead of a
farce. Sondheim recalls that

Jerry said I should write a baggy pants opening and told me not to indicate any
movement: "Let me do it," he said. So I wrote "Comedy Tonight," a totally neutral song, a
list song, a do-it-yourself lyric which is not interesting lyrically – it's an endless list of
adjectives . . . The new song allowed Robbins to show off, which is exactly what he did.
His staging was spectacular: it was what Jerome Robbins could do, which nobody else
before or since could equal.

"The opening ticked off what kind of show it was," Abbott says; "We were in
business."

Movement fused to the core of character and circumstance, dance conceived as dramatic action, acting that vibrates with a sense of the characters'
inner lives – Robbins introduced a new vocabulary into the musical theatre.
Galvanic and erotically charged, his dance dramas bristled with neurotic
undercurrents, modern ambivalence. Yet Robbins has not directed a musical
in twenty-five years. "Why do so many of the best people in musical theatre
leave?" Prince asks.

They get battered emotionally, and they don't want to let themselves in for more. With a new musical you're always shaping the material, and you're so susceptible to audiences and critics. Opera and ballet, in comparison, are safe; the productions have a scheduled run regardless of reviews. Unlike Broadway, they are a cloister. I stay in the commercial theatre because I have a short memory.

After *Cabaret* established his credentials as a moulder of the dark musical, Prince returned only once, with *On the Twentieth Century*, to the kind of musical in which he had trained under George Abbott. "Betty Comden and Adolph Green, who are like Abbott children, completely disciplined, supportive, and professional, brought me their finished book. After I read it I said, 'By God, this is an Abbott show!' Years ago I had done *The Matchmaker*, but I'd never done that kind of rough and tumble comedy again. I liked the challenge."

In 1932 Abbott had directed *Twentieth Century*, a play by Ben Hecht and Charles MacArthur based on an original piece by Bruce Milholland, from which Comden and Green adapted their libretto. A comedy of theatrical bad manners, *Twentieth Century* had also been made into a popular 1934 film starring John Barrymore and Carole Lombard as a down-on-his-luck impresario, Oscar Jaffe, and his former protegée Lily Garland, who has become a star of the silver screen. Fleeing from creditors after the ignominious closing of his latest fiasco, Oscar spends the play spinning a web in which to ensnare Lily while both are passengers on a train, the Twentieth Century, en route from Chicago to New York. The doors of Oscar's and Lily's adjoining rooms open and close with escalating frenzy as the two engage in a running battle of wit and invective that, like those of the sparring partners in Restoration comedy, indicates their mutual attraction.

"It was just fun," says Prince, taking time off (in 1978) from his "serious" musicals. "I wasn't troubled that the show didn't make any statement. It's the hardest show in the world to do. First, you've got to believe these people; you can't be silly, or send up the material. Then how do you stage it? How do you do a musical on a train?" Prince used his background with Abbott to sustain the show's tempo and to justify every opening and closing of a door and every element of physical comedy.

Although in story and characterization *On the Twentieth Century* represents a throwback to an older musical–comedy style, Prince and his team introduced a modernist concept in the show's surprising score. Instead of having a period flavor to match the thirties setting, Cy Coleman's score is primarily comic opera – the musical exaggeration provides a roguish comment on the overripe characters. Oscar and Lily are always on stage, consciously monitoring their performances, gauging the effects of their actions, and their lush operetta singing style becomes part of the comic

overstatement of their personas. "It would have been a terrific show if the
score had been entirely *opéra bouffe,*" Prince says. "But the musical material for
Imogene Coca [who played Letitia Primrose, a refugee from an asylum
masquerading as a philanthropist] was night club; it was musical comedy, and
not pretentious enough. Imogene was wonderful, but we should have
sacrificed her warmth and sweetness for music that had more pomp and so
was in keeping with the rest of the score."

Adding flashbacks and a dream sequence, Prince and his writers periodically opened up the show beyond the confining train setting, and a chorus of
tap-dancing porters who wove in and out of the action provided further
fluency. (Larry Fuller, the show's choreographer, recalls that "originally the
four porters weren't supposed to be dancers. Because they wanted the show
to be comic opera Comden and Green decreed that there should be no
dancing, and God forbid that there should be tap-dancing, which would be
too common!") Crisp, kinetic, extroverted, peppy – Prince consciously
directed *On the Twentieth Century* in the Abbott mold. "Except for this one
show my musicals haven't been like Abbott's. My taste is really quite
different from his. But he respects the kind of work I do – he loved *Evita,* and
said he wouldn't have known what to do with the material."

3 On the job

'"There's a danger in doing a revival of your own work, especially when it has been as imitated as this show," Prince announces to the company on the first day of rehearsals (January 26, 1987) for *Cabaret*:

You can end up being your own cliché . . . Visually our original production [which opened in November 1966] was enormously influential. At the time, we looked brand new: unless you want to count what Brecht and Weill did (they were there before us), a black box hadn't been used before in musical theatre. We also 'invented' the mirror, which we're going to use again.

Appropriately, since he has to see "what a show looks like before I can begin to direct – for me, set design is a form of co-authorship," Prince begins the first rehearsal by showing the company a model of the set. In what is clearly a carefully prepared puppet show Prince, with the help of David Chapman, who has adapted the late Boris Aronson's original designs, moves miniature set pieces on and off the model stage as he guides the company through the play, explaining how scene changes, lighting, and *mise-en-scène* help to define the mood and meaning of *Cabaret*.

Next Prince introduces his costume designer, Patricia Zipprodt, who is recreating her original assignment. As she holds up her sketches for the Kit Kat Klub performers she says, "The costumes are trashy. It's a trashy show." (Trashy, yes, as cut-rate Las Vegas glitter collides with German Expressionism.)

After the cast has seen the environment in which they are to be placed and how they are going to be dressed, Prince offers them another visual stimulus when he shows them an enlarged photograph of a group of disheveled protesters. "I brought in this photo on the first day of rehearsal twenty-one years ago," he says;

I asked the cast to identify where and when the photo was taken, and everyone naturally assumed it was Berlin in the early thirties because that's the time and place of our show. They were surprised when I said it was taken in Little Rock, Arkansas, in the mid-fifties: these aren't Hitler Youth but blond white kids snarling at black kids entering an integrated school, an image that is still relevant today, unfortunately. We've come a long way since 1966, and since 1930 too for that matter, but human nature doesn't change; what happened in Berlin at the time of *Cabaret* can happen here, and that's why the mirror is our metaphor.

Yesterday as I was walking up Central Park West in the snow, I saw a man on a bench huddling among his bundles, and I looked the other way. In Germany, in the thirties and

40

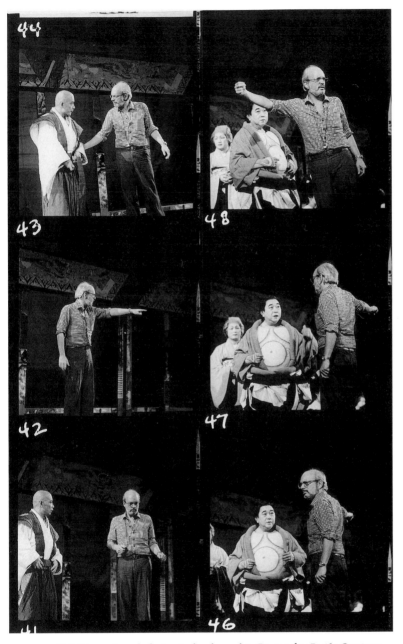

11 Hal Prince at work during tech rehearsal in Boston for *Pacific Overtures* (November 1975) (photos courtesy of Van Williams)

12 "We invented the mirror!": "framing" the audience in *Cabaret* (1966)
(photo courtesy of Van Williams)

forties, some people say they knew what was happening and looked the other way; others insist they didn't know what was going on. Judy [Prince's wife] and I were in Berlin recently, which hasn't changed much since Isherwood's description of it in *Berlin Stories*, and what happened to Germany under Hitler is still constantly talked about, which indicates palpable guilt. The question the play asks is, "What would you do?" This is a show about survival and about how most people unheroically look the other way in order to survive.

Outlining the curve he wants the show to have, Prince explains that

there's a trap in *Cabaret*. If you have Nazis on stage right at the start, as in the recent London revival and in the film, where is your trajectory? In Act 1 I want to indicate that these are people trying to have a good time; they're coping. I want to show that "just folks" became Nazis: I like the character of Fräulein Kost [the prostitute who boards at Fräulein Schneider's rooming house]; she's a fun-loving woman who got caught up in the Nazi groundswell because it brought her money and nice clothes – and there she was.

"We want dimensional, rounded characters," Prince warns. "In *West Side Story* we had a less experienced company than you, and Jerry Robbins got them to immerse themselves in the world of the rival gangs. Exactly that kind of identification is needed here too." He ends by reminding the company that "musical theatre is some of the best theatre we do in this country." When former opera diva Regina Resnik (cast in Lotte Lenya's role as Fräulein Schneider) laughs good-naturedly at his statement, Prince says that he has been working for years "to break down the barriers between opera and musical theatre – I was proud to see recently that in Sweden *Fiddler on the Roof* was at the Opera House – and if you don't believe in that, what are you doing here?"

Running true to form in his opening ceremonies today, Prince communicates a charged enthusiasm for the work ahead as he defines his visual and thematic concepts for the show. In his quick, high-pressure delivery, pride mingles with excitement, tension is cut by quips (as in his aside about how "remarkably unchanged" he and his collaborators all look twenty-one years later). Although he is not producing the show as he did in 1966, there is no doubt of who is in charge.

What follows here is a series of snapshots of Prince at work on *Cabaret*, from early rehearsals through final tech and the day after the show's first public peformance in Wilmington, Delaware, on February 26, 1987. Set in Berlin in 1929–1930, a city on the edge of nightmare, the action moves back and forth between two locations, Fräulein Schneider's rooming house and the Kit Kat Klub, as in traditional musical-theatre style it dramatizes two contrasting romances, in themselves non-traditional, between an American writer Clifford Bradshaw and British cabaret singer Sally Bowles, and between Fräulein Schneider and her beau Herr Schultz. Both affairs are doomed by the political catastrophe that overtakes Berlin.

The scene being rehearsed today (January 27) occurs early in the first act when Sally Bowles arrives unexpectedly at Clifford Bradshaw's boarding house asking to become his roommate. First, seated around a prop table, the actors – Alyson Reed as Sally, Gregg Edelman as Cliff, Regina Resnik as Fräulein Schneider, David Staller as Ernst, a young German of ambivalent sexuality whose Nazi affiliations are not revealed until a party scene at the end of the act – read through the scene. A free-for-all discussion follows in which the actors clearly feel entitled to offer their own ideas and to explore questions of action, motive, and subtext. A good talker, Prince also knows how to listen, and he has created a charged yet casual atmosphere which makes his performers feel that their problems can be examined.

"O.K., gang, now let's get up and do it," Prince says briskly. The scene begins with Clifford giving Ernst an English lesson. "You're already being a

Nazi," Prince tells David Staller, "so there won't be any surprise. You're giving the show away. Don't be so sinister; that comes later. Downplay the anger; make the English lesson start more casually and intimately. And remember, sexual attraction to Cliff underlies everything you say."

The lesson is interrupted by Fräulein Schneider announcing a visitor. "Sally should be behind the door at first, so her entrance is a surprise," Prince says. "When she comes in, and in fact throughout the scene, there should be an undertone of hysteria. Max [the man Sally has been living with] has thrown her out, but she's a survivor so there's bravado. But underneath, remember, she is fragile; we're building to the end, when she cries, which we've never done with the character before."

Sally's main action in the scene is to make prairie oysters, her favorite drink, and Prince spends much of the rehearsal in plotting a sequence of logical behavior. "Joe [Masteroff, the librettist] wants Sally to have a shopping bag from which she takes the eggs," Prince says, "but I don't think so. I want you to take the eggs out of your coat – they're something you always have with you, so you can whip up prairie oysters whenever you want to. The audience will love you when you take the eggs out of your coat. Don't look at Cliff as you're making the drink, just babble on: don't divide your focus." When Alyson Reed asks if she will really have to drink the concoction she's making Prince promises that he will drink it first to check for poison. ("When I directed *Turandot* in Vienna the entire company refused to walk on the set [a huge staircase almost as high as the proscenium], so I ran up the stairs, jumping up and down, to test their safety.") Without warning, Sally asks Cliff if he is homosexual. "You move away from her," Prince says, getting up and demonstrating.

When the characters start to sing "Perfectly Marvelous," a song that celebrates their kooky budding romance, Prince is careful to treat the music as a continuation of the action. "Make the singing more intimate and casual," he tells both his actors. To bind the song to the scene he gives both characters a series of actions, placing Sally at the desk pretending to type as Cliff defensively grabs his typewriter away from her. "You're surprised she's gotten through to you so soon, so it's all right not to look at her and to face front. Cheat a little, move downstage further so it's not all bunched up.

"O.K., guys, let's run it again so it begins to have a flow."   ⸱ ⸱

"Lay it on when you say *Frau* Bradshaw – like this," Prince demonstrates for Regina Resnik, his tone brimming with irony. "Don't pause there"; "put the coat down on that line"; "'reply' isn't a word people use in conversation, so don't underline it, toss it off conversationally"; "hold out your hands like that, to show Sally's green nails": Prince's instructions are filled with directives about gestures, emphasis, timing. The actors let him get away with line readings because, like Abbott, he has achieved a preeminence that may well be intimidating, especially to young actors, though it may be that his commands go unchallenged because as he demonstrates what he wants he becomes something of a delightful ham, defining a movement or articulating a line with surprising panache. Also Prince builds up a reserve of good will because he never tells actors what to do when work on a scene begins – his orders seem to issue from spontaneous problem-solving as he literally thinks on his feet. As he moves through the actions of a scene, standing in for each of the actors, handling props, exploring the space, he seems to receive cues from his body. Though the process might seem mystical, with Prince it is entirely pragmatic, a way of insuring both the logic and the rhythm of the scene.

That he does not bring a pre-determined *mise-en-scène* to rehearsal is especially notable here, since he is staging a revival. His assistant director and long-time associate Ruth Mitchell has the original prompt-book and refers to it when they hit a snag, when something about the set or a prop or the way the actors are placed is puzzling, but Prince seems to be approaching the material as if for the first time. Later he's to encounter problems with Joel Grey, recreating his original role of the Master of Ceremonies, whose statement of "As I remember, twenty-one years ago we..." becomes a refrain. "You *can't* remember exactly what you did twenty-one years ago," Prince says, as his own fresh, on-the-spot directorial choices bypass the pitfalls of reconstruction.

Today (January 30) Prince is staging a climactic scene between the older lovers at the beginning of Act ii. Fräulein Schneider comes to the fruit shop of Herr Schultz (Werner Klemperer) to break off their engagement. The scene bristles with unspoken tensions, a rumbling subtext, as Fräulein Schneider works up the nerve to say what she feels must be said while Herr Schultz tries to conceal his mounting apprehension under a cheerful facade that begins to crumble. Prince's main objective, it becomes clear, is to protect the scene from the pathos and sentimentality that both actors keep edging toward. "Don't make it just pity," he tells Resnik. "Fräulein Schneider has a healthy sense of irony, so work on making her crusty; I know I'm asking the right person for 'crusty.'"

Typically, Prince walks through the scene to feel for himself the characters' physical responses to each other. "The reason Schultz moves upstage when she says something has changed is to pretend that nothing has changed"; "you shouldn't be next to her when she says, 'But if I fall'"; "take it a few steps over, darling, so we don't play center – I have to take everything off center." "Peel her an orange as you are singing to her," he tells Herr Schultz. "When you sing, you're getting somewhere with her, you're beginning to persuade her, she's bending: maybe she won't break off the engagement. So you have to be more aware of her. This is the one moment we think he's persuaded her."

"*Dismiss*, darling," Prince chides Resnik. "That's the key word here, don't throw it away." A line reading by Prince follows, accent properly placed: "I saw we can no longer *dismiss* the Nazis."

A sudden act of violence – young Nazis throw bricks through the Jewish proprietor's shop window – disrupts the courtship. (The upstage action, seen in deep focus through the shop window, is the first time in the show that the Nazi menace directly invades the characters' lives.) Prince plots the movement of the crowd. "Let me filter in about three more people before the guys break the window. Watch the boys, you act as if you aren't there," he tells one of the onlookers milling outside the window. "Watch the boys, you see they are up to something. The boys should be jolly in their mischief, and after they hurl the bricks they should move up to the door, to challenge Schultz when he opens it." Prince takes the crowd through their action several times, until it begins to look real to him. "You can't look like extras; a little drama is unfolding behind the windows and I have to believe it."

"Hey, guys, do it from the top of the scene; let's go back and get this far. You'll do it perfectly this time."

This afternoon (February 9) Prince is staging a song, "What Would You Do?", which he feels contains the kernel of the show's message. The young lovers are arguing – Sally wants to return to the Kit Kat Klub, Cliff is increasingly angered by her obliviousness to politics – as Fräulein Schneider enters to announce her broken engagement. She has come to return the fruit bowl that was their engagement present to her. "As you sing," he tells Fräulein Schneider,

you have to divide your attention between your innermost self and the two young people. Take it right inside, yes, that's terrific! Remember that in the song you are *provoking* these youngsters who don't understand.

Cliff, you should walk away, almost involuntarily, when she sings, "What would you do, my brave young friend?" It's a hard message for a young person. Keep your hand on the fruit bowl, Regina. You're right not to move to him here. Move up slowly on him at the end of the song. "Go on, tell me, I will listen, what would you do if you were me?"

In the song when she says she's not at war with anyone – "*not anyone!*" – it's Joan of Arc. Say it loud, don't sing it. At the end of the song, confront Cliff once again: impale him! *Make* him move downstage away from you.

What's important here is what's going on in the room: relationships make a difference.

Now let's motivate her exit. Wait a few beats before speaking, then turn upstage: start the speech with your back to the audience, then when you feel it, turn on him: "What other choice have I?" When she says she regrets returning the fruit bowl she turns to Sally because she figures that this is something dimwitted Sally can understand. [Prince goes over to hug Alyson Reed as he says this.] Then take a pause before her final line, "I regret everything." Get rid of any sentiment on "I regret everything." There's no self-pity here. It's strong, it's a fact! (She's wrong, you know. If she went off with Schultz, if they just got up and left Germany, they'd have a life. They're both very resourceful. Ninety-eight percent of people would do what she did, and they're wrong. They know it's the easy way out and they'll pay for it.)

Resnik is having trouble with the speech; her timing is off and she keeps looking nervously to Prince. "You're trying to get it too much from me," he says, cutting the cord. "I don't care what you do as long as you *feel* it."

"Good! You felt something there," he says when in one of the run-throughs she releases her focus on him and begins to play the scene.

In the day's final run-through Resnik performs the song beautifully, observing her character's relationships to Sally and to Cliff, and to the fruit bowl, yet endowing her movements with an inner life. Rather than seeming like an actress obeying the commands of her director she creates a strong illusion of Fräulein Schneider's defeat. "That's heartbreaking, darling! Terrific! Let's leave it alone now," Prince says, visibly moved.

This morning (February 15) the scene is the charged final encounter between Sally and Cliff that precipitates Sally's return to the cabaret and Cliff's departure for America. "Everything Cliff says makes perfect moral sense; everything Sally says makes perfect emotional sense: that's what I love about a good scene like this." For Prince again it is the conflict on a personal level that embodies the political realities; the psychological subtext is always the starting point. "Cliff, make it impossibly difficult for her to be seductive. Sally, ride over each one of his roadblocks: his position is so clear and negative. Try to break down his wall. She's ready to fight in this scene; for Sally the goal is 'I've got to get out of here.'"

Prince wants both actors to explore the feelings, the web of entangled, ambivalent emotions, that underlie the words:

Cliff's words say one thing – when he tells Sally to face up to what's happening in Berlin – but his actions say another. There is a side of Cliff that doesn't want to face reality, and when you play that the scene has some energy. Sally has bravado on the surface but she's a trembling thread underneath: she's just had an abortion and she's shaky. She's on the edge of hysteria, very close to a scream.

Prince cautions Alyson Reed not to play for sentimentality. "Don't feel so sorry for yourself; I'm not going to feel so sorry for you if you do."

Like giving line readings, the kind of textual analysis Prince offers today – his examination of motives, of the characters' hidden agendas, of the contradictions between words and feelings, between actions and intentions – may correspond to the cliché image of the autocratic director as puppet master. However, while his work is grounded in practical matters – attention to props, the stage picture, spatial relationships, beats and tempo – one senses that Prince brings to rehearsals the results not only of a close literary analysis of the play but of the ways in which the material is important to him on a personal level. Becoming impassioned about the characters and the dark history that overwhelms them, he makes the kinds of connections to the material that he encourages in his actors.

Characteristically the break for the actors is only a change of pace for Prince, conferring quickly with Ruth Mitchell before going to the phone. At the moment (February 1987) Prince is juggling two other productions, *Roza* and *The Phantom of the Opera*, while also laying the groundwork for a theatre of his own to open in Astoria (a project that did not work out). As he makes a good half-dozen calls during the fifteen-minute break, Prince is in constant movement, pacing and gesticulating – a high-powered Broadway wheeler-dealer at accelerated speed.

I've been surprised that three weeks into the rehearsal period Prince has yet to work with Joel Grey. That the director and his star appear not to be crossing paths is a peculiarity not only of *Cabaret*'s structure but of the piecemeal way that musicals are assembled. As director Prince is in charge of the book scenes, while in a separate room choreographer Ron Field and his assistant Bonnie Walker work with the ensemble on production numbers. It is only later in the rehearsal schedule that Prince looks at the choreography; since he is not a choreographer he must rely on Field's expertise, and the split of responsibilities can (and has) led to temperamental clashes: Prince fired Field from *Merrily We Roll Along* (1981), though they appear to be on good terms now.

Joel Grey's numbers are the best part of the show, and that Field rather than Prince is working with Grey would seem to dim the director's luster. But like everyone else Field is working according to Prince's master plan. When Field shows Prince the dance numbers, Prince responds as he has in the book rehearsals, treating musical staging as an inherent part of the dramatic fabric. (As actress Mary-Lou Rosato says, "Hal works to keep the *play* as the centrifugal force; he won't allow the audience to relax into the atmosphere of musical comedy. He's true to the heart of classic theatre while not forsaking the traditions of musical comedy.") "The sense of challenge in the cabaret dance doesn't read," Prince says, asking for more work on a thematic through line so that dance becomes part of the action rather than a *divertissement*.

The final technical rehearsal in Wilmington (February 25): the heat is on. Prince wears a whistle, which he blows whenever the show needs to be stopped. Moving from one side of the house to the other to test sound levels and sight lines, Prince is wired. Lyrics that can't be heard; an overbearing orchestra; lighting that doesn't have the right atmospheric effects; a set change that isn't fast enough; costume touches that don't work ("I don't like the hats in the 'Two Ladies' number; tomorrow night: no hats!") – Prince is a vigilant and impatient trouble-shooter, demanding immediate adjustments. Working on the "button" for "Tomorrow Belongs to Me," an *a capella* song that begins innocently but builds into a hymn to the Nazi youth movement, Prince says, "I want a count of four followed by a black-out. I want the singers to disappear into *total* blackness: that's the point. Then we have the blinder lights, which have to blind; that's why they're called blinders." The "button" is rehearsed time and again, until the absolute precision Prince demands has been achieved. When the timing is finally mastered – the song ends, the actors turn upstage into a black abyss as the blinders at the foot of the stage light up – the moment is a startling visual premonition of the darkness that is to envelop Germany.

A difficult scene, in which two doors must open and close in exact counterpoint, is also done many times, until Prince is satisfied. "There's no scene here if the timing is even a fraction off!" Whenever a cue is missed, Prince blows his whistle.

Moving about the house for short intense conferences with writers, musicians, lighting technicians, and Ruth Mitchell, Prince is edgy and mercurial, a study in volatility. His explosions are brief, often followed by a hug, and never personal. "I'm reasonably well-liked on the job," Prince says, and indeed being well-liked is clearly important to him. "Let's go, gang!" "Great, guys! Terrific!" His sports-coach lingo creates a democratic spirit in which the captain and his players are united by an exhilarating common aim.

If Prince has a short fuse when something goes wrong he is equally quick to offer praise for a job well done. "It was sensational, guys," he says at the first post-opening rehearsal. "I love the show more now than I did twenty-one years ago: it's fleshier, it has more substance, and it was nice to see some real life in the group scenes. This hasn't felt like a revival." The cast applauds – Prince's enthusiasm is a reward worth working hard for.

The kind of bond that Prince establishes with his actors is apparent in a post-opening party he hosts in his suite. The evening shifts from manic post-performance excitement to a mood of true confessions. Alyson Reed talks about her depression following the disappointing reviews for the film version of *A Chorus Line*, in which she starred as Cassie. "I came back from Los Angeles feeling depleted, to find a fan letter from Hal about how much he enjoyed my work in the film; I burst into tears." Nora Mae Lyng (Fräulein Kost) mentions how Prince's backstage praise three years ago after he had seen her in a performance of *Forbidden Broadway* "changed my life. It kept me going all through a difficult time." (Prince blushes.) Prince tells Gregg

Edelman that his work "reminds me of my favorite actor, James Stewart: you have that same quality of simplicity and honesty."

It is obvious that Prince has become something of a father for the younger actors, all of whom are a little awed by the chance he has given them. Prince responds with candid personal comments:

> I can make a connection between my early "success" and my nervous breakdown at fourteen. I didn't sleep for three months; I wandered the streets muttering to myself, often carrying on imaginary conversations with theatre people whom I pretended I knew and worked with . . . out of that breakdown I created the person I wanted to become; by the time I was twenty, I'd begun to meet the people I'd conjured up at fourteen. Imagine being in the same room with Richard Rodgers and Oscar Hammerstein, Irving Berlin, Moss Hart, Sidney Kingsley, Lindsay and Crouse — and George Abbott.

On November 3, 1986, less than a month after *The Phantom of the Opera* has opened in London, Prince begins rehearsals for *Roza*, a new musical with a score by Gilbert Bécaud and book and lyrics by Julian More. As with *Cabaret* and *Phantom*, Prince prefers the more limited role of a director, because of its responsibility for what he sees as the creative core — the acted scene and the dramatic integration of the musical and choreographed elements — to the economic control of the producer. After a series of Broadway failures, he is relieved to be developing a musical for a non-profit regional theatre (*Roza* opens on December 16 at Baltimore's Center Stage). "Broadway gets bleaker and bleaker," Prince says, "and so I'm happy working on a show that I'm *not* thinking of in terms of Broadway." However, his backers, the Producers Circle, clearly had Broadway in mind — and indeed *Roza* did finally open on Broadway on October 1, 1987. Even in the early days of the project Prince said that developing *Roza* in the regional theatre made good economic sense in Broadway terms. "We're doing *Roza* in Baltimore for $500,000; we could open on Broadway for one million dollars, or for a million and a half, which shaves off several million if we had gone direct to Broadway." As he and his Broadway team left for Baltimore, Prince asked, "What is so obscene about the marriage of the commercial and not-for-profit theatre?"

"It's taken us nearly five years getting here," Prince announces to his company on the first day of rehearsals. Typically, throughout the long gestation period, Prince has worked closely with the show's writers. When Gilbert Bécaud originally approached Prince with the idea of doing a musical based on Romain Gary's novel, *La Vie devant soi*, which had been the basis of a film, *Madame Rosa*, starring Simone Signoret, about a former prostitute who runs a house for the children of prostitutes, Prince had said no. "I hated the movie, which I thought was sentimental and negative." But Bécaud, who had loved *Sweeney Todd*, was determined to arouse the director's interest, and Prince finally agreed on condition that he select the librettist who would also write the lyrics (Julian More).

At Prince's suggestion More wrote a first draft that mixed past and present time frames. "But it was clear that it was pretentious," More says. A second Prince concept, to do the show as a serious play in a *Folies Bergère* style, also didn't work. "We decided then to do it directly, without any frame," More says:

It was the best way of treating the material. I also had to get rid of the literary conceits that are part of Gary's novel, which is superb, a *literary* masterpiece, told by Momo [the boy who becomes Roza's favorite, a surrogate son] in the first person. I simply had to throw out the whole concept of the book and tell Momo's story simply and directly.

At each step in their progress Bécaud and More brought their work to Prince, who took a central role in shaping the final script. As More notes,

Hal helped me to find the arc of the story: in Act I, Roza takes care of Momo, while in Act II their roles are reversed. Hal has musical ideas too. At first "Don't Make Me Laugh" [a duet sung by Roza and Lola, a transsexual prostitute who lives in Roza's apartment building] was slow; he said that was wrong, it should be bright. We had a terrific row over Momo's song, "Life is Ahead of Me." Our original English producers [the show was to have been done in London with Angela Lansbury but the producers couldn't raise the money] thought it was a hit, but Hal doesn't care about having hit songs in his shows; talk to Kander and Ebb about "Cabaret". At one point he threatened to leave the show if we didn't take out the song, which he thought was just too sentimental. But we changed its place, from the end of Act I to early in Act II, where it becomes more aggressive and more real: the future *is* ahead of him now.

Once he has agreed to direct *Roza*, Prince begins to collaborate on the set design. "I get rhythm out of the way a show looks, and my failures have usually been when I haven't known what a show should look like," he says. Five months before the first day of rehearsals, Prince calls a meeting to introduce his designer, Alexander Okun, and Okun's model of the set to key members of his *Roza* production team, lighting designer Ken Billington, choreographer Pat Birch, and Georgia Brown, his star. "I asked for the impossible," Prince says, "and I got it." On a sharp slant Okun has constructed the set of the apartment house where Roza lives; in addition to Roza's apartment the set contains parts of the apartments of four of her neighbors connected by a serpentine stairway that winds and curves, rises and falls, from one side of the model to the other. "It looks like a print by Escher, doesn't it?" Prince crows. "That comes from the illusion that's created of the stairs going down as they go up. Most of the action, in Roza's room, is to be played three flights up, and yet that room is lower than the other apartments which are actually on lower floors." Okun's dazzling set is a visual trick that typifies Prince's love of illusion, making the audience see something that actually isn't there.

At the first cast meeting Prince makes his traditional opening comments, explaining how the project has evolved and why they are doing it:

13 Alexander Okun's "Escher" set for *Roza* (1987) (photo courtesy of Van Williams)

This show is about a community, the people who live in this crazy house. My image is Saroyan: odd people in an odd house, all "virgins," all innocent. Gilbert took me to Belleville [the section of Paris where the play is set]; during the day you see Jews, North Africans, Arabs all living together in loud and energetic harmony, in the spirit of our show, and at night there's a blend of different kinds of ethnic music. We've lost a sense of community and family as we isolate ourselves in front of our televisions, and this show illustrates what we've lost. Your job is to establish a sense of camaraderie, and you're here because we sensed it would be easy for you. Slick I'm not looking for; joyful is what I want. The show's spirit is informal and congenial.

After the reading Prince is unsettled. "Hearing the show today I can see where I disagree with the authors," he tells me. "This was Gilbert's last performance of his songs, and his tempi were too slow, and there's too much underscoring; I can't even tell where the scenes are. Gilbert performs the songs so sentimentally, which goes right against my grain."

At the final technical rehearsal in Baltimore, Prince uses his whistle frequently. Bécaud's appealing score, a mélange of European disco and North African rhythms, is presenting acoustical problems as a synthesizer and amplification threaten to overwhelm lyrics and dialogue. "This is a show, not a rock concert," Prince warns his sound designer. And because the cast includes several children with scant stage experience Prince delivers impromptu lessons in diction and projection: "'Reward' has a 'd' on the end; I want to hear it"; "'People' has two syllables."

His directions consistently emphasize physical detail and an anti-sentimental note that counteracts the show's moist qualities:

You can cheat on that line: look front when you say "some day" – and say it bitter.

Lola's dress has to go. It's too Jean Harlow. And Lola needs a bigger hat.

The make-up for Roza in Act II makes her look cute, when she should look like death.

The pinspot on Roza in the opening is pompous. I hate it. It looks like what I would do: people will say, "Oh, another dark Hal Prince musical," when that isn't the show. Let's make the lighting there more real.

That move looks phony.

Roza, keep moving during the song; wash the little boy as you sing, so that we have a continuing reality.

At a production meeting the morning after the first preview Prince is prepared to make major changes in script and action, again concentrating on maintaining a harder edge:

The opening number ["The World is Full of Crazy People,"] is embarrassing, a musical comedy introduction for a show that isn't *Guys and Dolls*. [It is cut completely.] The characters are introduced like a regulation chorus; it's all too frivolous, wrong for the tone of the show.

The dialogue between the Katzes at the beginning sounds like leftovers from *Fiddler*: it has to go.

We have to cut Roza's first journey down to the basement; the audience doesn't know what's going on.

"Live a Little" [Roza's death-bed song in which she passes on her philosophy of life to Momo] is gooey, and how many times does she need to sing it, for Christ's sake!

At the end of the Baltimore run another production meeting pinpoints adjustments that will be needed before transferring the show to Broadway. The most notable aspect of Prince's comments is his sensitivity to flaws in the structure of the show and his accuracy in predicting critical reactions.

In New York we're going to get our heads handed to us if we have a black character who's a pimp and a drug dealer. We need to rethink the character. [N'da became Raoul, a black bargain-basement travel agent.]

We need to know what every single character in Roza's building does. We need to flesh out all the supporting characters; all it takes is a few lines. [New York critics unanimously complained about the undeveloped ensemble.]

I have to keep the trajectory in mind: does the show have too much Abbott shorthand? Should some points be repeated, for clarity? [Critics commented on the lack of a narrative through-line.]

"Life is Ahead of Me" is a pop lyric imposed on the show. We need to enrich the lyrics, make them more personal, less rock and roll. You don't want to read reviews about a Bobby Darin lyric.

Other changes accent "a limboesque, fairy-tale quality" by subtle alterations in costume, setting the action back a decade to the early 1970s, and show Prince's consistent commitment to the dramatic justification of musical elements.

You need the burst of a production number in each act, but we have problems with both production numbers. The party in Act I is our "Once a Year Day" spot, but right now we have a party without a full scene: we need to add about ten more lines. In Act II we need a better cue into the voodoo number [in which the neighbors, led by Lola, try to cast a spell that will restore Roza's health]. I'm embarrassed by the voodoo, but I think if we focus on Lola then we protect ourselves. [Prince's solution was to end the number comically, with Roza awaking from her faint to ask what all the nonsense is about.]

In Act I Momo searches for his mother; in Act II, when he finds out his father killed his mother, the boy doesn't react. It's dangerous to have a dramatic scene at this point but we have to do more with it, though I want to avoid Momo crying, "You killed my mother!"

The show's ending arouses heated debate. After Roza dies in her basement hideaway Momo returns to the apartment, where Lola is waiting for him. As Momo starts to light a cigarette, Lola, his "new" mother, takes it away from him. "That's a curtain!" Prince says, while Julian More argues that "there's no rite of passage. The boy is stuck with another fucking mother." (Prince's instinct for the theatrical moment prevails.)

Part of Prince's reluctance from the beginning has been his feeling that his directorial values are antithetical to the "lifegiving, extemporaneous, joyful quality" of a basically conventional, inherently sentimental star-vehicle like *Roza*, which requires "pulling on heart strings, small responses – I haven't done a musical like this since *She Loves Me*." His uncertainty about the show's Broadway prospects were all too justified. Although business and audience response in Baltimore were strong and regional reception in Los Angeles – where the show ran for a healthy nine weeks – was equally encouraging, in New York *Roza* opened to a chorus of hostile reviews and closed after twelve performances.[1]

Interviews with some of his colleagues confirmed my own responses watching Prince at work on *Cabaret* and *Roza*. What follows is a composite portrait of how his co-workers react to Prince on the job, at auditions, pre-production conferences, rehearsals, and post-opening pep talks.

Joanna Merlin, Prince's casting director from 1970 to 1985, recalls that

"Hal phoned me out of the blue with what he said was 'a crazy idea.' 'How would you like to be a casting director?' he asked me. He was operating on instinct, which is how he casts: 'I chose you because you're a Jewish mother who likes actors,' he told me. He was right." Choosing a "Jewish mother" like Merlin helped Prince set a tone for his auditions, widely known for their friendliness. "Hal shows a respect actors aren't used to," Merlin says; "he has much respect for talent, and he is so gracious, that we would get calls from agents whose clients felt they had gotten the role because Hal had been so enthusiastic."

"He makes you feel good even if you don't get the part," says Dorothy Collins. "When I auditioned for *She Loves Me*, Hal jumped over chairs to tell me I was the most vulnerable person he had ever seen on stage. And when, seven years later, I auditioned for *Follies*, he jumped over chairs again. This time I got the part!"

"Hal auditions everyone, including stars, for his shows," Merlin reports. Although some of his musicals have had big-name performers none of them (with the exception of *Roza*) qualifies as a vehicle. "Hal and Steve were the stars," Merlin says, "and so they didn't need any others. Most directors aren't involved in the total concept of a show as Hal is, and he isn't willing to relinquish control to a star." The only time Prince has had problems with actors has been with such well-known performers as Madeline Kahn in *On the Twentieth Century* and Ben Vereen in *Grind*: "Actually, when I cast her, I thought Madeline Kahn was Bernadette Peters," Prince says;

I had gotten the two of them mixed up. At any rate Kahn gave a terrific performance opening night and the audience gave her a standing ovation. When I went backstage she said, "You don't expect me to do that every night, do you?" and I knew we were dead. She didn't have the stamina, and I've always thought she ruined our chances for a long run.

Remembering his conflicts on *Grind*, Prince snaps that he isn't in business "to construct vehicles for Ben Vereen."

Like George Abbott, Prince has always preferred taking a chance on newcomers rather than relying on established personalities with presumed box-office appeal. "He could have gotten a television name to play Nora [in *A Doll's Life*] but he picked me because he thought I was the best one for the job," says Betsy Joslyn. "No one but Hal Prince would take a chance on an unknown kid like me," says Maureen Brennan, a college junior from Ohio when Prince cast her as Cunégonde in his 1973 revival of *Candide*. "At the time I'd never even seen a Broadway play! But he saw an essence in me that he wanted for the part."

Once he makes his choice Prince maintains his belief in the performer's ability to play the role. Except for the original lead in *Merrily We Roll Along*, an actor without any professional experience, and Mary Ure in *Love for Love*, replaced by Glenn Close, Prince has never fired anyone. "My reviews when *Evita* opened in Los Angeles were disastrous," recalls Patti LuPone. "They said I was the reason the show was a failure. The producers wanted to fire me, but Hal wouldn't let them. I was paralyzed with fear, but he told me I had whatever it took to play the part."

Having evolved his concept for a show over a period of months and sometimes years before the first day of auditions Prince knows what he is looking for; as with Maureen Brennan, he casts on "essence", relying on his instincts about an actor's ability to fulfill his vision of the material. "Casting is seventy-five percent of the director's job," says Len Cariou, who worked for Prince in *A Little Night Music* and *Sweeney Todd*, "and I think the secret to his success is to cast very strongly."

Choosing actors who match his concepts is a form of protection for Prince, who says he knows very little about acting technique. He allows actors to bring in their own choices, which he then edits. "He always knew the moment something was wrong," says Dorothy Collins. "When he told me he trusted my instincts I felt freed, and because of that I was the best I could be. He's a wonderful listener, and you can bend his ear. Ego doesn't get in the way with him — I had an opposite idea from him for one scene, and he said to go ahead and try it." "He knows exactly what he wants but he'll let you do it your way," the late Hermione Gingold told me:

He left me alone because he saw I was right for the part [of Madame Armfeldt in *A Little Night Music*]. I can't really imagine anyone else playing that part, can you? I thought he'd be slick, this famous Broadway showman. But he isn't; he's very gentle with his actors — he yells at his crew but never at actors. I don't know if it's good for the actors to have someone as nice as Hal, who's a darling. He's the exact opposite of Stephen Sondheim, who also knows what he wants but doesn't ask nicely. I'd dry up in front of him, as I used to do in front of Noël Coward.[2]

"Hal doesn't stifle your creative contribution," says June Havoc, who was reluctant to accept the role of Mrs. Lovett in *Sweeney Todd* because she thought she would have to imitate Angela Lansbury. "But Hal chose me because he wanted *me*. If I was doing something unusual, and he liked it, I got to keep it. He's very open and brash with you and you don't have to be polite with him."

"He gives you his whole concept and expects you to work it out," says Barbara Baxley, a Method-trained actress directed by Prince early in his career, in *She Loves Me*.

Unlike Elia Kazan, who could be a teacher, a therapist — whatever the actor needed — Hal expects you to be a grown-up. He doesn't want to hear about the actor's personal problems in working out a character; he just wants you to get up and do it, and he'll tell you when you haven't found the right way. With Hal it's rotten or it's great, and he lets you know.

"You don't personalize as much with Hal as with a Method director," says June Havoc, a long-time member of the Actors Studio. "He's less analytical, more external, than the Method folks. He'll give you a line reading, he gives you pieces of business. There's more *doing* with Hal, less talking." "The so-called Method actors would have problems with Hal's fast-paced rhythm," Joanna Merlin recalls. "Hal needs to hear what the play sounds like, and to see what it looks like, so he gets everybody up on their feet and stages it quickly." "He wanted us off book fast," says Maureen Brennan. "He'd block a scene and then he'd expect it to be memorized." "Once a scene is set, he's pissed if you ever change it afterward," Barbara Baxley says.

Prince's drive and enthusiasm galvanize his actors. "You work to please him," says Lonny Price (*Merrily We Roll Along*), "because when you do it the way he wants it, when you hit it, his face lights up. He's like a kid with a new toy." "When I worked out an exit I was having trouble with – 'I want it high,' he told me – Hal hit the ceiling he was so happy," Barbara Baxley remembers. "His reaction made up for all my worry-warting."

Despite his reputation as a director of icy musicals, and his own distaste for sentimentality, Prince himself, as Dorothy Collins says, "is the antithesis of cold and impersonal." "He is manic-depressive every thirty seconds, with tears followed by laughter," says librettist Joe Masteroff. "I used to think it was phony; I don't anymore." "Hal is very emotional, though he often manages to hide it," Joanna Merlin says, while Ann Morrison, who played the female lead in *Merrily We Roll Along*, says that "he is a real feeler; he would often say, 'this doesn't *feel* right.'" "Hal's direction has a spiritual quality that comes out of a rather strange naiveté," June Havoc observes. "I think he is an innocent who goes his way through life and art with a glow you can't help but feel and that makes you blossom."

Prince's responsiveness to actors is part of his general pattern of making colleagues feel that they are an important and creative part of a team effort. Once he communicates his concept he permits collaborators to go off on their own. "He's a benign watcher-over," the late librettist Hugh Wheeler said; "we'd meet for discussions, then I'd go off and write the libretto as a play, with areas I thought would musicalize well; Steve Sondheim would usually spot other areas, good ones, that I hadn't thought of. Sometimes Hal and Steve may have been in some conceptual upper air, but they really let me go my own way."

"Once he saw what he was getting from us, he gave us enough freedom," says Franne Lee, who with her then-husband Eugene Lee designed the sets and costumes for five Prince shows.

"He involves the choreographer completely," says Larry Fuller, who has worked on six Prince musicals:

As we would go over the script together, he would give me his concept, indicating what should be accomplished in the musical numbers. This kind of close collaboration accounts for the seamless quality of his shows. Then during rehearsals we worked in separate spaces, and at the end of the day we would show each other the work we had done. He was open to letting me critique what he had done.

"Hal can be intimidating," Joanna Merlin says, and his quick flare-ups can be awesome, but co-workers recognize that Prince's dedication to a project overrides any temporary impasse. His commitment filters through an entire company. "We were all so proud to be working together on *Sweeney Todd*," says June Havoc. "It was a love affair and that always comes from the top." "On *Follies* we felt joined at the hip," Dorothy Collins says. "There was a family feeling backstage at *Merrily*," Ann Morrison remembers. "He was 'Uncle Hal,' and we felt he loved us as if we were his own children." "Hal's dedication and force at every rehearsal affected everyone," according to Barbara Baxley:

In being exuberant he allows you to release yourself. He's active, as actors must be active. He's never bored, so the actor is never boring. Every half-hour he would crack us up with a joke. Maybe he had to, because so much energy had been built up, maybe he did it as a conscious technique: I don't know. But I do know that *She Loves Me* was the most joyful company I've ever been in.

Prince is known for his loyalty to colleagues even in the face of defeat. "During the long disastrous preview period for *Merrily*, he gave us pep talks every night," recalls a grateful Ann Morrison. "And after the show opened he apologized, saying that he had given us a good show but that he had not given us a hit." "The morning after *A Doll's Life* opened to negative reviews Hal called me to apologize for not giving me a hit," says Betsy Joslyn. "And the second night he came to the theatre to cheer us up. He made us laugh. He could have not shown up at all."

Joe Masteroff notes that "Hal is in the business of being popular. He likes to be surrounded by people who say, 'Yes, you're wonderful, Hal.'" This may be, but clearly being well-liked helps Prince as well as his collaborators to function effectively. In the mid-seventies the *New York Times Magazine* rejected three assigned articles (by Mel Gussow, Susan Braudy, and Gerald Walker) on Prince because the writers couldn't find a lively story. (Prince says "they simply found me boring, and I'm proud of that, particularly in these days.") "At the time Prince was so powerful that people were afraid to say anything bad," Joanna Merlin suggests. But is there really anything "bad" to say? As June Havoc says, "Hal has such a beautiful life with his family — you never hear anything about Hal."

4 Musical metaphors

Cabaret is a genre landmark, a show like *Of Thee I Sing* or *Pal Joey* or *Carousel* which significantly expanded the musical's range both in style and subject. At the same time its links with Prince's other work can be seen in his choice of collaborators. The composer John Kander and lyricist Fred Ebb had written the score for *Flora, the Red Menace*, while the librettist Joe Masteroff had written the book for *She Loves Me*; and his designer, Boris Aronson, was to work on five future Prince musicals. With Prince supervising, Masteroff "wrote and rewrote over the course of many meetings (we must have had three thousand)" while Kander and Ebb "must have written fifty songs, most of which Hal rejected." *Cabaret* was a show "written by a committee." Masteroff's libretto is based on Christopher Isherwood's *Berlin Stories* (made up of two novellas, "The Last of Mr. Norris" and "Goodbye to Berlin") as well as on the lame play that John van Druten adapted from them. Van Druten confines the action in *I Am a Camera* to the rooming house where Isherwood's *alter ego*, Clifford Bradshaw, lives and tries to write as he absorbs atmosphere and acquires experience in a city on the edge of political, moral, and economic collapse.

In opening up the action beyond Clifford's flat, and in opposing the private world of the rooming house to the public world of the emblematic Kit Kat Klub where Sally Bowles works as a singer, *Cabaret* forcefully connects Isherwood's characters to the historical pressures that are to overwhelm them. In *I Am a Camera*, history rumbles in the wings, while in *Cabaret* it is transfigured into a vivid on-stage metaphor.[1]

Once they had decided to divide the action between the cabaret and the rooming house Masteroff and Prince had to select which of Isherwood's many characters to focus on. Van Druten's play "starred" Sally Bowles, Isherwood's kooky ingénue. "Hal told me right from the beginning that he didn't want this to be a musical about Sally Bowles, whom he feels is the least interesting character in *Berlin Stories*." Nonetheless, as a gamine always unlucky in love, a rotten singer who lives by her wits and her sex appeal, Sally is a character made to order as a musical heroine – "we never had any thought of discarding her," Masteroff says. "Sally and the character based on Isherwood had to be in it; the problem was who else to include. Early on we knew we wanted Lotte Lenya, yet the character she would play, the landlady Fräulein Schneider, didn't have much of a story. I loved the fact that the character was still there, in exactly the same place, after the war: she was a survivor." With Lenya's interest to spur him, Masteroff decided to build up the landlady's role by eliminating the part of Natalia Landauer, the rich Jewish heiress (played by Shelley Winters in the 1955 film of *I Am a Camera* and by Marisa Berenson in the 1972 film of *Cabaret*). "Natalia, like Cliff and Sally, could leave Germany at any moment, which is not inherently thrilling, yet Fräulein Schneider and her boyfriend Herr Schultz were Germans – they had to stay. For me, the subplot therefore becomes more commanding than the main plot."

With two romantic couples as the focus Masteroff's book in general outline conforms to the structural conventions of the Rodgers and Hammerstein musical play: Sally and Cliff are the squabbling young lovers based on the Laurey and Curly archetype from *Oklahoma!*, while Fräulein Schneider and Herr Schultz provide the comic subplot based on the *Oklahoma!* model of Ado-Annie, Will Parker, and Ali Hakim. As in *Fiddler On the Roof*, however, the historical background darkens the comedy and romance and thwarts a happy end.

Prince had a trick up his sleeve, a concept that in a stroke overturns the Broadway formula and sentimentality underlying Masteroff's well-written book. From the outset it was Prince's intention to slip the standard-make libretto with its regulation (if off-beat) pairs of characters and Kander and Ebb's book songs through which the characters express their feelings, into a frame, a limbo world presided over by a sinister Master of Ceremonies. "The figure of the Emcee was drawn from Hal's experience when he was stationed in Germany during the Korean War," Masteroff notes. "Hal knew right from the start how he wanted the character to be played – and he insisted on casting Joel Grey."

"We had two shows – my book, and Joel's fifteen minutes," Masteroff recalls:

Fred and John had written a number of cabaret songs, then I wrote book scenes. At first the songs were placed higgledy-piggledy throughout the show, although it emerged that the songs reflected the book scenes: there were a lot of wonderful accidents. It never occurred to me that when you put the two shows together you would have a new kind of musical, but Hal knew.

Beckoning the audience with a conspiratorial smile, and a song and a dance, the Emcee is a cocky lord of misrule. "He metaphorically represents the Depression," Prince says. "He starts out as a pathetic, self-deluded entertainer who gradually turns into an emblem of the Nazi mentality." Performed "in one," the place where filler material is staged to camouflage changes of scene, the Emcee's songs are set in a limbo area that is distinct from the worlds of both the rooming house and the cabaret. His numbers comment critically on the characters, linking their unconventional sexuality, money problems, and political cowardice to Berlin's general moral collapse. Functioning as ironic signposts, framing and pointedly disrupting book scenes, the limbo routines, like the songs in *The Threepenny Opera*, use musical interludes in a self-conscious way to isolate and to enlarge the show's themes. As they fulfill the entertainment imperative of musical theatre the comment songs also create intellectual detachment.

To underline the observation framework that the limbo numbers establish Prince introduces on-stage observers, a device that has since become part of his stylistic signature. Joe Masteroff remembers that the motif was "an accident. We needed the time for scene changes. Two girls from the cabaret lingered as they went up the spiral staircase stage left while the scenery changed, and Hal liked the way it looked and decided to keep it. It wasn't something that we had thought of before we put the show on stage."

In the 1986 London revival directed by Gillian Lynne observation was insistent, with cabaret girls and oversized dummies placed near the wings and on an upstage balcony to oversee the action. In Prince's revival, on the other hand, as in his original production, observers are used sparingly: two cabaret dancers picked out in an exquisite half-light on the spiral staircase watching Cliff and Ernst in the rooming house; the Emcee at the top of the stairs overseeing scene shifts from the cabaret to the rooming house. Prince, who has been criticized for using observers too often, is now defensive about the technique, commenting that "we did exactly what we did twenty-one years ago, but it was a new staging device then and so the observers were singled out; they seemed more prominent than they really were."

"There must be two worlds on that stage," Prince insists: the "real" world of the rooming house and the Kit Kat Klub, and the limbo area presided over by the Emcee. To create a clear physical separation between the two, Prince wanted a curtain of light like the one he had seen in the summer of 1966 at the Taganka Theatre in Moscow. But the technology for it was not available; and in the revival, as in the original production, the limbo numbers are played in front of a glittering rain curtain which approximates the same effect.

The limbo numbers – "Two Ladies," "Tomorrow Belongs to Me," "The Money Song," "If You Could See Her (The Gorilla Song)," and a chorus line that opens Act II – are intended to surprise and even to disorient the audience, to jar them out of the identification that the realism of the book scenes promotes. The Emcee also frames the historical action with the menacing invitation of "Willkommen," which opens and closes the show and is set within the "real" world of the cabaret itself.

"Two Ladies" follows a scene in which Sally and Cliff decide to become roommates. As the Emcee cavorts satyr-like with two tarts he embodies a

14 and 15 Al Jolson meets Brecht: the Emcee (Joel Grey) in the limbo area, performing numbers that comment ironically on the world of *Cabaret* (1966) (photo courtesy of Van Williams)

minatory eroticism: sex laced with dark premonitions. "Everybody in Berlin has a roommate; some people have two people," he croons insinuatingly. Immediately after a scene in which Cliff unsuspectingly becomes a courier for the Nazis when he agrees to carry parcels between Berlin and Paris for Ernst, the Emcee appears in limbo as a strutting pimp who sells girls of many nations at high prices: "Money makes the world go round." "If you could see her through my eyes, she wouldn't look Jewish at all," the Emcee tells us as he shows off his fiancée, a gorilla. Pointedly, the number follows the scene in which Fräulein Schneider breaks off her engagement to her Jewish suitor.

Borrowing vaudeville trappings, and performed before the curtain, the usual venue in musical comedy for "pure" song and dance, the limbo numbers overturn the conventions of musical-theatre staging. In top hat and tails, picked out of the enveloping darkness by a pinpoint spotlight, the Emcee looks like an affable entertainer, eager to please us. But through a sly sleight of hand the insignia of American show business are transformed into social and political satire: Al Jolson becomes Brecht. The way *Cabaret* mimics and reverses the forms of musical entertainment is typified in the dance number that opens Act II, as a regulation chorus line, kicking their legs with mechanical precision, becomes a Nazi goose step led by the Emcee in drag.

Joel Grey's "fifteen minutes" (actually 33 minutes 51 seconds), then, provide *Cabaret*'s central motor. Rivetingly staged and performed, the Emcee's numbers place song and dance in a frame which changes the way we read the characters and situations "inside" the play. In Prince's concept, the moral darkness of the Emcee's limbo world gradually overtakes the "real" world in which the characters try in various ways to serve, cope with, or evade Nazism. With their increasing menace the limbo numbers are a reminder of the larger world outside Clifford Bradshaw's rooming house that is on a collision course with a catastrophic destiny.

In preparing his trajectory for the show Prince set up deliberate contrasts not only between the book and limbo scenes but also between the show's two acts. In Act I "the characters are trying to enjoy themselves during hard times," he says, in a city that is both alluring and oppressive. In Act II, the tone noticeably darkens as the Nazi takeover disrupts the characters' lives. "If you have Nazis from the start where does the show have to go? You've given everything away. When Ernst is revealed as a Nazi at the end of Act II – when he wears a Nazi armband to Herr Schultz's engagement party – that should be a shock."

In theory Prince's trajectory makes thematic as well as theatrical sense. With the tilted mirror that "invites" the audience into the show with their disfiguring reflections Prince means to insinuate a connection between the contemporary audience and the Berliners of 1930. "It *can* happen here,"

16 German Expressionism by way of Orson Welles: Prince cut this
menacing image during *Cabaret*'s out-of-town try-out (1966) (photo
courtesy of Van Williams)

Prince told his cast, and to support that claim he presents Nazis and Nazi
collaborators as more or less regular folk, indistinguishable from the crowd.
Floating the show on the idea of the banality of evil and thereby playing
against the stereotype of the demonic Nazi is a challenging and fresh
approach, but one filled with traps. With all these likable characters, plus
Kander and Ebb's appealing songs, Prince clearly wants to give his audience a
good show before he lowers the thematic boom. But in making Isherwood's
characters at home on the musical-comedy stage – the world in which his
characters are "having a good time" is closer to George Abbott than to Berlin
before the Third Reich – Prince is in danger of making Fascism attractive.

"In 1966 the show was soft at the center," Prince admits, feeling he could
go "only so far with a Nazi musical." So he made compromises "with my eyes

wide open." Corrected to some extent in the 1987 revival, these concessions to popular taste involved the treatment of the leading man and of three supporting characters, and two musical numbers.

If Isherwood's *alter ego* is problematic as the hero of a musical it is not only because of his sexual ambiguity but because Isherwood, at the time he wrote *Berlin Stories*, was shielding his own homosexuality and therefore presented the character in soft focus as a passive observer ("I am a camera") of a bewitching *mise-en-scène*. In none of the *Berlin Stories*, nor in any adaptation, does the character emerge as a vital actor in the drama of his own experience. The portrayal of Clifford Bradshaw in the original *Cabaret* as a pleasant innocent, wide-eyed in Babylon, was notably pallid, and compounding the lightweight musical-comedy performance of Bert Convy was a song, "Why Should I Wake Up?", which was a salute to an American ostrich, oblivious to history, and which in context was startlingly superficial. As Berlin hurtles toward disaster, Convy would croon about how happy he is in his cocoon with Sally.

Prince "felt at the time that audiences had enough to handle – two doomed romances, Nazis, Sally's abortion – without inflicting Isherwood's homosexuality on them as well." Joe Masteroff notes that "in the original stories the character really had no sex; in 1966 our Cliff was heterosexual; in Bob Fosse's film he was bisexual." In the 1987 revival "Why Should I Wake Up?" is replaced with the more urgent "Don't Go," Cliff's plea to Sally to stay with him. Yet Cliff reluctantly admits to his homosexuality. His earnestly willed affair with Sally is a subterfuge, a commercially shrewd cover-up of the non-sexual attachment of Isherwood's odd couple, a homosexual and a woman unlucky in love who turns to Clifford–Christopher as a refuge from heterosexual catastrophe. However, making Cliff disdainful of his sexual past while presenting two minor homosexual characters as silly, flitting queens, is hardly the way to tell the truth about Isherwood.

"Along with *Evita*, *Cabaret* is my sexiest show," Prince says, adding that he means "sexy in the sense of seductive, not pin-ups." Yet it is not the hero's sexuality that heats up the show – Cliff is a square who remains self-protectively detached from the cabaret world's sexual enticements – it is the Emcee's. Like a naughty child acting out primal instincts Joel Grey's Emcee is indeed alarmingly "seductive"; at the New Year's party, dressed in diapers, he does a lubricious bump and grind; in "Two Ladies," he's polymorphous-perverse; in "The Money Song" he's an incarnation of after-hours sleaziness, a huckster who gives sex a dirty name. By contrast sex in the book scenes is tame. If anything, Prince keeps too great a distance between Cliff's ambiguous desire and the lure of Berlin night life.

Like Isherwood's stand-in, the Jewish Herr Schultz as well as the Nazis

Ernst Ludwig and Fräulein Kost are also soft characters. In the revival Prince removed the comic Schultz patter song "Meeskite," which was littered with ethnic stereotypes. Yet while Prince's concern to avoid satanic Nazis is valid, his two emblematic Fascists remain too ingratiating. With her bevy of handsome sailors and her raffish laughter Kost comes straight from comic opera, and Ernst is too thinly developed to function as anything other than a narrative device. Similarly, two production numbers which appear in the revival as well as the original – a telephone dance that follows "Don't Tell Mama," Sally's first cabaret song, and a dance in Schultz's fruit shop during the climactic Act I engagement party – may fulfill Prince's strategy of showing the characters "trying to have a good time," but Ron Field's choreography stays closer to Las Vegas than Berlin. Unlike the limbo routines, where song and dance have an ironic function, even in the revival these two ensemble dances are presented in a straightforward musical-comedy style that, in context, is inappropriate and irrelevant. Rather than furthering the story or enriching atmosphere, the energetic, conventional show dancing seems to be included to give the audience a respite from the play's serious purpose.

With both Fräulein Schneider and Sally Bowles, however, Prince was able more fully to fulfill his revisionist intentions. Particularly in the original production his concern to protect the book scenes from becoming saccharine was helped by Lotte Lenya's presence as the landlady. With her severe, wizened face and harsh voice Lenya played the character as an earthy pragmatist, stoic in the face of apocalypse. "We wrote every word and lyric for her," Joe Masteroff says;

We told her, "If anything on that stage isn't right, tell us, you're the expert, you were there." She loved the role, which allowed her a range from broad comedy in Act I to tragedy in Act II; it was her one great success without Weill. She said she'd do the role when she heard "So What," which she said had the feel of a Brecht–Weill song.

Aiming Cabaret higher than a Jerry Herman Great Lady musical, Prince was determined to keep the role of Sally Bowles from becoming a showcase for a Broadway diva. With her hoydenish, off-center, spunky personality Sally could certainly be turned into a big starring role, but like Berlin Stories Prince wanted the show to be about a place and a time rather than a study of one particular character. He also wanted a Sally who doesn't sing well. In any realistic sense Liza Minnelli's Sally is too talented to be working in a dingy Berlin bar, though as Masteroff says, "You can't really have Sally untalented. The average audience isn't sophisticated enough to know that someone who can really sing is singing badly on purpose. If Sally can't sing, you have no show."

Prince's original Sally Bowles, Jill Haworth, belted her songs in a brassy, cutting style. Playing Sally as a hardened adventuress, a singer who clearly was never going to become a star, Haworth was exactly the sort of unsentimental leading lady Prince was looking for. And while by design she was no Liza Minnelli, she delivered on the title song, as any Sally would have to. In Prince's staging of "Cabaret," the narrative and its frame come together for the first and only time in the show as Sally during the number steps into the limbo area. With this symbolic movement Prince underlines the song's irony, for in context Sally's invitation to "come to the cabaret" is positively chilling. Far from being intended as a celebration of good times, "Cabaret" is the ironic theme song of a social and political dimwit, a no-talent loser, who blindly capitulates to Nazi darkness. Yet thematic intention clashes with the heft of musical performance: "Cabaret" may well be a premonition of Sally's fateful irresponsibility, but it is also a show-stopping eleven o'clock number, and for most audiences performance is likely to trample politics. "It's certainly possible to interpret the song as a negative statement," Masteroff says, "but in performance the song really takes over and becomes a celebration."

Part conventional book musical, directed for fleshy psychological realism, part ironic Brechtian *Lehrstück*; part Broadway sentimentality, part Georg Grosz-like satire, *Cabaret* has a split focus. It is a schizophrenic show in which the spiky metaphoric frame and the literal narrative are sometimes at cross-purposes. In his film Bob Fosse eliminated the book songs, a choice dictated not only by the medium's demand for greater realism than the stage but by the fact that music doesn't really sit comfortably on the book scenes. Despite Prince's efforts to integrate action and song in these scenes, the conventional use of song pales beside the debunking limbo numbers. In the film all the songs except "Tomorrow Belongs to Me" and (glaringly) "Maybe This Time" are protected by a performance framework: the music is on stage, which in *Cabaret* is where it really belongs.

For all of Prince's compromises with his eyes "wide open," *Cabaret* in 1966 was a courageous show which introduced a new visual and thematic vocabulary to the American musical. If in 1987 *Cabaret* was no longer innovative it was still eminently playable.[2] "We realized during rehearsals that what worked then still works," Joe Masteroff says. *Cabaret* is the "most imitated and influential" of Prince's musicals. His use of a symbolic frame and of observers, his resistance to the acting and singing conventions of musical theatre, his use of music to provide social comment, his refusal to construct the show as a star-vehicle, his filmic punctuation, his expressionist motifs (the tilted mirror, high contrasts between light and dark, the blinder lights and the black-box setting, the spiral staircase), provided a rich fund of ideas that for the past two decades have helped significantly to renovate both the structure and substance of musical theatre.

Prince's next show, *Zorbá*, confirmed his evolving aesthetic of musical drama. Like *Cabaret*, *Zorbá* had a literary pedigree in the Nikos Kazantzakis novel, which had been the source of a popular 1965 movie starring Anthony Quinn, and the libretto also pivots on a contrast in age between paralleled romantic couples: Zorbá courts Hortense, a faded French courtesan who reminisces about her youth, while Zorbá's young partner Nico is paired with a young widow. As in *Cabaret* as well, both affairs end tragically.

To give the characters the needed mythic dimension, Prince placed them within a frame which, as in *Cabaret*, significantly boosts the show's dramatic and musical texture. *Zorbá* is presented as a story performed by a group of musicians who play the leading roles and function as a chorus. "The stage is bare, and the background neutral. The whole company is seated in two rows in a semi-circle, bouzouki-style"[3]: *Zorbá* begins then with a group of performers, a theatrical company, suspended in a blank space that acquires definition only when the performance begins. "Want me to sing?" an anonymous company member asks the audience. What follows – the story the company enacts – is *Zorbá* the musical. As in *Cabaret*, the frame weaves a performance motif throughout the show, shrewdly underscoring the fact that the musical is an inherently artificial and theatrical medium.

"Observing became more important in *Zorbá* than it was in *Cabaret*," Prince says. As sideline spectators, the chorus reminds the audience that it is watching a re-enactment, a tale. But – as in Greek tragedy and, closer to home, as in Rodgers and Hammerstein's experimental *Allegro* – the chorus also pushes the characters to their destinies, sings the thoughts a character is unable to utter, points a moral, or at times participates in the action directly, surrounding the widow when the enraged father of a suitor she has spurned kills her, becoming the vultures that dismantle Hortense's hotel.

Like *Cabaret* too, *Zorbá* was strikingly designed. Prince, who always conducts a thorough research of the venues in which his shows are set, visited Crete and Mykonos, and the staging recreated his impressions of the peculiar color and light of the Greek islands, the stark white of the rounded buildings as against the funereal black of the people's clothes. Memorably *Zorbá* was presented in severe chiaroscuro. And just as their *Cabaret* score succesfully fuses Broadway and Weill's Berlin, Kander and Ebb's *Zorbá* score adapts Greek folk music to the expectations of West 44th Street. Bouzouki and Broadway ballads blend in a skillful pastiche.

Even so, "There were problems with the show we never quite solved," Prince says. "I think it was too dark for most Broadway audiences. The revised version with Anthony Quinn [produced by Michael Cacoyannis in 1985] was more upbeat than ours, and for that reason less authentic." For the revised *Zorbá*, for instance, Ebb changed the opening lyrics of "Life Is" from

"Life is what you do while you're waiting to die" to "Life is what you do till the moment you die" and with Kander wrote two new notably sentimental numbers: "The Mine Song," a village celebration in which the ensemble sings that "the voice of your heart is the sound of tomorrow," and a song for Zorbá in which the character declares that "woman is like a fresh spring . . . you drink till you are dry."

Despite its abrasions, ultimately Prince's concept is too soft to fulfill the demands of its source. The drama of *Zorbá the Greek* is an inner one, Nico's struggle between the world of intellect in which he feels safe and the life of desire that Zorbá embodies, and to sustain a larger-than-life dimension the characters (as well as the show itself) require a continuous musical texture that is darker, more "fateful," more propulsive, than Kander and Ebb's rhythmic and tuneful song catalogue. A relentless fate, atavistic revenge, failed romances, the ravages of age, the community as a reactionary force – the play's essential material, the elemental battle Kazantzakis dramatizes between sex and repression, with Zorbá as a life-affirming primitive in combat with a community one step above savagery in the evolutionary scale, requires a weightier musical idiom.

Above all, however, the show's lack of popularity was due to misunderstandings about Prince's intentions. "I think people in 1968 expected another *Fiddler*. We probably made a mistake in casting Herschel Bernardi and Maria Karnilova, both of whom New York audiences identified with their roles in *Fiddler*; and we had the same librettist." Nonetheless, for all its undernourished ingredients *Zorbá* marks a significant effort in Prince's campaign to create a musical-theatre framework within which to dramatize substantial themes.

5   A little Sondheim music (I)

Twenty-one years after they first met Prince and Sondheim produced *Company*, their first "concept" musical. Prince then produced and directed five other Sondheim musicals, presented *Side by Side by Sondheim* (an anthology of the composer's show music) on Broadway (1977), and asked Sondheim to contribute some lyrics for *Candide* (1973). The failure of *Merrily We Roll Along* in 1981 temporarily ended their collaboration. "Steve and I got sick of each other after having worked together for so long," Prince says. "We had to go off in separate directions." But, rumors to the contrary, they have remained personal friends and Sondheim says firmly, "My goodness yes, we will work together again." Prince mentions a forthcoming project, typically eager to talk about its concept, while Sondheim, equally typically, says "Please don't say anything about it, nothing's definite yet."

Prince galloping ahead while Sondheim holds tightly onto the reins; Prince the affable public-relations man, glibly articulating concepts and trajectories, Sondheim leery of publicity; Prince relishing the activity of the rehearsal process, Sondheim disliking it: out of the fusion of their temperamental dissimilarities they have become modernism's answer to Rodgers and Hammerstein – the makers of the self-reflexive musical. Prince says their collaboration has thrived on "creative abrasion," and while Prince seems to be gregarious and Sondheim seems to prefer solitude, it would be naive to petrify them into complementary masks of comedy and drama, with Prince cast as the high-powered extrovert to Sondheim's misanthrope. Both are stagestruck showmen weaned on a romance of the Broadway big time that they have never outgrown and that helps to explain their drive for continued achievement, and for critical as well as popular acceptance. In terms of their record they qualify as theatrical elder statesmen, but both cloak their hefty egos in an appealing modesty.

Prince tends to dismiss his reputation: "I guess after all these years people in the business look at me the way I looked at George Abbott forty years ago. They see someone who's successful, Broadway's former 'boy wonder.' Yet that isn't how I see myself at all." For all his renown, Sondheim, too, has some lurking insecurities. "If you're talking about financial success you're talking to the wrong guy," he says;

Most of my shows were money failures. And most of my reviews have been negative . . . My friend [the late] Mike Stewart didn't believe me when I talked about the hostility to my work but after he attended a preview of *Merrily We Roll Along* he said, "You're right, they *are* out to get you" . . . I think Hal and I have come in for such hostility because we're mavericks and yet we aren't starving.

Prince and Sondheim both operate out of a contradictory combination of confidence and uncertainty. "No one has taken more chances than Steve and I," Prince says, yet both he and Sondheim are unsure about how their work will be regarded by posterity; Sondheim shrugs – "I'm not going to know" – and adds that no musical except *Porgy and Bess* is likely to endure for generations to come, while Prince wants very much to leave an artistic legacy. Both decry the power of the press; Sondheim maintains that "musical theatre is the only art form that is criticized by people who are totally ignorant about the subject . . . Only the *Times* review counts, and the other reviewers know that; it's what explains their vituperativeness."

Despite their complaints about critics, audiences, and the hothouse pressures of putting on a show on Broadway, both acknowledge that in the world of commercial theatre success on Broadway is still the ultimate validation. "It's all about imprimatur," Sondheim says:

The producers of *Big River* wanted to open on Broadway, though they felt that with its country-and-western score the show had little chance of succeeding. They felt the show did have an appeal for rural audiences, however, and that it would help to sell it in the provinces if they could advertise *Big River* as coming direct from Broadway. That still counts.

Prince and Sondheim have learned to play the Broadway game, conforming to the customs of the country, because despite their strong wills and their definite ideas about the kinds of shows they want to create they are both born collaborators. "I had no idea that James Goldman was going to rewrite *Follies* when we began planning for the [summer 1987] London production," Sondheim says, "or that I would end up writing four new songs to replace four discarded ones. But of course I went ahead because he's my collaborator." Significantly, Sondheim describes himself not as a composer-lyricist but as a "collaborative playwright." Typically he would not begin work on a score until after "two to four months of meetings in Hal's office" and until the libretto had acquired a "perceivable structure and tone."

"I'm an imitator," he says. On both *Company* and *Merrily We Roll Along* Sondheim took his cue from librettist George Furth's "bright, sharp, no-nonsense dialogue." His score for *Follies* was written to complement James Goldman's "arch, larger-than-life characterizations. Hal and I were the only ones who liked that book. It's what we both love about the theatre, precisely that it *is* abstract and larger than life." That the late Hugh Wheeler was a "naturalistic writer" changed the thrust of *A Little Night Music*, which became

17 Stephen Sondheim and Hal Prince backstage on the opening night of
Merrily We Roll Along (November 21, 1981) (photo courtesy of Van
Williams)

"the kind of show that Hugh could write rather than the sort of highly
theatrical piece I had in mind."

When he reports that "nobody respects the writer's work more than Hal
Prince – and I mean the sung as well as the spoken word," Sondheim is clearly
speaking about himself as well. He brings to his lyric writing a "passion for
words" and for the ways language creates style. (Amazingly, however,
Sondheim is not a reader. "The novel is an invitation that never took," he
says. "I always get defeated by prose style." Sondheim's interest in words as
independent entities, separate from "prose style," is reflected in his skill in
crossword puzzles, which he concocted for *New York Magazine* in 1968–9.)
Maintaining that he likes dialogue but "can't write it, it comes out stilted
whenever I try," Sondheim subjects the librettos he works from to the kinds

of literary evaluation "we all learned in English class." "Nothing in the theatre lasts that doesn't have either poetry or characters," he says. "There is very little poetry in the musical theatre, and not that many shows with real characters either. I like to think that some of the shows I've worked on fall into that category."

Contrary to the popular impression that Sondheim is intent on eliminating plot, he in fact savors a good story. ("I'm good at thinking up plots but I can't write them," he says.) A good story is what attracted him to *Sweeney Todd*, the only one of his projects that he forcefully initiated. "It has a terrific story," he says, "which will probably keep it around longer than any of my other work. When I saw Christopher Bond's version I was immediately hooked. Bond had succeeded in telling the story where other versions had failed because he gave Sweeney a motivation. The other versions are just blood and gore."

While Prince was raised on such George Abbott musicals as *Call Me Madam, Wonderful Town, The Pajama Game*, and *Damn Yankees*, Sondheim served his apprenticeship as a lyricist for such composers as Leonard Bernstein (*West Side Story*), Richard Rodgers (*Do I Hear A Waltz?*), and Jule Styne (*Gypsy*). Like Prince, Sondheim had valuable on-the-job training, but before he began to work on Broadway he had the good fortune to have had Oscar Hammerstein as a neighbor and mentor.

"More than any lyricist before him Oscar created characters and told a story," Sondheim says. "Oscar's lyrics are miniature dramas wedded to the shows for which they were written. He stressed clarity of thought, and in his work thought is always more important than rhyme." When Sondheim tried to mimic his teacher's sentimentality, Hammerstein told him to be true to himself. "'I believe in wind and willow trees; you don't,' he told me." Although not sharing his teacher's rhapsodic romanticism, Sondheim none-theless feels much closer to Hammerstein than to Richard Rodgers's first partner Lorenz Hart, whose caustic wit, topical references, ingenious rhymes, and resistance to sentimental pieties would seem closer to his own tempera-ment. But Sondheim disparages Hart's work while allying himself with Hammerstein's model of writing lyrics that serve character and story. His objection to much of Hart's wit is that it is often a display of virtuosity for its own sake rather than an integral part of a narrative. About his own work Sondheim is often least satisfied when he settles for sound rather than sense. "When Maria in *West Side Story* sings 'I feel fizzy and funny and fine,' that character doesn't have a lot to say."[1]

"When I was developing the score for *A Funny Thing Happened On the Way to the Forum*," Sondheim recalls Burt Shevelove, the show's co-librettist, asking "'Haven't you ever heard of Cole Porter?' Burt said the songs in the show should 'savor the moment' like a Cole Porter song rather than necessarily helping to advance the plot or define character." But when Sondheim does mimic a Porter style, as in a list song like "Pirelli's Miracle Elixir" in *Sweeney Todd*, it is for a reason that serves the play rather than simply to "savor the moment" or to parade his word-juggling skills. "'Pirelli's Miracle Elixir' isn't really Porter-like because Porter never had a dramatic function to accomplish."

After Hammerstein and Burt Shevelove, a third major impact on Sondheim's lyric writing came from Arthur Laurents, the librettist for three of his early shows, *West Side Story*, *Gypsy*, and *Anyone Can Whistle*. "Arthur taught me subtext, an invaluable lesson," Sondheim says. "He taught me how to imply, and how to make words and intention collide: a character sings one thing but actually means something entirely different, or a character's words contradict his actions." Writing songs with a subtext that suggests a character's undercurrents, the ambiguities and ambivalences that bind a character to a dramatic event, is a way of countering the tradition of the song as a "number": "Most of the early show songs were written as vehicles for singing stars," Sondheim says with evident disapproval.

On his work as a composer Sondheim is less open in acknowledging influences and models. Instead of specific instructors, he admits to having a strong imitative facility. "I'm a pasticheur," he says. "I can imitate virtually any style of music after hearing it briefly."[2] The Sondheim canon is thus filled with musical quotation and parody, from the Broadway show music in *Follies* to the Orientalia of *Pacific Overtures* to the Ravel waltzes of *A Little Night Music* to the movie music of the Golden Age ("the film scores of the forties were my true literature; I know every note of every score of every Bette Davis and Joan Crawford movie," he says). Sondheim scores also mimic an environment (the New York sounds that permeate *Company*) as well as an art form (the "pointillist" score of *Sunday in the Park with George* that parallels Seurat's painting technique).

As he constructs his scores to meet the specific requirement of each new libretto Sondheim's variety of musical mood and style is indeed prodigious. Yet in Sondheim's work there are distinctly personal harmonic, rhythmic, and melodic qualities that underlie the patchwork of reference and mimicry. While "dissonant" and "unmelodic" are the two adjectives with which Sondheim critics typically brand his work, neither is really accurate. Sondheim is "dissonant" (which is critical shorthand for music that seems cacophonous or "difficult" or depends on counterpoint) only for dramatic heightening, to suggest inner tension and conflict between characters or to anticipate or underscore climactic moments. "What people mean by 'unmelodic' is really that they're unfamiliar with it," Sondheim says. "It means the tune isn't immediately hummable, but I do feel that with exposure you can hum almost any musical composition." On a first hearing, and assigned to their place in a narrative structure, Sondheim's songs may not boast the ripe bountiful tunefulness of the work of older Broadway masters like Irving Berlin or Richard Rodgers – his concern is with dramatic values rather than melodic simplicity or accessibility. But on the Sondheim anthology albums, where his songs are presented *as songs* rather than as elements of a musical play, melody is abundant.

Prince remembers that "in 1954, when we produced *The Pajama Game*, the week we opened we had a hit song on the radio, Rosemary Clooney's version of 'Hey There.' Of course that meant a lot to us at the box office. By the early sixties that kind of cross-over was no longer a realistic possibility."[3] But even if it were, song-plugging would undermine the musical-theatre aesthetic Prince and Sondheim were evolving. Just as the director has turned away from the big number that can be easily lifted from its theatrical context, so the notion of writing hit songs contradicts Sondheim's sense of himself as a collaborative dramatist responsible for helping to sustain a show's story, characterization, mood, and concept.

To undercut the feeling of a song as an entity that exists apart from the play, Sondheim often interweaves dialogue with his lyrics. "I ask the librettist to give me dialogue at the spot we've picked for a song, and then I mix the two." Another way in which he erodes the convention of straightforward song performance is in the copious stage directions which accompany his lyrics. "Directors are usually grateful for the suggestions for movement and action that I notate," he says. "When they ask if they have to follow my instructions exactly I say no, but even if they don't I've given them ideas, a blueprint for action." Although Sondheim insists that he does not want to direct – "I wouldn't know what to do, where to move the actors or what the set should look like: all the things Hal is good at" – his instincts about how to stage a song are surely those of a director. For "The Worst Pies in London," Mrs. Lovett's first number in *Sweeney Todd*, it was Sondheim's idea to have the character punctuate the lyrics by swatting and smashing bugs crawling around her kitchen: her apt low-comedy antics help to unite song and story.

As a lyricist, his collaborative skill is apparent in the way he adapts his style to the work of the librettists for *West Side Story*, *Gypsy*, and *Do I Hear A Waltz?* To serve Leonard Bernstein's symphonic score for *West Side Story* Sondheim wrote in a pitch of fevered romanticism not evident in his later work; his lyrics for Jule Styne's *Gypsy* score have a punchy Broadway brass, while to abet Richard Rodgers's mellifluous melodies for *Do I Hear A Waltz?* he wrote with a lush sentimentality tinctured by intermittent irony. But at the same time that he was demonstrating his flexibility Sondheim was also experimenting with his commitment to songs as an integral part of a show's development of plot and character.

18 Beginning at the top: Sondheim's first Broadway assignment was as lyricist for Leonard Bernstein's *West Side Story* (1957). Setting by Oliver Smith

In his concise libretto for *West Side Story*, Arthur Laurents created a suitably stylized diction for the rival gangs. The Jets and the Sharks speak a made-up slang peppered with expletives like "frabbajabba" and slick be-bop phrases like "womb to tomb" and "sperm to worm." George Abbott's initial reaction, that this isn't the way young hoodlums really sound, is exactly the point. The kids talk in staccato bursts that suggest a nervous urban rhythm – Laurents writes dialogue that seems ready to spring into song – echoed in Sondheim's lyrics. While some of his phrases like Maria's "it's alarming how charming I feel," may be too sophisticated and others are uncharacteristically sticky ("Oh, moon, grow bright, / And make this endless day endless night"), at its sturdiest Sondheim's work complements the drive of Laurents's book, Bernstein's score, and Jerome Robbins's direction: the best of his lyrics demand to be danced to.

Revealing his fondness for counterpoint, some of his lyrics are written *against* the text in order to create dramatic tension. At the beginning of Act II, for instance, Maria sings "I Feel Pretty," a conventional ballad transformed by context – the character does not yet know what the audience knows, that her lover Tony has killed her brother – into tragic irony. The sweet, trilling lyric plays against the audience's awareness of doom. Placing a romantic song in a setting that changes the song's statement is a technique that became characteristic of Sondheim's later collaborations with Hal Prince.

"A Boy Like That" is another powerful example of how Sondheim enfolds a song within a dramatic purpose. At the beginning of the song Anita berates Maria for continuing to love Tony: "A boy like that, who killed your brother," she hisses. By the end of the song, through the persuasions of music and lyrics, Maria has succeeded in changing Anita's mind as she makes Anita aware – as she makes Anita *feel* – the strength of her love for Tony. In a conventional musical so crucial a transition would be entrusted to dialogue rather than lyrics, but in charting an emotional progression in this Hammerstein-like musical scene Sondheim claims for lyrics a dramatic status equal to that of dialogue.

Gypsy marked the end of a tradition rather than, like *West Side Story*, suggesting possibilities for a new one. Working on a standard backstage story, and tailoring his material for a star, Sondheim nonetheless succeeded to a remarkable degree in pursuing his goal of writing songs that are like playlets rippling with subtext. "Some People" has all the earmarks of a big top-of-the-show "here I am" number designed to spotlight Ethel Merman's Mama Rose as a brash broad fired by ambition. "What the song is really about, though," Sondheim points out, "is Rose's effort to convince her stubborn disapproving father to give her eighty-eight dollars" so she can leave a dreary small-town life to pursue a career in vaudeville for her two daughters. "This gives the performer something to play – a dramatic purpose," says Sondheim, who objects to stranding a performer on stage with nothing to do *but* sing. In "Small World," Rose sings to a man she's just met about how much they have in common. Her honeyed words paint a picture of domestic serenity that Rose is incapable of fulfilling: "It's a con song," Sondheim says.

The Act I finale, "Everything's Coming Up Roses," is a raucous number that showed off Merman's clarion voice and sent the audience into the intermission in a pumped-up state; but in context the song is not – or at any rate is not *only* – a celebration of the spunk and determination that musical-comedy characters typically exhibit. Sondheim intended it as "a deeply insensitive song: Rose is being completely self-centered, ignoring the feelings of her daughter" as she plans their theatrical future. Louise (who will become Gypsy Rose Lee) and her agent Herbie beg Rose to give up show business so they can become a normal family but Rose's excitement escalates to manic proportions as the song offers a new twist, the Merman show-stopper as a form of nervous breakdown. "It was a protected scene in which we had Sandra Church [as Louise] and Jack Klugman [as Herbie] doing the acting, responding in horror to Rose, because we weren't sure how much of an actress Merman was. Actually she turned out to be better than we expected," Sondheim recalls.

Dramatizing emotional collapse through a song, a technique Sondheim employs triumphantly in *Sweeney Todd*, is the core of the show's most famous number, indeed one of the most acclaimed numbers in musical-theatre history. In the climactic "Rose's Turn," Sondheim's fragmented, repetitive lyrics vividly depict the character's collapse. Sondheim claims that "the song allows for the reconciliation between mother and daughter at the end; seeing her mother falling apart, Louise can now forgive her." The idea is challenging, but Sondheim's estimate of what the song accomplishes is not entirely correct. Lyric and music may dramatize Rose's crack-up, in which the character finally acknowledges her selfishness – "I did it for me!" However, the actual performance of the song, a virtuoso turn by Merman in her one and only dramatic role, becomes a salute to the star's magnificence. Rose is a monstrous character, a vulgar driven woman who has turned her talentless daughter into a stripper, but the demands of the scene as performed compel audiences to applaud the singer herself rather than booing the character, as she deserves. Although "Rose's Turn" tells us that the singer is a crass, washed-up old woman, ultimately the song functions as a celebration of the performer's energy: Merman would regularly get ovations at the end of the number. ("Originally the number didn't have an ending," Sondheim recalls. "It's all wrong to give her that big finish, but when Oscar [Hammerstein] came to see the show out of town he said we had to end the song because the audience was waiting to applaud Merman and when we didn't let them they weren't able to listen to the crucial last two pages of dialogue.")

Despite its frequently unconventional use of song, and despite Sondheim's claim that *Gypsy* "says things the audience doesn't quite want to hear," the show is deeply conventional in its belief in star quality – Merman's, which played havoc with the script's implications, and, within the show itself, Gypsy's.

Sondheim wrote both music and lyrics for two pre-*Company* shows, *A Funny Thing Happened On the Way to the Forum*, with a book by Burt Shevelove and Larry Gelbart, and *Anyone Can Whistle* (1964), with a book by Arthur Laurents. While the latter show is an attempt to find new forms, *Forum*, with a more traditional structure, posed almost as many challenges. "It's a one-set musical," says Sondheim, "and it's the best farce ever written – it's hard to write music for a farce." Pseudolus, a slave, is promised his freedom if he can procure a courtesan for Hero, his master. On this initial premise the *dramatis personae* – masters and slaves, captains and courtesans – are thrown into a narrative vortex of masquerade, mistaken identity, mistiming, and steadily accelerating confusion that is magically untangled to provide universal happy endings. In this masterfully constructed farce plot, what can music accomplish?

"The songs are there to 'savor the moment,' which is what Burt Shevelove asked for," Sondheim says, "and which is why in Act II when the action speeds up there are fewer songs." In a sense the music periodically intercepts the swift plotting to reveal character or simply to present a vaudeville turn on a subject suggested by the action. "The score and the book don't match," Sondheim says. "The book is high-style low comedy; the lyrics are witty in a salon way." When they sing, therefore, the characters don't quite sound the way they do when they talk; the small breaks, the fissures, between song and dialogue help to set the music in a frame of its own, apart from the action proper. In song the characters produce puns and clever turns of phrase not allowed them in their dialogue. While in the plot the characters continually lose control, of events and sometimes of language, in a number of the songs they claim a victory over both through Sondheim's virtuosity. In "Free," for instance, Pseudolus speculates (brilliantly) on what life will be like once he has attained his dream of freedom. "All my verse will be free," he puns. "Freedom is the necessary essence of democracy," he sings, with metrical flair. In "Everybody Ought to Have a Maid," a male ensemble often clobbered by the plot triumphantly tosses off a series of clever rhyme schemes ("skittering, flittering, littering" is "answered" in a following chorus by "wriggling, jiggling, giggling, and wiggling"); internal rhymes ("dustbin," "just been"); and deflating alliterations ("graceful as a grouse"). More than any other song in the show "Pretty Little Picture" is a set-piece, entirely detachable from the mechanics of plotting, that showcases Sondheim's dexterity: "The bong of the bell of the buoy in the bay, / And the boat and the boy and the bride are away."

Sondheim's signature is apparent not only in verbal acrobatics but also in the way the songs consistently mock emotion and sentiment, and the way lyrics comically contradict the characters' true feelings. Unlike *The Boys From Syracuse*, a comparable farce for which Rodgers and Hart wrote haunting romantic ballads like "You Have Cast Your Shadow On the Sea," *Forum* contains not one straight-faced song. Philia, the courtesan and inamorata of Hero, sings "I'm lovely, lovely is the one thing I can do," to a melody that is itself genuinely lovely. ("I wrote myself out of a hit with that song, because

19 Witty lyrics for a low comedy: a troupe of vaudevillians (John Carradine,
Jack Gilford, David Burns, and Zero Mostel) tell us "Everybody Ought to
Have a Maid" (*A Funny Thing Happened On the Way to the Forum*, 1962)
(photo courtesy of Van Williams)

20 Breaking the musical-comedy song form: Mayor Cora Hooper (Angela Lansbury) and henchmen perform "Me and My Town," an extended commentative number in Sondheim's *Anyone Can Whistle* (1964)

the comic lyric undercuts the melody," Sondheim says.) In Act II, the song is reprised not by the oblivious young lovers but by a slave, Hysterium, dressed up as a courtesan and Pseudolus, assuring him/her that "you're lovely." There's a fly in the ointment even in "Pretty Little Picture," as Pseudolus interjects "Hear the whips on the galley slaves!" into the lovers' fantasy of getting away to an enchanted isle.

Lyrics repeatedly reveal the characters' lack of self-knowledge. "I'm calm," shrieks the perennially hysterical Hysterium. It's "Impossible," Hero and his father Senex sing as each contemplates the distinct possibility that the other is having an affair with Philia. "That Dirty Old Man," sung by Domina, Hero's mother, about Senex, his father, also dramatizes ambivalence, a state Sondheim enjoys placing his characters in. "Just wait till I get my hands on him!" Domina wails, then tenderly sings, "I'll hold him, / Enfold him." To depict the singer's schizophrenia, Sondheim introduces abrupt rhythmic and melodic shifts.

A would-be marriage of musical comedy with theatre of the absurd, Arthur Laurents's libretto for *Anyone Can Whistle* mixes a soggy romance between a repressed nurse and a free spirit, a story about a fake miracle, and a political satire on a corrupt lady mayor and her henchmen. As in his play *The Time of the Cuckoo*, Laurents's fable is about the awakening of a frozen woman, though here (appropriate for a musical) the lady learns to whistle. But Laurents doesn't make his people speak like characters who sing, and weighed down by its long-winded libretto and its thematic diffuseness, the show can probably never be made to work.

Sondheim maintains that *Anyone Can Whistle* (a nine-performance failure) is the first musical to use "musical-comedy style for non-traditional subject matter," and correspondingly his music and lyrics form an assault on musical-comedy precedents. His score has two kinds of songs, those with simple lyrics in which the characters express their feelings straightforwardly, and those which alter the shape of the standard thirty-two-bar AABA format. Ironically, some of Sondheim's sweetest music and lyrics – including the hero's theme song, "Everybody Says Don't," which celebrates rule-breaking (perhaps reflecting the way the authors felt about their show) – are embedded in a show that tries hard to avoid musical-comedy formula. "I guess *Anyone Can Whistle* is my most sentimental piece," Sondheim concedes.

In deliberate contrast, the other songs – "Me and My Town," "Simple," "The Cookie Chase" – are "difficult." Interwoven with dialogue and dance and marked by steep harmonic and rhythmic shifts, the songs are prolonged production numbers. "Me and My Town" is a presentational, commenting number in which the mayor protests that she and her town "just want to be loved." Performed as a parody of a night-club act, the song changes gears in mid-section to become a tuneless patter between Cora and a line of bantering chorus boys. Similarly "Simple," which is almost the length of a one-act play, prefigures the use of the mirror in *Cabaret*. The mad hero mistaken for a doctor conducts interviews for determining who's crazy and who isn't: at the end of the confusion he has orchestrated, members of the cast who have been certified as mad sit in theatre seats applauding the audience. With several melodic strains intertwined and dialogue continually eroding the boundaries of the lyric – it is sometimes hard to find the song amid all the action – the number, fragmented, split, changing its contours, spills directly into and helps to structure the action, blurring the barriers between the spoken and the sung word.

A cacophonous musical catalogue that includes a *Swan Lake*-like ballet theme, a waltz with dissonant underscoring that has classical echoes, and a refrain, "lock 'em up," sung to a stately melody, the climactic Act III "Cookie Chase" is even more chaotic than the ironically titled "Simple." Recalling the résumé of musical and lyrical fragments that constitutes "Rose's Turn" and looking ahead to *Sweeney Todd*'s symphonic "City on Fire," "The Cookie Chase," like "Me and My Town" and "Simple," declares war on the conventional structure and use of song in the musical theatre.

6   A little Sondheim music (II)

Prince says that "if at some point in every rehearsal period I don't say this is the most pretentious thing I've ever seen, I get worried." Borrowing techniques from film and from a variety of historical, avant-garde, and foreign theatrical styles, the Prince–Sondheim team may not always have fulfilled their thematic intentions but each time out they have succeeded in shattering preconceptions about the Broadway musical.

Their six musical collaborations can be grouped into contemporary and period pieces: *Company, Follies,* and *Merrily We Roll Along* on the one hand, *A Little Night Music, Pacific Overtures,* and *Sweeney Todd* on the other. The three modern musicals have a distinctly New York flavor, and while their subject matter may be traditional (*Follies* and *Merrily* are about show people, *Company* examines love and marriage, Manhattan-style), in tone and form the shows were subversive. Prince and Sondheim are clever termites, boring from within as they discover fresh ways of making musicals.

Company and *Follies* have been called plotless (Sondheim defines them as "in the twilight zone between a revue and a book"), while *Merrily* has a reverse chronology. "I'm attracted to stories that present difficulties in the telling, and I'm often interested in getting away from the linear and the naturalistic," Sondheim says. "Our motto is that content dictates form and breaking form is therefore connected to the story you're telling: we never started out by saying, 'Let's do a non-plot musical.'"

If the collaborators worked variations on the linear Rodgers and Hammerstein musical play they also challenged their predecessors with the variety of mood and point of view they introduced into their work. Yet despite the attack on sentimental cliché that has informed almost all of their shows, underneath the cool surfaces of their work, the uplift and romanticism that supplied the motor for the old-fashioned musicals struggle to be released. It is the resulting conflicts between modern ambivalence, irony, skepticism, and self-reflexiveness on the one hand and show-business schmaltz on the other that give their work its distinctive sweet and sour pungency.

If *Cabaret* was half of an experimental show, *Company* went the entire distance. "In a good musical, the book and the songs are one piece," Sondheim says,

85

and in *Company* we wanted a total texture ... My music and lyrics grew out of the way we commented about the characters in conferences; before I began to write I absorbed the play's ambience and atmosphere, its style of speech. I don't make the characters speak, but I try to mime or echo or enhance a story or characters invented by somebody else. With *Company*, I collected musical ideas from the sharp rhythmic vitality of George Furth's dialogue.

The material that evolved into *Company*'s revue-like vignettes of what Sondheim calls "the total possibility and impossibility of relationships and the isle of Manhattan" was originally conceived as a series of one-acts about marriage. When Furth encountered structural problems, Sondheim took the plays to Prince for advice, though "it never occurred to me that there was a musical in these pieces."

Furth's Manhattan is very much like Woody Allen's, an enclave of privileged characters exhausted by trendiness and ambivalence, but where Allen's satire is mixed with genuine affection for his characters and their milieu, Furth shows little compassion for his puzzled people trapped in relationships they do and do not want. A bachelor observes the marital bad manners of five couples who represent a cross-section of upper-middle-class Manhattan mores circa 1970 that, Sondheim says, "has begun to date around the edges." The first couple Robert visits, Sarah and Harry, are classic New York neurotics: she has an eating problem, he has a drinking problem, and their relationship bristles with hostility (expressed by Sarah trying out newly learned karate techniques on her husband). Couple number two, Peter and Susan, are getting a divorce, which will enable them to live together more peaceably. Couple number three, Jenny and David, are trying to keep up with youth by smoking marijuana. Amy and Paul, couple number four, are planning to marry after having lived together for years. Joanne of couple number five dominates her third husband Larry and wants to have an affair with Robert.

To Prince, "A guy observing and not participating – that's dangerous: it's *I Am a Camera*. Robert isn't the narrator, he's the leading character." As in "Rose's Turn" in *Gypsy*, the play's climactic action – what choice will Robert make? what has he learned from the company of his friends? – is expressed through song rather than dialogue as Sondheim literally steals the show from his librettist. Will Robert marry, commit himself to a relationship, or maintain his bachelor's freedom? At one time or another in the show's evolution, Robert chose each of these options, and this comparison was reflected in an uncertainty about what kind of song best expressed the show's intentions; "Being Alive," the number that was eventually selected, was the third one Sondheim wrote.

The first rejected song, "Marry Me a Little," in which Robert decides on a safe marriage with the partners jealously guarding their independence, defines a witty, urbane posture, one that has in fact become emblematic of Sondheim's customary fondness for ambivalence. (*Marry Me a Little* is now the title of a Sondheim songfest comprised of numbers dropped from shows.) The second attempt, "Happily Ever After," proclaiming Robert's wish to escape from the threats of marriage, to fly free, is the manifesto of a misanthrope. Prince felt, correctly, that neither offered an appropriate resolution, although both songs certainly reflect aspects of Robert's character; but the affirmative simplicity of the final choice ignored the play's ambiguities. "Being Alive" may be the most impassioned song Sondheim has yet written, a cry for

> Someone to hold you too close,
> Someone to hurt you too deep,
> Someone to sit in your chair,
> To ruin your sleep . . .

> Someone to crowd you with love,
> Someone to force you to care,
> Someone to make you come through,
> Who'll always be there, as frightened as you,
> Of being alive . . .

In an interview in 1976 Prince said that "the audience wanted a hopeful song," though he "didn't believe in it for a second."[1] Indeed, the character's eleventh-hour resolve does not seem to spring from his temperament or his experience in the show and betrays openly careless dramaturgy: when Joanne proposes an affair by saying, "I'll take care of you," Robert replies, "But who will I take care of?" as if realizing for the first time that he has arranged his life so that he wouldn't have to be responsible for anyone. Robert is so repressed that his instantaneous transition from habitual bemused distance to "being alive" is not credible. Although in 1970 the creators couldn't suggest that Robert's partner would be a man, their reluctance to join him to the heterosexual mating dance is underlined in the show's final ambiguous image, when, after his song, Robert mysteriously fails to show up at the surprise birthday party his friends ritualistically prepare for him each year. "He's trying to tell us something," Amy says. But what is the message? The play ends with a spotlight on Robert smiling. Who is the joke on, his friends or us?

"Is *Company* for or against marriage?" is a question Prince and Sondheim are still regularly asked. George Abbott recalls that Prince told him he could take his choice, while Sondheim says it is about relating "in a mechanized society; audiences mistook our saying that marriage and relationships are *difficult* for relationships are *impossible*."² "No show is about only one thing," Sondheim says. "On *Company* we all had a different idea but we agreed on tone and why we were writing it." If, as Hobe Morrison reported in *Variety*, *Company* "doesn't make its point clear,"³ the ambiguity was intentional, part of the Prince–Sondheim assault on musical-theatre banality. In a crucial way whether or not the show is for or against marriage (and the reviewer who wrote that "*Company* is really no more anti-marriage than a war film is anti-peace"⁴ seems accurate to me) is less important than its double-edged tone. "We wanted a show where the audience would sit for two hours screaming their heads off with laughter and then go home and not be able to sleep," Sondheim says.⁵ As Walter Kerr reported, "the mood is misanthropic, the view from the peephole jaundiced, the attitude middle-aged mean . . . a highly original stance for a Broadway musical to be taking,"⁶ or as John Lahr wrote, "To confront the betrayals of middle-class life . . . is to strip the musical of a crucial ingredient of its former appeal: romance. In *Company*, no one dreams, only survives. *Company* is an urban ghost dance."⁷

At the time, then, *Company*'s tone seemed refreshingly, disturbingly iconoclastic, a riposte to the unshakable good will of the Rodgers and Hammerstein shows. Yet Prince, ever respectful of commercial reality, pulled back from making the show the pitch-black comedy it might have become. Steering a tricky course between satire and affection, Prince wanted to crack the conventional musical-comedy surface without dismantling it altogether:

In rehearsal we made a commitment to examine the characters with emphasis on their neurotic, compulsive behavior. As a result, our first preview in Boston was serious business – too damn serious. So, on the next day, I told the cast: "You know everything you need to know about these characters. Now think of it as an upside-down cake and play for comedy." That was all I had to say. The next performance was extremely funny.

Appropriately, then, the acting style Prince worked for was one that remained within a musical-comedy tradition, light and presentational. As Prince realized, the performance of a musical has to protect its stylized activities of singing and dancing. Acting in musicals has evolved its own conventions, which are different from those for straight plays. When it is not well done, a musical-theatre performance can seem tinny and hollow; solid musical-theatre acting, on the other hand, should not have the same weight as acting in a drama: different from if not always larger than life, musical acting is acting in a frame, performing with traces of self-consciousness. Creating a character in a musical comedy or musical drama requires supercharged energy and size – going out there and selling musical theatre itself.

Avoiding undue psychological complexity, Prince's actors delivered their punch lines with their awareness as much on the audience as within the scene.

Although the show is about what Robert sees, it is an ensemble piece on which Prince imposed a unified performing style: cool, wry, detached, as if all the actors were slightly outside their roles, commenting on their follies the way Sondheim's music comments on character and situation.

Furth's light social notation – *Company* goes hardly deeper into its milieu than a Neil Simon gagfest – and self-conscious dialogue keep the show anchored within the musical-comedy format. Conforming to the Broadway tradition of smart-alecks for whom wisecracks and one-liners are a way of life, Furth's characters are theatrical stick figures lacking flesh and dimension. The language they speak belongs on a stage. "Sara Lee is the most phenomenal woman since Mary Baker Eddy," Sarah announces. To whom? To the characters in the scene, her husband Harry and her visitor Robert, or to the audience? Kathy, one of Robert's peripheral girlfriends, declares, "Some people have to know when to come to New York, and some people have to know when to leave."

These arch, articulate characters are written to provoke laughter from the audience; they are theatrical figments who would be unable to perform what Sondheim calls "the Rodgers and Hammerstein kind of song in which the characters reach a certain point and then sing their emotions. All the songs had to be used, I'm sorry to say, in a Brechtian way as comment and counterpoint . . . We had our songs interrupt the story and sung mostly by people outside the scene."[8] In most of the songs the performers address the audience rather than each other and as a result the music usually stops the show, pulling us out of emotional involvement in a scene in order to provide a running, generally acerbic gloss on character and action. Singers stand above or apart from the acted scene, evaluating the characters the way the characters are continually scrutinizing the subjects that transfix them – themselves, one another, marriage and relationships. Except for Robert, each member of the company is part of a fluid chorus that moves in and out of scenes.

After Sarah's karate sequence the action freezes while the company, led by Joanne, sings an ironic ode to marriage, "The Little Things You Do Together," a Sondheim list song that grows increasingly bitter ("looks you misconstrue together," "children you destroy together," "becoming a cliché together," "getting a divorce together"). While Jenny and David press him to get hitched, Robert's three girlfriends appear in a spotlight to sing, "You Could Drive a Person Crazy," a litany of Robert's faults, his distance, his teasing, all the qualities, in short, that make him a poor marital prospect. With the three singers grouped around a microphone and then bowing to the audience when they are finished, the song is presented frankly as a number, a performance, which stops the scene: once again the actors freeze as a song supplies a stinging commentary. At other points the relationship is reversed: scenes serve as an ironic counterpoint to the songs. While Robert is in bed with April, a stewardess, the women in the company sing of their sadness that he has no one to love – and in faking it with April Robert is indeed quite alone. Similarly in Act I, scene 5, a girl appears on a park bench to sing "Another Hundred People," a frenetic anthem to Manhattan:

> Another hundred people just got off of the train
> And came up through the ground
> While another hundred people just got off of the bus
> And are looking around
> At another hundred people who got off of the plane
> And are looking at us
> Who got off of the train
> And the plane and the bus
> Maybe yesterday.

Delivered in fragments, the song structures the scene: after each chorus, the singer observes encounters on the bench between Robert and April, then Kathy, and finally, after one last reprise of the entire song, she herself has a scene with him.

The separation of character from action is also reinforced by Michael Bennett's choreography. As we hear Robert's and April's inner monologues while they are making love, their feelings are expressed by the gyrations of a dancer who appears at the opposite end of the stage. Like most of the songs, this expressionistic "Love Dance" interprets what the audience sees. In fact, the show is so conscientious about distancing feelings, the characters' as well as the audience's, that when emotions erupt they seem misplaced, disproportionate. "Being Alive," Robert's attempt to break free of the world of brittle sophistication, overpowers the action which presumably has provoked it. The same discrepancy between text and song is evident in "The Ladies Who Lunch." Joanne's observation – "Look into their eyes and you'll see what they know:/Everybody dies" – is too dark for the character, the scene, and the show. As John Lahr noted,

Elaine Stritch's grating toast [the song, like the entire part of Joanne, was written for the actress, whose patented growl can be heard in every syllable the character utters or sings] lacks real poignancy and texture because in *Company* she is only a caricature singing about a condition for which the book merely sketches broad contours. The drama is in Sondheim's words; but the scene cannot support the song's truth and becomes merely melodramatic and facilely bitter.[9]

Company was Sondheim's first "concept" score. With its repeated busy signals, jittery stop-and-go rhythms, and suggestions of traffic, Sondheim's musical mimesis vividly evokes the show's mythicized Manhattan. Orchestrator Jonathan Tunick says the score "has a lot of city sounds, mechanical sounds . . . it has a very contemporary urban sound that's very influenced by pop music."[10] Significantly, Sondheim wrote the title song (the opening number, reprised in fragments throughout the show) only after he had seen a model of Boris Aronson's set, and the set's vertical steel girders are reflected in what Sondheim calls the "verticality" of his score. For Prince too the set inspired his own work. He called for a skeletal abstract impression of the city's towering glass and chrome and steel – a cool, impersonal visual match for Furth's dialogue and Sondheim's lyrics. Elevation, which has since become a Prince trademark, was a crucial part of the design: the set was built on levels, with movable platforms connected by flights of stairs to suggest the high-rise apartments in which New Yorkers live on top of each other. An elevator that lifted and lowered characters from one level to another became the show's technological trademark. To underline the insistent verticality of the Manhattan setting, Prince and Aronson experimented with slides of tall buildings and elongated shadows projected against a cyclorama. Prince notes that "on Broadway we had six hundred slides while on the road we had only forty; the number of slides didn't seem to make any difference. Audiences were only subliminally aware of them, which was what we intended."[11]

"Theatre should avoid the kind of specifics that movies demand," Prince feels, and unlocalized rooms suggested by one or two pieces of movable furniture allowed for fluid movement from one level to another. Freed from realistic clutter and from maintaining an illusion of real space and time, Prince could give *Company* the kind of swift tempo (part of his inheritance from George Abbott) that is thematically appropriate to New York neurotics who use constant movement as a way to avoid looking within. The multi-leveled set also enabled Prince and Michael Bennett to find visual metaphors for the characters' detachment from Robert and from each other: the company arranged on upper levels observing a solitary center-stage Robert became the show's visual leitmotif. Like Sondheim's score and Aronson's set, Prince's theatrical choreography was "conceptual."

For the book scenes "we flooded the stage with light, a technique for comedy I learned from George Abbott," Prince says. "And we shortened the playing area by moving in the scaffolds: you don't want characters in a comedy stranded on a vast empty stage." But for the songs Prince used spotlights to accent the singers and to place the actors in the scene in semi-darkness. With his fluid lighting plot and shifting sets, and his actors in perpetual motion as they crossed from one "apartment" to another and climbed up and down stairs, Prince created a kinetic, unstable field within which to portray mercurial Manhattan manners.

21 "I'm Not Getting Married Today," Amy (Beth Howland) wails as Paul
(Steve Elmore), her groom-to-be, prepares for the ceremony while a
commenting chorus perched on Boris Aronson's scaffold observes the scene
(*Company*, 1970) (photo courtesy of Van Williams)

As with *Company*, Prince had a crucial impact on the structure of *Follies*, although he did not begin to collaborate on the show until after Sondheim and librettist James Goldman had been working sporadically for nearly five years. Goldman's first draft, called *The Girls Upstairs*, was a basically realistic treatment of a theatrical reunion of a group of disillusioned middle-aged characters who engage in verbal and physical assaults. "It was a melodrama in which you wondered who was going to shoot whom," Sondheim recalls. "It was a 'who will do it?'" To Prince, "a straight-on realistic musical always seems to me a contradiction in terms. I wasn't remotely interested until I started to wonder about where the characters come from ... I asked for young counterparts to the middle-aged couples." "Hal told us to use the material in their heads on the stage, and to stop thinking in realistic terms and instead to consider the simultaneity of past and present," Sondheim says. "He said we'll use space and atmosphere ... With Hal prodding us we began to think in surrealistic rather than naturalistic terms — Hal likes everything on stage to be larger than life, and really so do I."

These suggestions of interweaving past events into the present action to make the characters confront their younger selves aimed at creating what Prince calls "a Proustian fracturing of time." A reunion of Follies girls provides an eerie symbolic frame against which the characters' follies — their self-delusions and misjudgments — are enacted.[12] And the show's logo, a Follies girl as a cracked Miss Liberty, suggests national and political dimensions that the play does not sustain, but nonetheless reveals the thematic reach for which Prince was striving.

Guided by their belief that "content dictates form," Prince and Sondheim realized that *Follies*, like *Company*, demanded an unusual structure. "Hal told us not to tell a story but to maintain a tension," Sondheim says. "You can have a story, though, without having a plot, and *Follies* does have a story, many stories, but it has no plot: it's Chekhovian, everything happens underneath the surface." A series of confrontations in which the characters' masks are peeled away layer by layer, the fragmented, vignette-like structure compares with *Company*. And like *Company* too the action unfolds cinematically, with the theatrical equivalents of fades, parallel editing, deep focus, and shock cuts.

But if the original melodrama of attempted suicides or murders has been eliminated, the show still has a definite dramatic arc as the two central couples arrive at the reunion, fall deeper into delusion and then depart after their follies have been exorcised. Prosperous, successful and handsome, Benjamin Stone looks bitterly at his cosmopolitan career and passionless marriage to Phyllis, who has turned brittle and caustic. Sally, who lives with the illusion

22 The past and the present intersect at the Follies reunion: Sally (Dorothy Collins) observes an encounter between Young Sally (Marti Rolph) and Ben Stone (John McMartin) (photo courtesy of Van Williams)

that Ben is the man she should have married, is equally dissatisfied with provincial Phoenix, Arizona and her two-timing second-level salesman husband, Buddy Plummer.

With their interlocking fantasies, these are probably darker and more embittered types than any earlier musical had ever attempted to depict. "They are all tragic characters," says Dorothy Collins who played Sally, the most deluded of them all. "Sally's fantasy about Ben was just that, all in her head, in her imagination. I can't believe there was ever even a romance. Yet she was so excited to get to the reunion that she came without Buddy; by the end her dream was shattered. There are a lot of women like Sally, with 'if onlys' running their lives."

Prince feels "there are more ideas in *Follies* than in any show I've worked on – emotional ideas that kept revealing new layers; we kept scratching and we kept finding. *Follies* examines obsessive behavior, neurosis and self-indulgence more microscopically than anything I know of" – and not surprisingly, given the genesis of the show, Prince "very much identified with the middle-age crisis the characters confront." Indeed (as with *Cabaret*, or *Company* where the "thirty-five-year-old Bobby was me, making my decision to marry") establishing emotional involvement with the material was an essential basis for Prince as a director: "Fellini had asked me to do a musical of $8\frac{1}{2}$ and I told him I couldn't because it was his story. I did *Follies* instead – that was my autobiography."

Yet despite the theatrical archness and the sting of much of the dialogue, the sophisticated cynical veneer that Prince and Sondheim were drawn by, Goldman's book ultimately can't carry the show. Too often the characters, who "sing more naturalistically than they speak," as Sondheim says, define themselves in flat bathetic terms: "I don't know who I am," Ben announces; "Someday I'll have the biggest goddamn limousine," his younger self declares. As a character study *Follies* is more often platitudinous than penetrating and, like most musicals, cannot sustain serious literary analysis.

Even so, as a theatrical event – the truest way after all to gauge the effectiveness of a performance art like the musical – *Follies* was a genuine masterwork of the American lyric stage. In performance *Follies* had a validity and a vitality that it cannot begin to claim on the page. Sondheim's score does more than serve the material, it transforms it. For the climax Sondheim takes over as a "collaborative dramatist," resolving the dramatic action in a dazzling series of songs which perform the kind of crucial dramatic function that the composer-lyricist had been experimenting with in "Rose's Turn" in *Gypsy*. In the ironic seven-song Follies sequence – there is a song for each of the four central characters in which they expose their vanities, preceded by an introductory song, and one number for each of the young couples –

23 and 24 "A Proustian fracturing of time": former Follies stars perform once again, accompanied by images from the past. Hattie Walker (Ethel Shutta) belts "Broadway Baby"; Vincent and Vanessa past (Michael Misita, Graciela Daniele) and present (Victor Griffin, Jayne Turner) dance "Bolero d'Amour" (Follies, 1971) (photos courtesy of Van Williams)

Sondheim fulfills the book's thematic intentions. In releasing the pressures that have built up both within and between characters, this musical collage accomplishes the classical dramatic functions of recognition and transformation. Musical performance operates as a psychic release, a therapeutic acting out of self-delusions that leads the characters to a dawning self-awareness.

Sondheim's score is designed to "contrast two different kinds of music, the book music and the atmosphere created by pastiche. I patterned each Follies song after a specific style; the book numbers [expressing emotions that are too strong to be contained within dialogue] are meant to be quite distinct from the show music." Among the composers Sondheim "quotes" are Friml–Romberg ("One More Kiss"), Irving Berlin ("Beautiful Girls"), DeSylva, Brown and Henderson ("Broadway Baby"), Jerome Kern ("Loveland"), George Gershwin ("Losing My Mind"), and Cole Porter ("The Story of Lucy and Jessie"). Of the show music which is not part of the climactic "Loveland" sequence, some numbers – "Broadway Baby," "Ah Paree," "Rain on the Roof," "Bolero d'Amour" – are simply decorative, with the old stars appearing out of the dark to perform their turns. Other spots – "One More Kiss," "Who's That Woman?" ("the one genre piece . . . a Hollywood forties number," as Sondheim says) – have an ironic connection to what is happening on stage. The lyrics of "One More Kiss" – "dreams are a sweet mistake / All dreamers must awake" – comment on the characters' romantic delusions, while those for "Who's That Woman?", performed by the present-day women and their young counterparts, suggest the follies of youth and the poignancy of time's flight.

But it is the songs in the show within the show that carry the main thematic burden. It is here, in the Follies within *Follies*, that past and present, fantasy and reality, and the show's two musical idioms, collide. The ultimate backstage musical, *Follies* comments on the old revue style in transforming its staples, and the interaction between past and present that forms the dramatic situation also describes the show's connection to the history of musical theatre. Possibly America's first revisionist musical, the show's full impact depends on a shared awareness among creators, performers, and audience of past musical-theatre styles.

Where musical performance in the Ziegfeld era was its own justification, in this latter-day Follies it is double-edged, intensely self-regarding in its use of music as metaphor. Ironic without ever descending to the crudeness of camp, the Prince–Sondheim "Loveland" is both tribute to and obituary for a musical-theatre style their own movement helped to make obsolete.

Its first three songs – the introductory "Folly of Love" ("Time stops, hearts are young, / Only serenades are sung / In Loveland, / Where everybody lives to love") and "The Folly of Youth" which includes "You're Gonna Love Tomorrow," sung by Young Ben and Young Phyllis, and "Love Will See Us Through," by Young Buddy and Young Sally – present an airy world of dewy-eyed innocents who imagine they can live on sentiment and hope, which is mocked by what we know has happened to the lovebirds. Then in turn the present-day "lovers," Buddy, Sally, Phyllis, and Ben, each perform a song whose style mimics twenties idioms but whose content echoes an earlier book number. Thus Buddy's "God-Why-Don't-You-Love-Me Blues" evokes his earlier song, "The Right Girl," to express the destructive ambivalence of desiring women beyond his reach while disdaining the ones who want him, while Sally's "Losing My Mind" in which she at last admits her despair is the Follies' "response" to her book number, "In Buddy's Eyes." The latter song is loaded with Sondheim irony: as Sally pretends to Ben that she married the right man and prefers the pleasures of her quiet suburban life, she is really revealing its terrifying emptiness and trying to punish Ben for having turned her down thirty years ago. According to Sondheim Dorothy Collins is "such a good actress that you could hear the subtext" while Dorothy Collins recalls that she "nullified the lyrics about how wonderful her life was by gestures and how I looked: that pink dress designed for Sally, which was so wrong but really helped to communicate what was going on underneath the lyrics."[13]

In her book number Phyllis asks Ben

> Could I leave you . . .
> Leave the quips with a sting, jokes with a sneer,
> Passionless love-making once a year?

But beneath her accusations is a genuine passion for Ben, and her Follies number, "The Story of Lucy and Jessie," reflects her ambivalence in the war between "juicy" Lucy (a young *alter ego*, naive and eager and drab) and "dressy" Jessie (her present self, imperious and "cold as a slab"). In "The Road You Didn't Take," Ben regrets what success has done to him while his Follies routine presents a man who rejects material success for the values of "Live, Laugh, Love," which he so clearly lacks. Stumbling on the lyrics, he is unable to complete the song because it isn't really his —

25 "Loveland": the gala introduction to the ironic "Follies" within *Follies* (photo courtesy of Van Williams)

26 Ben's "turn": "Live, Laugh, Love," with Ben (John McMartin) out of step, on the verge of a collapse that is to end the Follies (photo courtesy of Van Williams)

Some get a boot
From shooting off cablegrams
Or buzzing bells
To summon the staff.
Some climbers get their kicks
From social politics –
Me, I like to love,
Me, I like to . . .

Ben's breakdown abruptly ends the sequence:

The Follies drops begin to rise, and bit by bit we're back on the stage of the Weismann Theatre. Not literally, however. We're inside Ben's mind, and through his eyes we see a kind of madness. Everything we've seen and heard all evening is going on at once, as if the night's experience were being vomited. Ghosts, memories and party guests – all there.

They stand on platforms which are moving insanely back and forth, they mill about the stage, and all of them are doing bits and pieces of their scenes and songs.[14]

With dawn, and the restoration of order, the two reunited couples move upstage hand in hand, facing the morning light as their younger selves call out to each other "soft and faint, as if it were all spoken years ago."

As in *Company*, the tentative, ambiguously upbeat ending has greater theatrical than psychological validity. Prince sees the show's trajectory as "showing where the characters came from, their fall into different kinds of madness, and their path back, though for Ben there really was no path back — we compromised on that one." But the show's descent into mania and obsessions, areas of character drawing that the musical never entered willingly before, is too steep to allow such a quick retreat into a semblance of the characters' return to normality.

Follies' dark tone could have been predicted from Prince's first visual concept for the show, a famous 1960 photograph by Eliot Elisofon of Gloria Swanson standing in the rubble of the demolished Roxy Theatre. Prince wanted a *mise-en-scène* of nightmare rather than festivity, and Boris Aronson's abstract, multi-leveled set created a cavernous, spectral environment. If the *Company* stage was foreshortened and bathed with light to supply the appropriate mood for a comedy, the *Follies* stage was an immense black box in which the characters were often stranded. "Thank goodness there aren't many laughs in *Follies*," Prince says, "because we could never have gotten them on that stage."

To suggest emotional distance or different time frames the characters were often isolated by a spotlight, separated at opposite ends of the wide Winter Garden stage, or placed on different levels. The eerie limbo quality was enhanced by a chorus of ghostly showgirls dressed in black and white who glided silently through the play, unseen by the characters.

Prince's final decision to run the show without a break underscored the momentum of his and Michael Bennett's staging. "The show never stopped moving," Dorothy Collins remembers. "From up in the balcony we were told it looked like a chess game. Music and dialogue flowed into each other; there was often movement upstage during songs; a dolly with a band kept going in and out of the action." Partygoers filtered behind and to the sides of the central action, gesturing and talking in counterpoint to the unfolding drama between the two main couples; groups of characters emerged out of and then returned to the surrounding darkness, as platforms slid forward and back to change the shape of the central playing area. Ceaseless activity, cross-cutting between groups on either side of the stage, and fades between past and present action propelled the characters through the show's arc of arrival, breakdown, and departure.

27 Reconciliation at dawn in the demolished theatre (John McMartin and Alexis Smith). Setting by Boris Aronson; lighting by Tharon Musser (photo courtesy of Van Williams)

Prince "didn't want any seeming separation between the actors and the characters they were playing" – and *Follies* was cast like *Sunset Boulevard*. Ethel Shutta, once a Follies girl, had starred with Eddie Cantor on stage and screen in *Whoopee!*, while Mary McCarty, who had starred in Irving Berlin's *Miss Liberty* in 1949, was returning to Broadway after a long absence. Fifi D'Orsay had been a minor star in Hollywood in the thirties, and Yvonne de Carlo was a strikingly apt choice for Carlotta Campion, the Hollywood diva of the forties and fifties. Of the four principals, only John McMartin, who played Ben, had no prior associations for the audience, though facially he resembled Prince himself. The other three brought once well-known personas from film and television: Alexis Smith had faded from the screen by the early sixties, Gene Nelson hadn't been in movies since *Oklahoma!* in 1955, while Dorothy Collins was one of the icons in television in the fifties, the Lucky Strike girl on "Hit Parade."

Although the relationship between book and reality was oblique – and Dorothy Collins's case was typical: "*Follies* didn't really use my 'Hit Parade' persona, though Sally had the 'cute' look; she thought she was adorable" – awareness of the performers' careers changed and deepened the response to them in *Follies*, and helped audiences to "read" the play. Yvonne de Carlo's persona even helped to mould her character's one song, "I'm Still Here": "When you have Yvonne playing the role, that's the song you write," Sondheim says, and it appeared late in the show's development as a replacement for "Can That Boy Fox Trot!", "a one-joke song that wasn't working" during the Boston try-out. Astringency tinged with sentiment, "I'm Still Here" is a distinctly Sondheim-like mix that was also a perfect correlative for the singer:

> I've been through Reno,
> I've been through Beverly Hills,
> And I'm here.
> Reefers and vino,
> Rest cures, religion and pills,
> But I'm here.
> Been called a pinko
> Commie tool,
> Got through it stinko
> By my pool.
> I should have gone to an acting school,
> That seems clear.
> Still, someone said, "she's sincere,"
> So I'm here.

Dorothy Collins remembers that "Yvonne did things the character would do. It was appropriate – in character – that she often forgot or got mixed up on

28 "The show never stopped moving": Prince's multiple-focus staging, with groups of partygoers surrounding a central image, in this scene Stella and Max Deems (Mary McCarty and John J. Martin) (photo courtesy of Van Williams)

the lyrics of the song, and one night, when she didn't feel like doing the 'Who's That Woman?' number she just sat on the edge of the stage – again, exactly in character."

Returning to the big time in triumph after career setbacks, Yvonne de Carlo, Alexis Smith, Dorothy Collins, and Gene Nelson performed with a poignancy that perhaps can come only with age but that had not at any rate been permitted them in their heyday. The vulnerability they brought to their roles, and the continuity between real life and the theatre which their presence created, endowed Goldman's libretto with unexpected and almost unrepeatable dimension.

For the first and only time in his career Prince shared directing credit with his choreographer. Like his mentors Bennett twisted the traditional vocabulary of the Broadway musical into ironic variations: in staging "Side by Side" in *Company* he grouped Manhattan neurotics into an unlikely regulation chorus line while in *Follies* he also quoted from the dance styles of earlier periods, adding a knowing modern overlay. With present-day characters mirrored by their young *alter egos*, his show-stopping choreography for "Who's That Woman?" provided a potent visual metaphor for the passage-of-time theme. *Follies* was not a Michael Bennett show — "Michael wanted us to bring in Neil Simon," Sondheim recalls. "We wanted something darker and more removed from reality while Michael kept moving us in a more commercial direction. But we believed in our concept, and we stuck to it."[15] However, when Bennett went on to conceive musicals of his own the influence of Prince was clear. His best work, the superb *A Chorus Line* and *Dreamgirls*, contains echoes of the scenic abstractions, the scaffolds and platforms, the filmic handling of time, the continuous kinetic movement, and the love of physical metaphors, that mark *Company* and *Follies*.

7 A little Sondheim music (III)

The Prince–Sondheim period musicals are based on traditional theatrical styles: in story and score *A Little Night Music* recalls the romantic operettas of the Viennese school; *Pacific Overtures* imitates Kabuki; and *Sweeney Todd* is a Grand Guignol melodrama. For each show the collaborators faced the challenge of finding a production style that was reasonably true to its source and that at the same time was acceptable to Broadway audiences.

After the commercial failure of *Follies* Sondheim recalls, "we wanted to do a romantic château-weekend musical" – and when the rights to Anouilh's *Ring Around the Moon* were refused, they adapted Ingmar Bergman's *Smiles of a Summer Night* to present various sorts of follies in terms of love. While, unlike *Company* and *Follies*, *A Little Night Music* has a traditional plot (Sondheim feels "that's why it was a success"), he and Prince, true to form, wrapped it in a presentational frame. A quintet of wry musical commentators weaves in and out of the action, puncturing romantic reveries, introducing and reprising fragments of songs, providing transitions, and above all reminding the audience of the show's essential theatricality, the fact that a musical is *not* just like a play. Like the ghostly showgirls in *Follies* or the choral use of the acting company in both *Zorbá* and *Company*, the quintet is another Prince–Sondheim variation on the traditional musical-comedy ensemble.

Apart from *On the Twentieth Century*, *A Little Night Music* may be the only one of his musicals since *Cabaret* that Prince approached from a strictly craftsmanlike viewpoint. Unlike *Company* or *Follies*, the show is not set in a milieu that Prince could readily identify with nor did he discover a personal commitment to a theme as he did for other period pieces like *Pacific Overtures* and *Sweeney Todd*. But if the show was "mostly about making a hit,"[1] it was also elegantly conceived. Like Sondheim's score, Prince's fluid staging created interlocking patterns of movement as the characters circled and crossed each other in their mating dances. Complementing the way Sondheim used music to provide quick changes in place and time, Prince collapsed interior and exterior settings into a surrealist collage, with drawing-room sofas placed on a lawn, and created the effect of terse filmic cuts with movable, transparent and fanciful screens, painted with birch trees, which veiled one group of characters while revealing another. In Act II, with the action fragmented among many characters in a variety of indoor and outdoor

29 The quintet, commenting on and puncturing the lovers' follies in *A
Little Night Music* (Benjamin Rayson, Teri Ralston, Gene Varrone, Beth
Fowler, Barbara Lang) (photo courtesy of Van Williams)

settings, Prince's brisk pacing with its filmic transitions made the frantic
lovers seem like pawns on a chessboard, engulfed by a spinning machine-like
plot that lifted them up and hurled them to their proper and final places in the
intricate night waltz.

Like all Prince–Sondheim shows *A Little Night Music* is designed expressly
for the resources of the stage. Nonetheless, with Elizabeth Taylor as Desirée
and Len Cariou and Hermione Gingold recreating their original roles, Prince
directed a film of his intensely theatrical musical. "It was awful," Hermione
Gingold bemoaned. "Hal didn't have the control he'd had on Broadway. We
did it in Vienna, God knows why: it was supposed to be in Denmark, or one of
those cold places. For publicity I was asked to sing my number in Maria
Theresa's bed."

Opening the film with the actors performing on a stage and then shifting into real — filmic — space and time was a charming conceit, but realistic settings only made the songs seem disruptive. "The Glamorous Life" (for the film Sondheim wrote a new song with the same title) and "A Weekend in the Country," the show's two elaborate ensemble numbers which had a film-like structure on stage, are in fact beautifully assembled, but for the most part the film's editing — the intercutting within scenes and the transitions between scenes — is stilted and creates a sense of actual separation among the characters, who seem to inhabit their own individual frames rather than to collide, as they did on stage, within the same unifying *mise-en-scène*: an important point in this sexual rondelay.

Creatures of Sondheim's theatrical imagination, the quintet, of course, was eliminated, as were songs like "Liaisons" and "The Miller's Son" which

30 The night waltz that opens and closes the romantic rondelay in *A Little Night Music* (1973). Setting by Boris Aronson; lighting by Tharon Musser; choreography by Patricia Birch (photo courtesy of Van Williams)

supplied texture rather than plot advancement. Although Elizabeth Taylor has a dry wit that is apt for Desirée, she is too American and lacks the diction, the carriage, and frankly the class to be truly convincing playing a noted European stage actress at the turn of the century. That the film is in no way a reflection of the pace and texture, the lush, confident theatricality, of Prince's original production only underscores his affinity for the stage.

Like *Company*, *Pacific Overtures* was not originally supposed to be a musical. "John Weidman, a law student, brought me an idea for a play about Commodore Perry's entrance into Nagasaki harbor," Prince recalls.

It was factual and historical, and told from the point of view of Americans: it seemed like a teleplay. I wasn't interested in doing a realistic play, but the implications on progress fascinated me. I told Weidman to write it from a Japanese point of view. When he came back eight months later I told him it isn't large enough – the play was a confined series of scenes around a negotiating table in which the Japanese were hoodwinked by the mendacity of the American group. I felt the play wouldn't reach enough people. It needed to get beyond specifics; it needed size, and I realized then that music was how to give it size.

At first I was thinking in terms of a musical that utilized every conceivable theatrical style including mime and puppetry, and I wanted to tell the story in revue form. I felt that telling each episode in a different style would underline the universality of the theme: the desire to isolate yourself, to hold off the future, and the impossibility of that, which is touching and painful.

In his research on the history and art of the Commodore Perry era Prince kept discovering prints of Orientalized Caucasians which triggered the central concept:

We began to realize as we got deeper into the material that there was something about Kabuki that was so powerful and so clearly connected to the subject matter. I began to see a trajectory that took you from Kabuki to Ginza in the 1970s, which is as Western as you can get; in Ginza, which has a single, strident, vulgar image, the Japanese had out-imitated us.

Once Prince had decided on his approach he, his wife Judy, and Sondheim spent ten days in Japan attending theatre. "Because people expected us to be bored," Prince recalls,

they scheduled us for thirty minutes at a Kabuki or Noh play, but in fact we stayed much longer. One night we went to a Noh play that lasted over six hours, and we were enthralled. So much of performance art is artsy and without content, but this is not true at all of Japanese theatre styles. In a Kabuki house lights are left on at a certain level, and there's a constant traffic up and down the aisles: typically a show lasts eight hours. The traditional stories are familiar to the audience, who talk to each other almost in full voice. Obviously the Japanese have a very different perception from us of how to deal with theatre.

Nonetheless, Kabuki and the Broadway musical are both artificial performance arts with their own sanctified rituals, and linking the two styles gave Prince his richest chance yet for creating a show in the heightened, larger-than-life format that he favors. The Kabuki tradition of a professional storyteller as narrator supplied Prince with a ready-made frame, while doing the show as an American version of a Japanese impression of how the West had invaded Japanese history and culture wrapped *Pacific Overtures* in a box within a box within a box.

Once Prince and his collaborators had selected the Kabuki format they faced a major structural challenge. "We had to find ways of telling bits of history chronologically and we also wanted to tell a story."[2] When they first began to construct their scenario, Sondheim felt that the show was "closer to *what* it is about rather than *who* it is about. We've usually dealt essentially with characters, but here we're essentially starting with an idea: musicals usually don't deal with ideas."[3] Once the script was completed he realized it was "a story about two men" and that the show's "idea" emerges out of the experiences of these two emblematic figures, Kayama and Manjiro.

A minor samurai selected by the Shogun to repel Commodore Perry's invasion, Kayama gradually sheds the trappings of traditional Japanese culture as he becomes Westernized. His friend Manjiro is a commoner, a fisherman who has been to America and who offers advice about how to prevent the Americans from stepping foot on Japanese land, an act that would violate sacred decree. In contrast to Kayama, Manjiro returns to his roots, embracing conservative isolationist values as Western influences permeate the country. At the end of the play, he is among a band of reactionary samurai assassins who kill Kayama, who had become a symbol of dreaded acculturation.

Though indeed, as Prince and Sondheim claim, *Pacific Overtures* tells a story, a political allegory of the formation and break-up of a friendship, the two characters are as overwhelmed by the show as feudal Japan was overrun by the West. *Pacific Overtures* is that rare thing, a musical about an idea — specifically the necessity and the costs of progress. In earlier Prince musicals like *Fiddler On the Roof* and *Cabaret* the characters hold their own against a historical canvas, but in *Pacific Overtures* history is the star; as the revue-like scenes advance a thesis of Japan's manifest destiny, the background moves to the foreground, pushing the skeletal characters into the wings. As in *Fiddler On the Roof*, tradition is both celebrated — it provides communal security — and criticized: it can be dangerously insular. Yet the show says that progress, "necessary and unavoidable" according to Prince, comes at a steep price in personal and cultural dislocation. *Pacific Overtures* thus promotes the kind of thematic ambivalence — tradition is comforting/retarded; progress is necessary/painful — on which Prince and Sondheim thrive. "It's a good thing when an audience isn't quite sure what to think; that way you prod them to do a little thinking on their own," Prince says slyly. In this show, at least, the collaborators are closer to Brecht's *Lehrstück* than they care to admit.

A Kabuki musical with Brechtian touches and a thesis dipped in dialectic was obviously not destined to be a big hit. Prince concedes that

it could never be a popular show because of its form and its statement. And indeed we had an economic crisis, though never one of confidence. We tried out in Boston, where . . . I was faced with closing the show . . . or paying for it myself. But what you do in a show you do regardless of critics – you follow your impulse, and I felt the show *had* to come to New York; it had to be seen. I lost all the money I had saved, an irresponsible thing to do for a man with a wife and children. With *Evita*, I was able to make up for my losses on *Pacific Overtures*.

Typically, Prince was excited by the show's statement, "the terrible cost of removing the protection and structure of a traditional society" (which might serve as a paradigm of Prince's career in the musical theatre), while Sondheim put up "terrific resistance." "At first I just didn't see how it would sing," he says. Reluctantly, with nothing like Prince's gusto, he began his research. "I didn't do much," he admits;

I picked up an album in Japan, and looked at some Japanese theatre: how much do you need to know? I got a chapbook on Japan, a book of trivia which was more valuable than anything philosophical. I read two small books of haiku. And I looked at some instruments and studied some scales. For for rest I trusted John Weidman, who knows a lot. I'm good at imitation.

Despite his apparent diffidence, and guided by his motto that "a song has to be embedded in the material around it," Sondheim wrote a score that is inseparable from Weidman's libretto and Prince's production concepts. Like Prince's staging it skillfully blends "Zen and zap"[4] as suggestions of the percussiveness and chordal structure of Japanese music underlie Western harmony. As Sondheim said at the time, "We're not doing a thesis for a college. Basically we're doing a Broadway musical" which has an "impulse and ambience [that are] intrinsically Japanese."[5] As Prince kept the action moving at a New York clip (Japanese leisureliness would have been intolerable for American audiences), Sondheim's score mimics Oriental motifs while implanting them within a comfortably Westernized sound.

Prince and Sondheim were determined, however, to avoid being "merely" Broadway, and in freely adapting traditional elements of Japanese theatre they produced a show that is unlike any other Broadway musical. Among the foreign touches are the *hanamichi* (a stage running into the auditorium on which the actors enter), men playing women's roles, exaggerated clown-like make-up that obscures the actor's individuality, sets changed in view of the audience by stagehands dressed in black ("black to an Asian is the absence of color, so the stagehands would literally not be there," Prince says), and white lighting. Scenic designer Boris Aronson said at the time that "the Japanese artist has a peculiar way of seeing things: the white backdrops in *Pacific Overtures* are the way in which the Japanese depict clouds. Since this is a play

31 Prince, music director Paul Gemignani in the pit, and Sondheim at a rehearsal for *Pacific Overtures* (Boston try-out, November 1975), with the *hanamichi* running into the orchestra (photo courtesy of Van Williams)

about issues and not about people and moods, Hal and I decided on white lighting, which has a crispness, a simplicity, a directness."[6]

To give full value to the incantatory, sing-song quality of both Weidman's dialogue and Sondheim's lyrics, Prince decided on a highly inflected traditional acting style, at the opposite pole from American behavioral realism.[7] The oratorical performances heightened the connection between song and speech – *Pacific Overtures* did not cease being a musical whenever the actors lapsed from lyrics to dialogue. "The spoken lines are declamatory," Sondheim says. "There isn't a line in the show that isn't large. My lyrics are declamatory too – *Pacific Overtures* is my closest show to opera." When Sondheim heard the show performed by the English National Opera in 1987 he felt it "thrived on opera singers. The singers gave it a grandeur that befits the material and that comes from a tradition of five hundred years of performing Shakespeare."

To insure a performance authenticity and "to strip away the possibility of being pretentious," Prince insisted on casting Asians, recruiting in San Francisco and Los Angeles because "there just aren't that many Asian actors in New York." Since

all our actors were Asian except for one, who swore he was one-eighth Asian, I had to justify to our actors that we couldn't do a straight Kabuki, which would be inappropriate ... "This is the way it looks to us, as Westerners," I said to the cast. "It is our intention to interpret Kabuki with respect."

The rehearsal period was very collaborative: the actors were the ones with the tradition, after all, and they had a thousand things more than I could use.

Prince discovered that he couldn't give notes before a performance

because at half-hour everyone was meditating, working out some kind of exercise; this continued for the length of the run. We had a bomb threat by Caucasian actors who resented our casting Asians – there's no doubt that with Caucasians we would have had a better shot at a longer run, though we would have had a less artistic piece. And if we'd had women playing women we would have made it easier on audiences. We looked like a real Kabuki theatre; it wasn't clear that it was an American musical – from the outside of the theatre it looked like a visiting troupe, and that was dangerous. We're suspicious of Asians, less so now than when the play opened but still there is an alien feeling.

Also traditional was Prince's insistently horizontal movement, a departure from his usual interest in what he calls "elevation" – his recurrent steps, platforms, catwalks, and bridges. "The physical metaphor is always important to me," he says. "It informed why I conceived of *Candide* as a journey; I designed *The Phantom of the Opera* in deep focus because it's a play about distances and depth – depth gives you height. If you go horizontal, as I did in *Pacific Overtures*, you flatten everything out: *everything* in *Pacific Overtures* was horizontal, and that's true to Japanese theatre." Sondheim's opening number, "The Advantages of Floating in the Middle of the Sea," introduces the motif of sliding screens that Prince depended on throughout the show:

> Beyond the screens
> That glide aside
> Are further screens
> That open wide
> With scenes of screens like the ones that glide.

Painted to evoke the iconography of traditional Japanese landscapes, the gliding screens, as in *A Little Night Music*, function as an on-stage editing device, effecting cuts, dissolves and transitions between episodes and foreshortening the width and depth of the playing area while also "transporting the audience hypnotically into the realm of *ukiyoe*, 'the floating world' of the Japanese print."[8] As Martin Gottfried noted, "sliding is the show's staging and scenic scheme; the actors like the screens slide in screenlike planes."[9]

The sliding is reflected as well in Sondheim's score. "*Pacific Overtures* was

32 The Kabuki reciter (Mako) in front of Boris Aronson's Japanese curtain
(photo courtesy of Van Williams)

the first time I really tried to interweave themes extensively, a technique I used again on *Sweeney Todd*, *Merrily We Roll Along*, and *Sunday in the Park with George*, all of which have interrelated scores." But Sondheim stopped short of writing continuous music for the show. "Almost anything can be sung all the way through, but I like dialogue and I especially like John Weidman's dialogue for our piece. Let's call *Pacific Overtures* a ballad opera, with a series of set scenes."

Following Prince's arc ("it's only in Act II that a Western flavor appears"), Sondheim's score traces the progressive impact of the invading Western hordes on Japanese isolationism. The opening and closing numbers frame the show's trajectory: Sondheim's lyrics for "The Advantages of Floating in the Middle of the Sea" —

> In the middle of the world we float
> In the middle of the sea.
> The realities remain remote
> In the middle of the sea

— suggest the ordered and repetitive rhythms of a society bound by ancient customs, while in "Next," the finale, actors in modern dress recite a staccato litany of the effects of progress —

> Tower crumbles,
> Man revises,
> Motor rumbles,
> Civilizes.
> More surprises
> Next!

Prince and his choreographer Patricia Birch staged the opening with gliding horizontal movements that evoked the languor of "Nippon, the Floating Kingdom," while in "Next" the actors rotated the screens painted with sylvan landscapes to reveal modern chrome that creates an impersonal backdrop against which to announce the achievements of progress.

In Act I Sondheim stays close to his Japanese musical sources while in Act II he opens his palette to a broader tonal and melodic range. Sondheim based the form of "There is No Other Way," early in Act I, on the narrative models of Japanese theatre. In the song Kayama's wife, grief-stricken by the news that Kayama has been selected to represent the Shogun in an attempt to repel Commodore Perry's "four black dragons," dances her feelings while two observers sing; the first sings about her, the second expresses her words and thoughts. "Comment and internal soliloquy are built into the structures of Japanese theatre," Sondheim says. "The reciter sometimes talks to people on stage. I felt the elusiveness and the mystery of simultaneous comment were appropriate to the piece, and helped to keep the action fluid and unexpected, even if the form of the song was difficult for the audience so early in the show."

He used the Kabuki recital structure as the basis of another "cubist" observation song, "Someone in a Tree" (which Prince says is Sondheim's favorite song). The structural pivot of the show, placed at the end of Act I, the song is a report in triple focus of what happened during the historic encounter between Commodore Perry and the Japanese representatives. Instead of seeing the meeting, we hear about it from an old man who was there, a young boy (his younger self) who witnessed the event by climbing up a tree, and a warrior who stood guard beneath the Treaty House. The old man and the boy only see the encounter while the samurai only hears it – fused together their colliding recollections comprise a sight and sound spectacle. "It's *Rashomon* in five minutes," Prince says. "It's a *tour de force* that tells a complete story and is so complex it wears you out. Originally we had put together a scene in which we showed what happened – what the negotiations were like," Prince says, but he felt it would be more theatrical to present the event as a collage of musical recitations.

In "Poems," more obviously than in any other song, Sondheim demonstrates his imitative facility. ("The lyrics seem the work of a lover of Japanese poetry," wrote Martin Gottfried.)[10] "I will make a poem," Kayama says, as he and Manjiro walk to Kayama's house:

33 Broadway Kabuki: the reciter "in one," the ensemble upstage, Boris Aronson's white-cloud backdrops, and the screens moved by stagehands dressed in black (photo courtesy of Van Williams)

KAYAMA: Rain glistening
On the silver birch,
Like my lady's tears.
Your turn.

MANJIRO: Rain gathering,
Winding into streams,
Like the roads to Boston.
Your turn.

The short phrases, cryptic connections, and the imagery drawn from the natural world evoke haiku conventions. Yet Sondheim did not write the song as a display of his virtuosity (at least not only as a bravura set-piece) but to serve "a strong narrative use. Two people who don't know each other become friends as they make up these poems; by the end of the journey strangers have formed a bond that is to underlie the rest of the story. The

34 To approximate Japanese staging, Prince designed "everything in *Pacific Overtures* to be horizontal" (photo courtesy of Van Williams)

song was written to be *seen,* however – when you only hear it it seems not to have a function."

The Western intrusion is announced in an extended production number, "Please Hello," near the top of Act II. The song is the ultimate Sondheim pastiche, in which foreign ambassadors present their credentials (and their greed) in parodies of such national music styles as the French can-can and a Gilbert and Sullivan patter song. Taking over the space sanctified by Japanese tradition, the ambassadors made their entrances on the *hanamichi,* transformed by Patricia Birch's clever choreography into a vaudeville runway: sassy American show business collides with Oriental ritual in a witty visual paraphrase of the show's theme.

The transition on which the entire show turns is epitomized in Act II in Prince's favorite number, "A Bowler Hat" ("it's astonishingly simple – that's when you do it absolutely right"), in which Kayama and Manjiro sit on opposite sides of the stage. Kayama writes a series of letters to the Shogun, explaining changes in fashion and in his way of living. Between letters, Kayama's clothes, his writing implements, his glasses, even his posture, become increasingly modernized while at the same time Manjiro gets dressed with elaborate slowness in ceremonial robes for the ritual of tea. In the way that the song and the staging dovetail, "A Bowler Hat" is a model of the Prince–Sondheim collaboration.

Late in Act II, Sondheim sets his sweetest, most lilting, and most Western-sounding melody, "Pretty Lady," in ironic contrast to lyrics ("Pretty lady, how about it? / Don't yer know how long I been without it?") and context (Asian actors playing crude Cockney sailors mistake a Japanese woman in a walled garden for a geisha, and their actions lead to murder, a major incident between the United States and Japan, and internal conflicts between traditionalists and progressives). Prince used an authentically Japanese staging technique for Sondheim's misleadingly romantic Western-style melody. "In my studies I was intrigued by how Japanese theatre uses props – how little things loom large," Prince reports.

In "Pretty Lady," we used a little wall – I had seen these little walls in Kabuki – behind which stood a woman, who inspires the song. I noticed how the Japanese could take a playing area and reverse your vision of it, and following their lead I brought the wall downstage and reversed the position of the wall, so now the woman was in front of the wall, the sailors behind it. It was easy to do; it was getting the idea that was hard.

Subtitled a musical thriller, the Prince–Sondheim *Sweeney Todd,* with a book by Hugh Wheeler, is based on Christopher Bond's version of the 1830s legend about a barber who kills his customers and grinds them into meat pies. Where the other versions present Todd's rampage as unexplained bloodlust,

35 Japan in the modern age, with the reciter (Mako) in modern dress and with neutral modern panels replacing the Japanese motifs seen throughout the show (*Pacific Overtures*) (photo courtesy of Van Williams)

Bond's supplies its anti-hero with both a history and a motive: returning to London after fifteen years in prison on a trumped-up charge, Todd is determined to seek revenge against his nemesis, the lascivious Judge who has raped Todd's wife and adopted his daughter. When he misses killing Judge Turpin on a first try, Sweeney goes mad, deciding in a crazed epiphany that "everyone deserves to die." In league with his amoral landlady, Mrs. Lovett, who runs the pie shop that is downstairs from his tonsorial parlor, he becomes a killing machine; by the end of his spree the stage is as strewn with corpses as the fifth act of a Jacobean revenge tragedy.

When he saw Bond's *Sweeney Todd* in London in 1973, Sondheim "felt right away that these are characters who sing." But Prince, who does not share Sondheim's enthusiasm for melodrama and farce, had to be convinced:

I told Steve "I don't get it: it's a hoot and a howl, people's theatre, but why do it? It seems campy to me." Steve persisted, which is unusual – most of the time I have to drag him into a project. I told him that I had to find a way to do it. It seemed to me to be relentlessly about revenge, and I couldn't, then or now, afford to be interested in revenge. As a director I needed to see metaphor, to find some way of justifying the revenge. When I began to think of Sweeney's revenge as being against the class system that Judge Turpin represents I began to find a way to get inside the material: if Sweeney is victimized by the class system so is everyone else in the show. In a larger way I felt that by placing the action in its late nineteenth-century context we could say that from the day the Industrial Revolution entered our lives, the conveyor belt pulled us further and further from harmony, from humanity, from nature. All this hifalutin' stuff was acceptable to Steve and to Hugh and stimulating to our set designer, Eugene Lee, and I told them to go ahead with their own work and to ignore my metaphor. "We don't have to explain everything," I said; "the metaphor will be submerged in the material. Those who want to get it will get it," I assured them.

But to ensure that audiences understood the point his first concern was to create a scenic design which signalled the show's social metaphor. The show's choreographer, Larry Fuller, says that Prince's original idea was "a diorama, like a film set, of a London street that had buildings without fronts with rooftops seen in perspective. But Eugene Lee said that it wouldn't be possible to build such a set." Prince recalls that on a trip to Dublin he visited Kilmainham Jail,

which imprisoned everyone from Parnell to O'Connell, Collins and the other participants in the Easter Rebellion. It's a shrine now. The main cell-block room has a huge vaulted ceiling made out of smoked glass. In the middle of the room there is a high staircase from which a bridge, three stories high, spans the room. Eugene Lee and I based the *Sweeney Todd* set on this room.

Prince told his designer that he wanted "to set the whole show inside a Victorian factory that has a gritty glass roof which diffuses the sunlight." "Separating people from the sun" became his metaphor for "the incursions of the Industrial Revolution on the poetry within people. We purchased a derelict factory in Rhode Island, dismantled it and used it for the set." Evoking a twilight world of drab colors, the set and costumes together with the cold blue lights created a denatured *mise-en-scène* with a brooding symbolism. "It could be told in a naturalistic setting," Sondheim said when the show opened. "It could be a show about doors and walls and stuffy Victorian furniture. Hal turned it into something much more abstract, which affected how I thought about the songs."[11]

Spare and non-representational, with an upstage skeletal catwalk that raised and lowered, moving staircases, as well as a cyclorama of a slanted unpopulated London street and factory scene that changed color from blue to orange to red and was sometimes hidden by a black drape, the set created a sense of unnerving *absence*, a vast empty space crawling with shadows.

36 "What do they make in this factory? – A show called *Sweeney Todd*"
(1979). The Act II opening number, "God, That's Good!" with Mrs. Lovett
(Angela Lansbury) moving back and forth between her hungry customers
and Sweeney's barber shop (Len Cariou examines his new trick chair).
Setting by Eugene Lee; costumes by Franne Lee; lighting by Ken Billington
(photo courtesy of Van Williams)

37 Prince's scenic abstraction: creating a balcony for Johanna (Sarah Rice) out of a scaffold and stairs (*Sweeney Todd*) (photo courtesy of Van Williams)

Ladders, steps, and grids suggested a depersonalized environment that exposed the impact of the new industrialism. At the center of this minatory emptiness most of the action was played out on a central split-level unit, in which Sweeney's tonsorial parlor (furnished with a gas-chamber chair and a casket) sat perched over Mrs. Lovett's slovenly pie shop; the unit revolved to reveal two other settings, Mrs. Lovett's parlor and a bare wall with two openings, Mrs. Lovett's cellar door and the chute down which Sweeney's victims were hurled. "Part cathedral, part factory, part prison . . . and monstrously beautiful,"[12] this was the kind of set on which Prince could direct a *Sweeney Todd* he believed in.

If Sondheim was thinking in terms of Grand Guignol and Prince was mining the legend's social implications they nonetheless agreed on tone: their

Sweeney Todd was to be a dark musical relieved by a vein of black comedy, a bloodbath that would be suspended somewhere between melodrama and farce without ever slipping over into camp or generic send-up. Chills mixed with laughs, drama and comedy held in tense intimate balance – finding and then sustaining the show's tone, politically and through a unifying perform-ing and scenic concept, may well have been Prince's toughest challenge to date. Larry Fuller recalls that "it was blindman's bluff all the way through, searching for the right way to go . . . you have to believe there is a true danger; and on the other hand you have to have humor to relieve the heaviness."

By turns romantic and chilling, straightforward and ironic, Sondheim's score sustains the show's tricky dual tone. In an interview before the show opened, Sondheim described *Sweeney Todd* as a "musical thriller with roman-tic ballads and comic songs that tend toward a music-hall tradition. It is passionately funny and passionately intense. As a counterbalance to its gory material Hal moved the show toward the romantic."[13] "To make that kind of show work, you have to write romantic music," Prince says. "Our aim was to make the score as lush as we could." Many of the show's ballads, like "Green Finch and Linnet Bird," "Johanna," "Not While I'm Around," and "Pretty Women," are among the richest and most soaring Sondheim has yet written, while other numbers, "The Ballad of Sweeney Todd," "Epiphany," and "City on Fire!" and the underscoring are among his most sustained exercises in dissonance – music intended to be disturbing. "I wanted to create suspense through music," Sondheim says.

Like the startlingly shrill whistle that preceded each of Sweeney's killings, Sondheim wanted to write the kind of score that

can scare an audience. Hitchcock used Bernard Herrmann to write that kind of music – *Sweeney Todd* is my homage to Bernard Herrmann. As an example of how music can rattle an audience, think of the first ten seconds of *Jaws*, in which John Williams's double-bass scares the hell out of you. After that musical set-up you don't need Spielberg. The opening organ chords are based on "Kyrie eleison," and I drew on the medieval *Dies Irae*, from the requiem mass, because Sweeney is in love with death . . . The opening creates a rumble: something is about to happen. The dissonance is not quite resolved, which is creepy; the feeling is one of lifting and dropping the audience.

"Suspense musicals don't work because not enough music is used to sustain the suspense," Sondheim says. "To avoid that, I made music about eighty percent of the show." The extended musical development, with, as Sondheim says "its feeling of a score as opposed to a collection of songs," the leitmotifs and underscoring that build an almost unbroken musical fabric as well as the scale of the music and the production prompted some critics to label the show an opera, though Sondheim rejected this. "It belonged at the New York City Opera [where it was presented in 1984] which is an operetta stage, but it would never belong at the Met: grand opera requires a different voice and approach." Rather than imitating operatic models Sondheim designed his score to function the way "old movie scores do, with motifs used to re-arouse audience feelings, to identify characters and settings – the relentless underscoring in forties movies cues the audience's emotional response, which is what I tried to do in *Sweeney*."

To alert the audience that the show was not going to be a campy hiss-the-villain thriller, the authors realized that comic elements could be introduced only after an eerie and intimidating atmosphere had been solidly established. "When you see Eugene Lee's set, poured with chilling blue light, and hear the opening chords, you don't laugh," Sondheim says. Following Bond, Prince and Sondheim then introduced comic relief as a counterbalance. The show's tension between high drama and low comedy is sustained in its contrasting leading roles, which were specifically written for Len Cariou and Angela Lansbury: his intensity collided with her broad comic turns. Trembling with rage, alternately distracted and, when leaping into frenzied action, his face a glowering mask, Cariou played Sweeney without any apparent concession to the fact that he was in a musical, while as Sweeney's amoral accomplice Lansbury performed in a brisk presentational style that clearly aimed to please. ("Angela is juicy – you want to squeeze her, and that's important to the show," Sondheim says.) Following the lesson he learned from George Abbott, that melodrama and farce must be played for real, Prince told his actors that "in the past the credo that governed the work Steve and I have done has been 'less is more.' This time I want *more* than anyone has ever seen before: if you don't chew up the scenery, we're going to be in trouble." Following orders, Cariou says he and Lansbury

played the piece to its fullest. We didn't step back in the Brechtian sense; indeed, if we had the show wouldn't have had the impact on the audience that it did. We played it absolutely seriously; and what we were all most proud of was that we walked a fine line between melodrama and farce without dipping over into the farce area. You have to like a character in order to play him, and if a character is well-written, as Sweeney certainly is, there are always reasons to like him. It's easy to get behind a guy who's been thrown in prison for fifteen years for the wrong reasons. I identified with the man's basic motive: to reclaim his wife and daughter and to get even with his enemies. That was what had kept him going all those years.

In playing Sweeney sympathetically Cariou was observing Christopher Bond's original intentions. As Sondheim says, "Except for Bond's version the British dramatists always camped up the characters, but we wanted to avoid that. . . Our problem was to keep the audience from giggling, and when we accomplished that we felt we had done our job."

If Sweeney's hollow-eyed, sallow demeanor began to take on tragic inflections, Lansbury's Mrs. Lovett, with Raggedy Ann make-up and two thick braids, was a complementary embodiment of the comic spirit. If Sweeney still looked human, a man on the edge, Mrs. Lovett was a full-scale grotesque. The visual distinction between the two characters supported the split between drama and comedy on which the entire show pivots. Where Sweeney's dialogue and lyrics are consistently dark, filled with foreboding and demented passion, Mrs. Lovett's are lightweight. As Larry Fuller points out, "Mrs. Lovett's songs are musical-comedy numbers in a show that isn't a musical comedy." Her first song, "The Worst Pies in London," in which the character squashes bugs as she sings, is the first moment in the show in which Sondheim allows the audience to relax. In Act II, after she and Sweeney have become demonic conspirators, her inappropriate fantasy of bourgeois happiness breaks the rising tension:

> I can see us waking,
> The breakers breaking,
> The seagulls squawking:
> Hoo! Hoo!
>
> I do me baking,
> Then I go walking
> With you—hoo . . .
>
> In our cozy retreat,
> Kept all neat and tidy,
> We'll have chums over every Friday
> By the sea.

At the end of Act I Sondheim places Sweeney's drama and Lovett's comedy back to back: "after he misses his chance at killing the Judge, Sweeney goes mad; it's as if the man's mind snapped," says Len Cariou. "At that moment the character says, in effect, 'All right, fuck it, I'll get them all!' That's the only way to justify it on stage, to do it snap!" But the key element in making the moment credible was music, and Sondheim said it took a month to get the tone of it right. I had to motivate Todd from wanting to kill one man to wanting to kill all men, the moment at which we felt Bond's play was weakest. To demonstrate musically that his mind is cracking I switched between violent and lyrical passages, and had rapid rhythmic shifts, from quick to slow. His murderous vengeance announced to a chugging engine-like theme (the *Dies Irae* disguised) alternates with a keening threnody for his wife and daughter.

Slashing the air with his razor and spewing his misanthropy —

> There's a hole in the world
> Like a great black pit
> And it's filled with people

38 The recognition scene: Sweeney (Len Cariou) discovers that the mad beggar is his wife Lucy (Merle Louise), as Tobias (Ken Jennings), his hair turned white by what he has seen in Mrs. Lovett's cellar, descends into his own madness. "When no one in the audience laughed, I figured I had done my job," the librettist Hugh Wheeler said (*Sweeney Todd*) (photo courtesy of Van Williams)

Who are filled with shit
And the vermin of the world
Inhabit it —
But not for long!

— against percussive chords that echo his loss of control, Sweeney's musicalized breakdown builds a tension that "A Little Priest" immediately dispels: as Prince says, "the demonic glee of 'A Little Priest,' coming right after the demonic hatred of 'Epiphany,' provides a release for the audience." "A Little Priest" is Mrs. Lovett's epiphany in which she devises the money-saving scheme of using Todd's victims as the ingredients for her meat pies:

Think of it as thrift,
As a gift . . .
If you get my drift . . .
With the price of meat what it is.

The song is a music-hall turn filled with puns and *doubles entendres*, word play and rhymes:

MRS. LOVETT (offering another pie):

It's fop.
Finest in the shop.
Or we have some shepherd's pie peppered
With actual shepherd
On top.
And I've just begun.
Here's the politician — so oily
It's served with a doily —
Have one.

TODD: Put it on a bun —
Well, you never know if it's going to run.

"I got my cue [for 'A Little Priest'] from a stage direction in Bond's play," Sondheim recalls. "The song's comic spirit is an expansion of an emotional moment in Bond in which the characters giggle at their conspiracy. The comedy grows right out of the tension: you can be tickled *only* if you're tense — Hitchcock made a career out of that."

The startling counterpoint between "Epiphany" and "A Little Priest" defines Sondheim's approach throughout the show, as he sets up an abrasion between melody and lyrics and between songs and their dramatic placement that underlines *Sweeney Todd's* schizophrenic tone. One of his earliest ideas about the score was "to have a song where you'd expect to have someone killed, and it wouldn't happen, and then to reverse that by having a murder during a song that didn't prepare you for it. Both would be lyrical numbers meant to disarm you." Thus, as he relishes the prospect of slitting Judge Turpin's throat, Sweeney and the oblivious Judge sing "Pretty Women," a ballad with a sparkling melody. In Act II, Sweeney sings a reprise of "Johanna," a haunting ballad, as he dispassionately slices his customers' throats. "He's killing all those people, against that beautiful melody, which is a brilliant *double entendre*," Len Cariou says. "Singing that song with the intention behind it was such an exciting acting challenge – it was such good theatre!"

Sondheim delights in innocent-seeming songs in devious circumstances Mrs. Lovett and her dim-witted assistant Toby sing a romantic duet, "Not While I'm Around," in which they swear to protect each other. While Toby is sincere Mrs. Lovett is enacting a wicked charade, and after singing of her love for him she locks him in the cellar, where he goes mad when he discovers the ingredients of her meat pies. Sweeney's tenderest song, in lyrics as well as melody, is a hymn of praise addressed to "my friends," his "precious" razors:

> Well, I've come home
> To find you waiting.
> Home,
> And we're together
> And we'll do wonders,
> Won't we?

But not all of Sondheim's score is double-edged. For the juvenile romantic couple, the show's only unmasked characters, the sailor Anthony and Sweeney's daughter Johanna, Sondheim has written songs in both a romantic and a comic vein that express the characters' directness and passion. And the harsh, discordant musical fragments that Sweeney's mad disheveled wife Lucy sings express directly the character's emotional and physical dissolution.

Whether swooningly romantic or pitted with *double entendre*, whether straightforward or ironic, whether the melody flows into or sets up a counterpoint to the action, whether the lyrics reveal or disguise the characters' feelings and intentions, Sondheim's immense score always serves the play. Significantly, Prince notes about "A Little Priest" that "there's an element in the song of Mrs. Lovett wanting to please Sweeney. She's being coy. And that gives the song a tension that keeps it right in the show. It doesn't turn into high jinks." "God, That's Good!", which opens Act II, is a prime example of how Sondheim and Prince turn a song into a musical scene. "Steve wrote it as a dazzling *tour de force*," Prince says:

He had plotted out the song very carefully, noting who Mrs. Lovett talks to at which point; which customers are drunk, and so on. The customers were at various tables, and each customer had his own play going, singing individual dramas. "This is so complex the audience will go crazy," I told him, and I really had no idea at first how to stage the number. Steve said the customers should be hanging all over the set, but I said they must be around one long table so the audience has a single, concise image: an octopus of hungry, insatiable people.

However, because both collaborators felt that no matter how it was staged "God, That's Good!", which is expository rather than dramatic, a demonstration of how prosperous Mrs. Lovett's business has become, was not compelling enough to command undivided attention, Sondheim wrote the number so that it is continually interrupted by Sweeney, who is excited about the arrival of his new trick barber's chair. Mrs. Lovett goes back and forth between Sweeney and her customers, between two playing areas and two masks: her affected propriety as a capitalist and her conspiratorial exchanges with Sweeney.

"This isn't the Holy fucking Grail, it's only a show," a comment Prince made about another project, applies with special pertinence to *Sweeney Todd*. In strictly theatrical terms – its unified production style that maintains a balance between melodrama and farce – the show solves its challenges in triumph. The simultaneous action, the crowd scenes, the delight in creating theatrical illusion (a stepladder that suggests a balcony, a walk through London over steps and bridges and platforms placed by stagehands in full view of the audience), the observing chorus – *Sweeney Todd* is a bravura display of Princely manipulation; it's a show directed by a master showman.[14] However, in itself this showmanship demonstrates the problematic nature of the "concept" musical. As a spur to the inventiveness of Prince's staging, the factory setting not only provided the basis for the show's space and movement, but served as

a way to help the chorus members work out individual characters. Giving them an environment, the world of the factory, to fit into, dignified their assignments and gave them a sensory reality out of which to develop character ideas. I had chorus members come up to me to suggest details: one wanted to have a limp, another wanted to have a hunched back from working in a factory: this is exciting for a director. I can't stand seeing "here come the poor people on stage," as in *Oliver!* I think of choruses as an extra leading character, like the public in *Evita*. In *Sweeney Todd*, we had twenty different characters: it was *Marat/Sade*, and if they're unified, as in *Sweeney Todd*, that's what's valuable.[15]

At the same time, as a thematic symbol the factory is unconvincing. It remains simply a theatrical device. Responding to a frequent question, "What *do* they make in that factory?", Prince has a standard quip: "A show called *Sweeney Todd*." While conceding that the factory frame is not developed, Prince says that for him "the metaphor remains valid. I didn't feel the need to explain it within the show; I felt audiences could use their imagination a little, developing suggestions that we gave them." Even so, at the end of the play the cast pointed to the audience as they pretended to spot Sweeneys everywhere. Although Prince considered this direct address over-obvious, he agreed with Sondheim's view that it "was a valid way of saying that the need for revenge is a universal desire." But are there really Sweeneys all around us? A demonic dispossessed barber fixated on revenge who becomes a serial killer through contempt for his fellow man is surely not a figure of universal resonance. His story is too bizarre to stand the Everyman significa-tion that the creators seem to want to assign it – there is a good reason why the legend has been traditionally confined to the camp of Grand Guignol. Even supposing that Sweeney's tale does demonstrate that "the need for revenge is a universal desire," is this not a diminishing, even rather petty philosophic perception on which to rest a production of such magnitude? Prince's initial response that he couldn't "afford" to dwell on revenge was perhaps well-founded.

More promising as the moral archetype the show is searching for is the character of Mrs. Lovett, in whose rise to money is a satire and critique of capitalist enterprise such as Brecht and Weill might well have it portrayed in Berlin at the end of the twenties. As a bourgeoise with a criminal soul Mrs. Lovett is moral first cousin to the Peachums in *The Threepenny Opera*, guttersnipes who affect the manners of the moral majority.

But in his eagerness to create a meaningful musical Prince stretched the material to frame a perception about human nature and to sustain a contem-porary relevance that the blood-and-thunder legend cannot support (whereas for Sondheim "the show was always meant to be fun, like a horror movie, and I never looked for 'higher meanings'"). As a contemporary comment on a nineteenth-century theatrical tradition, *Sweeney Todd* is exemplary, a one-of-a-kind musical; as an attempt to cross Boucicault with Brecht, a musical satire that does for revenge what *The Threepenny Opera* and *Mahagonny* did for greed, lust, and hypocrisy, *Sweeney Todd* runs aground on its pretensions as well as the quaintness of its source material, for unlike Macheath and his fellows, who incarnated the mood of Germany on the eve of Hitler's ascension, Sweeney and Mrs. Lovett exist in a theatrical no man's land. Prince's ambivalence about *Sweeney Todd*, both at the time and in retrospect, can be seen as implicit recognition that the show derives from intellectualized statement rather than felt truth. "I liked the theatricality and politics and sheer impossibility of *Pacific Overtures*, but on *Sweeney Todd* I got up every day like a man who's been sentenced; I didn't know what I had. I didn't have confidence in it," Prince says. In a letter to George Abbott, as he was directing the London production, Prince wrote that "it's a relentless, exhausting show to direct – no fun at all. I can't tell whether it's the subject matter or simply that the material is so complicated (unnecessarily?)".[1] Prince's final comment to me about *Sweeney Todd* was, "We ran out of audience. After all, this was a show about chopping people up."

8 A few follies

"Until *Merrily We Roll Along* I really had what amounted to my own production team," Prince says. "I had my own design staff and a loyal group of investors. We were like a repertory company that just happened to be located on Broadway instead of the regional theatre." That ended when the ironically-named musical failed in November 1981, and until *The Phantom of the Opera* opened in London in the fall of 1986 Prince suffered a series of critical and financial failures: two other Broadway musicals, *A Doll's Life* (1982) and *Grind* (1985); an off-Broadway review, *Diamonds* (1985); and two straight plays, *Play Memory* by Joanna Glass and *The End of the World* by Arthur Kopit (both 1985).

Ten years earlier, in shows like *Company* and *Follies*, Prince had created a new musical-theatre architecture. "It's important to discern when you are merely repeating yourself, and when your choices are fresh," as Prince says; but now the artful techniques of earlier work threatened to descend into mannerism. For all their shortcomings, however, *Merrily We Roll Along*, *A Doll's Life*, and *Grind* are continuing evidence of Prince's commitment to a lyric theatre that strives to be both popular and provocative. All three shows are dark cautionary fables: sermons mixed with serenades. "*Merrily* is about wealth and success in terms of making art," Prince says. In Prince's original concept *Grind* was "my musical about violence." *A Doll's Life* takes on Ibsen as it fashions a scenario for what happened to Nora after she slammed the door on her husband and children at the end of *A Doll House*.

To Prince, for whom *Merrily We Roll Along* was "the most painful experience of my life," the problems with the production were primarily "the mistake of previewing in New York . . . where everybody could see and comment on what we were doing," compounded by scheduling that forced them "into rehearsal before everything was ready, and there was a loss of clarity." But beyond that the nature of the material provided a focus of attack for theatrical traditionalists, whose values had been challenged by all Prince's work to that point, while the experimental way in which he treated it was too far from Broadway staging norms.

As Prince recalls, the show came from his wife's suggestion of doing a musical about "what kids were thinking. Our two kids were in their teens at the time. I remembered the original Kaufman and Hart play, which I had loved as a youngster, and thought that it might provide the basis for our musical. I called Steve, who felt insecure about it, as I had felt uncertain about *Sweeney Todd*."

131

Kaufman and Hart's play is a surprisingly cynical melodramatic treatment of how commercial success corrupts a promising playwright, ruining his marriage and friendships as well as his talent. George Furth's libretto transposes the anti-hero's dilemma to the musical theatre and traces the erosion of a three-way friendship over a twenty-five-year period, from 1955 to 1980 – "our own time period," Prince says, referring to Sondheim and himself. The fates of the three friends – composer Franklin Shepard, who goes to Hollywood, lyricist Charley Kringas, who maintains his idealism, and writer Mary Flynn, driven to drink by her unrequited love for Franklin – are projected against the promise and demise of the Kennedy era. In the show's 1960 segment, the young musicians perform a comic song about the dazzling Kennedys; in 1957 their pledge to dedicate their lives to creative achievement takes place on the night that Sputnik is launched.

The musical retains the reverse chronology of the original play. "You can't do it in conventional time," Prince says. "To do that would be to undermine the ironic point, and because of its unusual form, telling the story backwards, beginning at the end, the show cannot be played in a conventional style." Prince therefore decided to reverse the usual practice of having older actors play younger characters by having kids without make-up enact the characters throughout the twenty-five-year span the show covered. "It didn't persuade the audience," Prince admits, but what he valued was "the raw commitment of kids, the fact that they're not slick or adept. When I did a reading of *Merrily* with entirely inexperienced youngsters I thought the show was terrific. On Broadway I wanted to retain that excitement of eager kids putting on a show." Lonny Price, who played Charley Kringas, says that

Hal wanted kids to act the story so you might think it was *someone else's* story and that what we see hadn't really happened to them – maybe they would be able to overcome the kind of defeat the play is about, maybe they would be the ones to change the world. That's an exciting concept: nobody else thinks like that. He felt that doing the show with kids gave it a twist so that it was not just about a rich man who's unhappy and who cares?

But whatever its moral value, carrying through such a concept reduced the show's capacity to communicate effectively to an audience. While the two leads, Lonny Price and Ann Morrison, who played Mary Flynn, were professional – a compromise with Broadway sophistication – most of the ensemble were literally raw, untrained, and inexperienced; the contrast showed up their lack of expertise. Even though Prince tried to compensate by cutting down the other roles during previews, as Sondheim says the 1934 play was "written for adults and so was ours: George Furth's brittle dialogue sounds better delivered by adults. We made a terrible error in casting kids."[1]

The problems were equally clear in stage movement since, according to the show's final choreographer, Larry Fuller, "Only five people in the ensemble were dance-trained; a few were not even movers. I put them in the back. For most of the numbers all I could do was a social dancing frame; the kids weren't capable of doing anything that thrilling." Ron Field, the choreographer on Prince's original team, who wanted to turn the show into the kind of slick dance musical that clearly violated Prince's deglamorized approach (which resulted in Field's replacement), "had tried to make them really dance and they didn't look good doing it, and I didn't have time to properly drill them. I redid one number, 'Hey Old Friends,' five or six times to try to make it stop the show, but it never got the reaction we wanted."

To protect his unvarnished concept Prince wanted a minimalist set. "Long before we did it I said there should be no scenery – I wanted the show to look like *Our Town*. Steve said to go ahead with that, but I got frightened. I didn't do what I thought was right; I didn't have the guts, and we opened previews with full costumes and scenery, and then when I realized this was wrong we spent previews getting rid of costumes and scenery." Lonny Price remembers that "Hal announced one day during previews that he had made a mistake, that the costumes were dwarfing our performances. 'Let's go to jeans and sweat shirts,' he said. He scrapped $200,000 worth of hand-made costumes: that's his kind of bravery." "Sweat shirts are what kids would design their costumes to look like," Ann Morrison says. "And visually this had more unity than when we started, with a different costume for every scene, which was just too much."

Prince ordered constructivist sets *à la* Meyerhold that suspended the action in a cheerless, unlocalized *mise-en-scène*. "It was an erector set, a big toy that bright kids might design," Lonny Price says. "But I never knew where we were: were we in a gym? In Frank's mind? The older Frank's mind? Hal was afraid that audiences paying Broadway prices wouldn't appreciate a set filled with ladders."

Yet as Prince says, "even when I stripped the sets and let the kids wear their rehearsal clothes – it became very Brechtian – nothing worked visually. *Merrily* was one of the rare experiences in my life when I didn't know what a show should look like. I still don't know what it should look like." Indeed, played on an abstract set in rehearsal clothes which labeled the characters (Best Friend, Rich Kid, etc.) and with dated legends on either side of the stage, the production's quasi-Brechtian bleakness undercut the impact of what Prince calls Sondheim's "warmest" score.

Perhaps the only successful element of the show was Sondheim's "melodic, joyful, old-fashioned musical-comedy score," as Prince describes it, "with new-fashioned requirements, with lyrics that are far more specific than the old-style shows required." Sondheim's score is another of his conceits: the music parallels the show's reverse chronology. "Like *Pacific Overtures* and

39 Rehearsal clothes in a Broadway musical: Ann Morrison as Mary, Sally Klein as Beth, Lonny Price as Charley, in *Merrily We Roll Along* (1981) (photo courtesy of Van Williams)

Sweeney Todd, the *Merrily* score is very much interrelated," Sondheim says. "Blocks of music are utilized in different contexts and time periods, to suggest the emotional colors underlying the relationships. The musical themes, designed to reflect themes in the characters' lives, are not developed but replaced: the musical approach is modular." Filled with repeated motifs, fragments of melody sung in varying moods by different characters, the score is "written backwards" to support the way the story is told. Beginning with the sardonic "Rich and Famous" and ending with the lyrical "Our Time," which evokes a feeling of youthful idealism – kids on a rooftop poised on the edge of making their way into a world of creative endeavor ("People were crying every night at that moment in the show," Lonny Price recalls) – the music mimics the narrative curve, the fall and rise of a three-way friendship. Like the title song in *Company*, the *Merrily* vamp is reprised in fragments throughout the show, providing a bridge between episodes, a musical equivalent of Brechtian placards.

However, what most of the criticism focused on was not the musical strengths of the show but the apparently self-indulgent reflexiveness of the material. "People think you set out to iconize yourselves, but you set out to do shows," Prince says, rejecting the criticism that *Merrily We Roll Along* was an autobiographical musical. "*Follies* was far more about ourselves: why didn't they accuse us there instead of on *Merrily*?" "Critics have tried to read autobiography into every one of my shows except *Pacific Overtures*, and it's nonsense", Sondheim protests.

Nonetheless the show inevitably invited comparisons between its characters, people who have become rich and famous in the musical theatre, and its creators, perceived by the public as being in the same category. Unlike their sour hero, Prince and Sondheim have neither deserted Broadway for Hollywood nor have they capitulated to commercial crassness. "I don't think either of us is in jeopardy of giving up what we want to do to be incorporated [which is what Franklin Shepard does]. We have a long enough record to prove that," Prince said at the time the show opened.[2] Indeed, unlike the show's somber statement about success contaminating artistic instincts, the careers of Prince and Sondheim demonstrate that with fame and riches come *increased* opportunities for artistic experiment. Given their record, in fact, *Merrily*'s statement that people in show business pay for their success and that "when you get there, there is no there there,"[3] is a show-business platitude that their own work happily contradicts. From the team that produced *Company, Follies, Pacific Overtures* and *Sweeney Todd*, that seemed an ordinary as well as an uncharacteristically smug thesis.

"*Merrily*" is about wealth and success in terms of making art: what is small about that?" Prince protests. Yet in working out this conflict in the context of the Broadway musical theatre, Prince and Sondheim invite the charge of parochialism. To move beyond the limiting autobiographical connotations, they needed the abstraction that metaphors had given them in earlier pieces – the kind of distance that Sondheim in fact found in his next (Pulitzer Prize-winning) work, *Sunday in the Park with George*, which supplies a broader and more protected framework within which to explore the same themes. Instead of the shallow Broadway/Hollywood setting, *Sunday* appropriates the creation of a great modernist painting, Georges Seurat's *La Grande Jatte*, as the canvas against which to examine the struggles of an artist.

Making art is the focus of Act I; Act II introduces success and money as obstacles in the artist's life – the themes of *Merrily* enlarged by an unexpected context. And while Sondheim and his librettist James Lapine courted a charge of overreaching (as Prince and Sondheim in *Merrily* made themselves vulnerable to being accused of looking down from on high at theatre professionals who succumb to commerce), reviewers and audiences for the most part accepted the metaphoric leap.

"*A Doll's Life* was far from perfect – its parts were not up to its demands," Prince admits. "I was condemned for doing it again – the neo-Brechtian chorus, characters watching the show from a catwalk, the narrative frame (of beginning and ending with a rehearsal of *A Doll House*) – and Betty [Comden] and Adolph [Green] [with their reputation for writing light comedy] were condemned for never doing this kind of show before."

Adding "a picaresque tale onto a classic play that takes place in a confined time period" was indeed, as Prince describes it, "dangerous and difficult." Defying historical and cultural probability, the flat-voiced libretto turns Nora into a cunning little vixen, a spoiled bourgeoise with an itch for money and power. To escape being a doll, she becomes like a man (Prince argues that "this post-Ibsen Nora who appropriates male values in order to succeed makes a telling point"), all too rapidly learning to do unto others as she has been done unto. Away from home, her body as freed as her capitalist instincts, she is transformed into a hard-nosed business woman. Betsy Joslyn, who played Nora, told Comden and Green that they had made her "just like the men she complains about. I wanted them to make her more charming and humorous; they had chosen me to play her – I'm funny, I love to joke – and yet they had me remain so somber throughout the show. Nora came off like Evita." Joslyn also felt that the ending, when Nora returns to her family, was unmotivated. "I felt she needed a crack-up in Act II, an epiphany like Sweeney Todd's that would justify and explain her decision to go home to her husband and children. I had to act between the lines, because Comden and Green hadn't written the transitions to make her real."

If the show foundered on the writers' shallowness, it nonetheless merits attention because of Larry Grossman's score, which demonstrates the degree to which (in his own words) "the Prince–Sondheim shows in the seventies – the Golden Age – took musical material to new places: I can't watch the old-fashioned musicals anymore, and it's hard for me to listen to those thirty-two-bar AABA songs, unless they're by Gershwin or Rodgers." Indeed, though it has a distinctively personal voice in its rich variety of waltzes, choral ensembles, recitative, melodic fragments, and leitmotifs, in its Wagnerian parody and extended musical scenes, and particularly in the way it weaves through scenes and in its occasional choral commentary, Grossman's score inevitably prompted comparison with Sondheim.

Set in a burlesque house in Chicago during the thirties, *Grind* has the kind of symbolically charged setting and the agitated social and political background to which Prince is attracted. In its ironic one-word title with multiple meanings and its metaphoric use of a theatrical form *Grind* recalled such earlier Prince vehicles as *Cabaret*, *Company*, and *Follies*: "Life is a grind, old chum," as one unfriendly critic wrote.[4]

Unlike *Sugar Babies*, a paean to old-time vaudeville, *Grind* was not

40 Prince's love of elevation, deep focus, and simultaneous action is
apparent in this scene from *A Doll's Life* (1982). An opera, "Loki and
Baldur," is performed on an inner stage as Nora's story proceeds stage left.
Setting by Timothy O'Brien and Tazeena Firth (photo courtesy of Van
Williams)

designed as a nostalgic tribute to a vanished form of entertainment. Rather, it was Prince's intention to quote burlesque style as a means of playing variations on the theme — violence — which had attracted him to Fay Kanin's original script, a screenplay called "This Must Be the Place." "All the violent acts — racial violence, a suicide, a homosexual getting beat up in the street outside the theatre — were to be done in a burlesque skit format. The revue structure would have made the theme of violence clear to an audience and would have given the show a unity of style and theme."

"I'm not trying to say that life is a burlesque show," Prince stated in a pre-opening interview. "Burlesque provides the trapping. The real grind is in the real world; inside the burlesque house, the grind is a performance. The theatre is a safe place and their employment gives the performers security."[5] The tensions of the "real" world seep into the theatre in a romantic triangle that develops as a black song-and-dance man vies with a refugee from the Irish Rebellion for the affection of Satin, the black headliner at Harry Earle's.

When it opened on Broadway in April 1985, *Grind* had neither the thematic nor stylistic thrust that Prince had originally planned. "What started out as me running things became me holding the floodgates," Prince explains. "I became an example of a human being who caves in to economic pressure. Eight producers were needed to raise the show's five-million-dollar budget, and because I felt I had to protect their investment I capitulated. I changed the story into a star-vehicle for Ben Vereen."

Larry Grossman, who contributed another strong score to a show that did not work, and who had suffered through star tantrums in 1970 on *Minnie's Boys*, a musical about the Marx Brothers — "Shelley Winters was an abomination on that stage!" — was appalled by the way Vereen "tried to force his Vegas act onto the show. Had a real actor played Leroy the balance of the show would have been restored. When he wanted his solo numbers in each act to be a Vegas routine we said, 'This is about Leroy not about you, Ben.'" However with so much money at stake, Prince says he "did the expedient thing." And Leroy's Act II spot, "A New Man," about the character's supposed reformation from a wise guy into a serious romantic partner, became a contemporary dance showcase aimed at appeasing Vereen's fans.

The problems were epitomized by the disagreement about "We All George," a song which both Prince and Grossman felt was "the centerpiece of the score." Ellen Fitzhugh's lyrics provide a mordant comment on race relations, satirizing the cliché that every Pullman porter seems to be named George:

LEROY: De porters on de B and O,
Y'know we all looks the same.
So de white folks long ago,

Dey come up wid one name –
So all o' us Porters
Don't haf t' keep rememberin'
"Is we Rufus or Clarence or Sam?"
Now it's easy as pie
Fo' us t' hie de hie
To be one name we all am . . .

ᴸᴇʀᴏʏ ᴀɴᴅ ɢɪʀʟs: We all George . . .

'All the black actors read the script with the number in it, and they all signed their contracts on that basis," Grossman says. "After the show was in rehearsal for two weeks they refused to perform it. After that, much of the show's courage was taken away. The number would have explained what we were trying to do." Prince was "amazed":

It was exactly as if Joel Grey had refused to do the gorilla song in *Cabaret*, which like "We All George" is not a number that says this is how we feel. The black actors told me I didn't

41 A vision out of Reginald Marsh: backstage at Harry Earle's burlesque house in *Grind* (1985), with Leroy (Ben Vereen) on the spiral staircase. Setting by Clarke Dunham; costumes by Florence Klotz; lighting by Ken Billington (photo courtesy of Van Williams)

know what it was to be black, yet I knew *exactly* what that number was. I'm Jewish and I responded to the number the way I felt about "if you could see her through my eyes she wouldn't look Jewish at all." Both are songs that *expose* prejudice, not condone it, for Christ's sake! When I cut the song . . . I felt emasculated. It was my weakest, most disappointing moment as an artist and as a human being . . . I should have dropped the show, or done it elsewhere, at a small theatre where my original scheme might have been accepted. A musical about violence doesn't belong on Broadway at this time.

Prince responded to the way failure seemed to have been built into the production of *Grind* because of the five-million-dollar price-tag that hovered over his head like the sword of Damocles by deciding to establish an off-Broadway theatre of his own, at the Astoria Kaufman Studios in Queens. Although plans for the Astoria project are uncertain at the present time, Prince is hopeful that he can develop an alternative to the hazards of producing musicals on Broadway. Prince notes that the Astoria project was conceived as

a factory where we could make musicals . . . All seats: twenty-five dollars, with none to the booth. Each show to be done for eight weeks; three new musicals and one revival a year. I would develop the scripts, the way I always have. If things go to Broadway, fine: I have always felt that art should pay for itself, and I don't like the unctuousness, the moral superiority, of art that doesn't earn money. There's a lot of compromise in non-commercial theatre too: look at Joe Papp, who floats his ship by putting on commercial vehicles like *Drood* and *The Pirates of Penzance*; only *Chorus Line* of the musicals he's developed was truly experimental.

At the same time, it would be dangerous and impractical – and only half the story – were I to turn my back on government partnership and private funding. In my six years on the National Council for the Arts, I think I was noisier than anyone about the logical marriage of not-for- and for-profit. Broadway could realize considerable help from government and private not-for-profit financing. This sort of thing happens all over the world effectively.

Astoria or its equivalent is not to be a clearing house for Broadway but a place to experiment in a way that I no longer can on Broadway because of economics. The literature that serves the country was created on Broadway; because of the pressures money imposes on our choices we're not influencing theatre the way we did. My new set-up, whatever form it may take, by significantly cutting the costs of producing a musical on Broadway, and by trying out experimental work that can't be produced directly on Broadway today, should help to revive Broadway as a theatrical influence.

9   Nights at the opera

"I have a hunch I'm probably in the best position to break down the whole fusty opera/musical theatre schism," Prince wrote in a letter to Beverly Sills, artistic director of the New York City Opera.[1] Indeed, as both propagandist and practitioner Prince has done more than anyone else to advance the idea that like the exchange between Fred Astaire and Ginger Rogers – "he gave her class and she gave him sex appeal," as Katharine Hepburn pointed out – the "high" art of opera and its more plainspoken popular cousin, the Broadway musical, have much to offer each other. Operatic models can help to release the musical from its conventions and, reciprocally, directors like Prince offset opera's custodial productions of sacred texts with a revitalizing theatricality. Prince has presided over this enlivening cross-fertilization not only in his career but also officially as president (since 1983) of the National Institute for Music Theatre (originally, before Prince's tenure, the National Opera Institute). As Prince defines them,

its priorities are to draw together . . . musical theatre and opera, to improve the quality of acting in opera, to alter the opera repertoire to accommodate American musicals (*Sweeney Todd* for one) and to encourage American composers and librettists to write musicals. We have an intern program and primarily give grants to singer-actors, composers, lyricists, directors, conductors. Throughout the year we have competitions for singers and annually an evening at Kennedy Center to award grants to the best of them.[2]

Despite – or perhaps because of – his musical-theatre background, Prince had a hard time breaking into opera, and it took six years of assiduous courtship before "Julius Rudel at City Opera called to ask if I would be interested in directing a new Israeli opera, *Ashmedai* by Josef Tal . . . Almost simultaneously Carol Fox at the Chicago Lyric Opera called me with an offer to direct *Girl of the Golden West*. And there I was, committed to two operas at the same time."

Musically untrained – "I can't read a note of music, but I *feel* it, and I am sophisticated enough to know what it is saying" – Prince approaches opera as drama. "Many people go to the opera and close their eyes and listen to the beautiful sounds. Some people think it is acceptable to have a diva who doesn't move. I can't go along with that."[3] As an avowed enemy of the star-vehicle, whether the star is Merman or Milanov, Prince treats opera

as if it's a play. I regard the lyrics as a playscript, and I approach an opera company the same way I would a Broadway company, sometimes to their amazement. We work

141

the same way as on a musical, beginning with a discussion of concept – why we are doing the piece – and working on matters of characterization and movement. Sometimes the singers resist or are surprised when I treat them like actors . . . I insist on having the chorus there at the first rehearsal.

Even so, he and his Broadway colleagues discovered that fitting into an opera company's schedule was quite different from rehearsal conditions on Broadway. "We were all frustrated working at City Opera," recalls Franne Lee, Prince's costume designer for *Ashmedai* and *Sweeney Todd*. "We could only rehearse two hours in the morning, and two hours in the afternoon, because other shows were being worked on at the same time." Larry Fuller, Prince's choreographer for *Silverlake* at City Opera, missed the

seven or eight hours a day for five or six weeks that you have on Broadway. At City Opera we could only get into the building two to four days a week. And you have to use the opera-house people; you don't cast for your own piece, so you can't be as exacting as in an individual commercial production. I couldn't bring in dancers who know my style. I come from an acting concept choreographically, but the dance ensemble at City Opera are opera ballet people who go out and do a ballet.

Divided between Puccini (*Girl of the Golden West* and *Madame Butterfly* for the Chicago Lyric, and *Turandot* for the Vienna State Opera) and modern pieces (*Ashmedai* and *Silverlake* for the City Opera and *Willie Stark* for the Houston Grand Opera), Prince's productions have been large-scale, always visually and sometimes dramatically daring. In opera, which he calls a "cloistered environment," Prince has indulged his epic tastes and experimented with a degree of scenic abstraction not always permissible on the commercial stage, while the opera form itself invites the grandiose conceptions he is partial to. If indeed his musical-theatre staging is often marked by its "operatic" tendencies, in opera Prince can fulfill outsized and sometimes visionary production schemes without fear that they will overwhelm the libretto.

While Prince helped to "fix" the new operas he directed, cutting and shaping their librettos as if they were new musicals headed for Broadway,[4] he has approached Puccini with reverence:

I wouldn't dare to touch or transpose a note; Puccini is a hell of a dramatist. In Verdi people enter and exit without motivation, which is unacceptable to me: that is never true in Puccini. I had trouble only with *Turandot*, which he didn't complete or rework the parts he had finished, and as a result the consistencies that are in the others aren't here. But *Butterfly* and *Girl* are based on plays by Belasco, another very good, very shrewd, showman.

Puccini's emotions are always where you want them for the actor. *Emotionally* the music is honest and authentic, and my three Puccini productions were notable for good acting. Puccini is always dealing with emotions, and he builds in pauses where there is nothing for the performer to sing: the singer at these points must *think*. Some opera divas don't know how to fill Puccini's pauses, but that is what you must do to play Puccini properly, to get full dramatic value from the music. His characters are thinking all the time, and you have to play this. Puccini anticipates my needs as a director. In *A Little Night Music*, for instance, I told Steve that I needed music to cover a character's cross to a window: Puccini always allows for that kind of consideration.

"What contribution can I make?" is the question Prince asks when staging an opera from the standard repertory. "I don't want to do *another* draft of an opera that has already been done so many times." If he cannot come up with a new concept, or if he has seen what he considers a definitive production ("Why compete?") he does not accept the assignment. "If you must do bread-and-butter operas, then why not make them dangerous, irreverent productions?", Prince wrote to Beverly Sills. "Why not wave the red flag at the classics?"[5] Although this sounds like a radical's rallying cry, in practice Prince's revisionism has remained within conservative limits – his modern operas have been more audacious than his approach to classics. Unlike Peter Sellars, for instance, Prince has not imposed shifts in time or setting on canonic operas. "There are no hard and fast rules about updating," Prince says:

Sometimes with Shakespeare I will see a new approach that clarifies the play: Orson Welles's Mussolini production of *Julius Caesar* did that for me. But updating cannot be an arbitrary device you use to keep an audience awake. I saw a *Madame Butterfly* directed by Ken Russell set in a whorehouse during the Vietnam War that featured a human size Coca-Cola bottle. I don't have any patience with that.

Instead credibility is his primary criterion:

Unlike Zeffirelli I don't want three hundred people on stage: that's what the audience wants, it isn't what a small opera like *La Bohème* demands. The absence of logic in Zeffirelli's second act, with people sitting out in the snow, was amazing to me. His movie of *La Traviata* is gorgeous but it isn't the story: courtesans don't give parties in palaces for a thousand people! I'd like very much to do a production of *La Traviata* because I've never seen one I believe.

Of his three productions of "bread and butter" Puccini operas, Prince's *Girl of the Golden West* was the most consciously revisionist:

It's always done as a cowboy-and-Indian Western, with a horse; bored opera audiences wait for that horse. I turned it into a horse opera without a horse, but I paid the audience back with a couple of mountain bears who rifled the garbage: my private joke. When I talked to my designers Eugene and Franne Lee I said, "This isn't a Western on the range; cowboys are on the range, this is about miners, who are on a mountain, where the predominant emotion is loneliness." The loneliness of being perched like a mountain goat on a mine is different from the cowboy on the range: the scale is different. It's the loneliness that provokes violence, sadness, mischief, the confrontations that drive the action.

"Our production was the American West, which is unlike the not-American way it is always done," says Franne Lee:

Traditionally the first act was set in an inn that was as big as the entire stage; the second act was the interior of the heroine's house that also took up the whole stage. What we did was to scale down the sets and to surround them with a sense of the wilderness, the threat of the outdoors. Scenically we wanted to suggest that the characters were vulnerable to the wilderness. In Act III, we created a mine, a hole in the side of a mountain, and instead of the heroine coming in on a horse she arrived on a mining car. In other productions the West was nebulous; we made it real.

Prince undertook *Madame Butterfly* because "while the music thrilled the opera always bored the hell out of me." Like his Cinemascope vistas in *Girl of the Golden West*, Prince's *Butterfly* achieved a notably cinematic fluidity in contrast to the often static quality of opera stagecraft. Turntables provided filmic dissolves as the action was played against interlocking interiors and exteriors. As with *Pacific Overtures*, Prince presented the story from a Japanese point of view and therefore incorporated elements of traditional staging: black-robed figures shifted the scenery, though he "decided not to use a *hanamichi*, because it would have called too much attention to itself." Similarly *Turandot* was staged as a spectacular Oriental fantasia in which his fetish for stairs, arranged in different monumental configurations for each act, reached climactic elevation.

If Prince wouldn't "change a note" of Puccini, he and his librettist Hugh Wheeler were fearless in their American adaptation of *Der Silbersee*, a 1932 Kurt Weill opera with an overweight libretto by Georg Kaiser. To Wheeler "It was a three-and-a-half-hour play with only sixty-four minutes of music. It just wasn't acceptable, though threaded through the morass of politics and philosophy was a rather sweet story." Where the original work was a play with music, the Prince–Wheeler redaction maintained a practically continuous musical underlining. "There wasn't enough musical material," Prince says:

We had to fill in. Weill's method, you see, was the opposite of Kaiser's; where Kaiser perorated, Weill was terse – too terse, actually. He developed the notion of encapsulated musical scenes that end before you're ready for them to end: he knew how to stop. I used that in *Evita*, the technique of stopping before the end of the scene, ending on a rise rather than a fall. This method of musical interruptus is frustrating and exciting for an audience.

In a simplified form, shorn of Kaiser's mystical and philosophical ambiguities, this Americanized *Silverlake* retained the parable of social injustice and redemption that contemporary Fascists had labeled "decadent." During a robbery, Severin, a hungry man who lives with a band of vagabonds at Silverlake, is shot by Olim, a police officer who becomes a sudden millionaire when he wins a lottery. At his newly bought castle Olim nurses an unsuspecting Severin back to health. By the end, Olim has shed his new wealth in order to join Severin and his cohorts in building a better world, a new community based on brotherhood. "It's a winter's tale, told around a fire," Prince says. "It's a very warm story, and so quite unlike Weill's work with Brecht. In telling the fable sparely my model was Kafka."

To lend this story with semi-magical elements an allegorical atmosphere Prince and his designer Manuel Lutgenhorst, a young German in his American debut, created mirrored movable panels that were at once reflective and transparent and were bathed in Ken Billington's otherworldly blue lighting. Moved by the actors the continually shifting, gliding mirrors, multiplying and imprisoning the characters as well as the audience – the mirror metaphor of *Cabaret* expanded exponentially – created a fluid sense of space and time as scenes and images melted into each other. "The panels are 'performers,'" Peter Wynne wrote,

that enclose the basic story in a complex and ever-changing environment. They can be mirrors, walls, or windows, or they can be doorways, cages, the towers of a bridge, a room in a hospital. Prince makes characters disappear and materialize at the blink of an eye – as they must in such a fairy-tale-like drama. The physical production is a living, magical thing.[6]

Prince's kinetic mirrored maze proved a fitting frame for Weill's restless mixture of high and low musical idioms in which jazzy syncopations, deadpan pop tunes, a waltz, a tango, and a fox-trot, are interspersed with densely developed arias and symphonic orchestrations. The contrasts between opera and music-hall in Weill's score were reflected in Prince's casting; imported to play Olim, Joel Grey sang and acted in a Broadway style distinctly different from that of his City Opera co-stars. Larry Fuller's choreography veered from comic Chaplinesque routines to "hard classically based dancing for a symbolic figure of Hunger that weaves throughout the show. In the original script he was an effigy," Fuller notes, "but Hal said to put him on the bonfire at the beginning and have the effigy come to life out of the fire. He represented various kinds of hunger – for power, sex, food, love."

A powerful physical production provided the motor for Prince's two other modern operas, both with political themes: Tal's *Ashmedai* (king of the devils in a Talmudic fairy tale) and Carlisle Floyd's *Willie Stark*, based on Robert Penn Warren's *All the King's Men*. Abstract settings created arenas in which the operas' demagogues enforced their will. For *Ashmedai*, a version of the Faust legend with atonal music created on a synthesizer, Prince and his designers, Eugene and Franne Lee, devised a stark background of movable bleachers from which villagers watched the story of how the king of the devils caused chaos in a country which had been at peace for five hundred years. In *Willie Stark*, Eugene Lee designed a barren no man's land: steep gigantic steps stretched across the entire width of the stage, with political slogans etched in marble against the rear wall. "*Ashmedai* was basically a

42 A Prince metaphor: Hunger (Gary Chryst) ironically trails a new millionaire (Joel Grey) in Weill's *Silverlake* (1980)

bare stage with bleachers and curtains that deliberately did not evoke any specific place, just as the costumes did not recall any particular place or time," Franne Lee points out. "The staging and scenic concept were really Oriental. I made up the devil figure with red clown hair, as in a European fairy tale; I gave the Queen an overstuffed costume that had no specific references: it was East meets West in a Grimm fairy tale." Prince wanted an "abstract, primitive look, like street-theatre" to serve his concept of the opera as a performance for villagers, with a juggler, knife-thrower, fire-swallower, and acrobats, and a king made up like a clown; and the success of this presentational style can be measured by the way reviewers picked up on precisely these points. Noting that "Prince managed to create a style of satiric stage movement and design that harks back to the epic German theatre of Piscator and Brecht,"[7] they also appreciated that "Broadway's Harold Prince, who has fully understood that opera – new or old – is, fundamentally, popular art, has turned *Ashmedai* into a nonstop dramatic circus" through a display of "directorial virtuosity, pulling out every trick from Pirandello to Buster Keaton."[8]

Helping to confuse genres, three Prince musicals have been staged for opera houses: Prince himself directed *Sweeney Todd* and *Candide* for the City Opera, while Keith Warner directed *Pacific Overtures* for the English National Opera. Surprisingly, since presenting musicals on opera stages is a political statement, complementing his injection of serious themes into the Broadway musical, Prince was at first reluctant to accept Beverly Sills's invitations to remount his two Broadway successes. And despite his campaign to blur distinctions between Broadway and opera, observing *Pacific Overtures* in an opera house showed Prince that transfers could not be made directly from one context to another. "I was more aware of talk in an opera house, and I felt the show was wordy, which I had not felt it was on Broadway: the laying out of the plot in the first part of the show was more detailed than it needed to be."

Of the three transported musicals *Candide* offers the strongest case for the kind of interbreeding Prince is eager to foster: in each of its three major and quite different incarnations, its 1956 Broadway premiere, Prince's 1973 revival, and his 1982 opera-house version, the show has provoked arguments about genre. "What kind of a musical *is Candide*?" is a question that has continued to be asked for over thirty years.

In 1956 both musically and thematically *Candide* seemed to be without precedent. At first it was billed simply as a musical, but when that designation seemed to mislead audiences the billing was changed to "comic operetta." The switch signaled a debate among the collaborators – composer Leonard Bernstein, librettist Lillian Hellman, and director Tyrone Guthrie – about what kind of a musical they wanted to present; in their uncoordinated production they seemed to be conducting their internal dissensions in public. Hellman's book and Guthrie's direction notably failed to serve Bernstein's vibrant and witty score. Indeed Bernstein was the only collaborator who apparently understood the show's source, Voltaire's satire on the popular eighteenth-century proposition, advanced by Leibnitz, that this is the best of all possible worlds. Bernstein's musical ideas, his conflations of classical and popular idioms, have a verve that evokes the spirit of Voltaire. Parodies of a trilling operatic style and of vocal overembellishment, symphonic orchestrations, and voluptuous melodies combine with driving rhythms in a score that crosses concert-hall decorum with Broadway showmanship to continue the kind of musical experiments Bernstein had conducted in his scores for a ballet, "Fancy Free" (1943), and for two Boadway musical comedies, *On the Town* (1944) and *Wonderful Town* (1953).

In the ballet, his first success, Bernstein announced his agenda of uniting classical and pop traditions: beginning with a blues ballad sung by Billie

43 Opera as circus: an on-stage audience, seated on bleachers, watches a fire-thrower, as a story about the king of the devils unfolds in *Ashmedai* (1976)

Holliday, his score slides from a jazz blues base to symphonic inflections as Gershwinesque syncopation collides with echoes of Copland and Stravinsky, two of the composer's acknowledged early influences. Both *Town* shows floated on the clever disparity between the composer's symphonic motifs which underlie romantic ballads and novelty dance numbers like congas and mambos and the light-as-air musical-comedy lyrics and librettos by Betty Comden and Adolph Green. Inspired by Jerome Robbins's premise for "Fancy Free," *On the Town* is about three sailors in New York on a twenty-four-hour leave. Its plot contrivances and breezy social comment conformed to genre regulations, but Bernstein's score and Robbins's vigorous dances made the show a musical-comedy landmark with "a new look and sound and movement" that drew Hal Prince to see it "at least nine times." "New York, New York, a helluva town,/The Bronx is up and the Battery's down," the famous opening number announces, setting a tone maintained by George Abbott's zesty direction. Written in five weeks, *Wonderful Town* lacks the youthful buoyancy of *On the Town* but it too converts Manhattan into an idealized musical-comedy playground, and the popular elements of both *Town*s absorbed Bernstein's "difficult" scores. *Candide*, based on a classic source, did not provide the same kinds of protection, and with its misguided original performance the show seemed suspiciously high-brow, as if refugees from the Metropolitan Opera were trying to invade Broadway.

To adapt Voltaire's racy story into a crisp libretto, Lillian Hellman was badly miscast. Insinuating contemporary McCarthy-era political references, her libretto is pious where Voltaire is Swiftian, and Tyrone Guthrie's overdecorated production with its primarily opera-house casting only enhanced Hellman's fraudulent high seriousness. "A really spectacular disaster," wrote Walter Kerr. "Candide goes on his odyssey with the tread of Oedipus lurching out of Thebes. Hellman's attack is academic, blunt and barefaced."[9]

Released from its production, the show's thrilling original-cast album turned *Candide* into a cult musical and spurred periodic hopes of a new staging. In 1973 Robert Kalfin of the Chelsea Theatre Center approached Prince to direct this long-awaited revival, an assignment Prince was reluctant to accept because he had thought the original was "awfully heavy-going and cold," a melange of disparate elements; as Sondheim said, "Lenny's score was pastiche, Lillian wrote a black comedy, Guthrie directed a wedding cake."[10] When he re-read Voltaire's *Candide* Prince was impressed by its "irreverent, prankish spirit," a quality altogether absent from Guthrie's production, but felt he could proceed only with a new libretto. Hellman refused to rewrite, and Prince hired Hugh Wheeler, who turned Voltaire's odyssey into a knockabout farce brimming with narrative improbabilities and sexual high-jinks. Never pausing to philosophize or to point a moral, Wheeler's lean

libretto with its cynical pokes at mindless optimism is true to the general
spirit of its source. His approach was to

re-read Voltaire and pick out what I thought were the most effective scenes. I did my own
architecture. I had a technical problem superimposed because the songs were already
written, and I had to service the music and lyrics. The original production had been too
long and so I tried to be concise. I treated the characters affectionately, which was easy
because that's what Voltaire did. Hal and I felt the picaresque structure needed a frame, an
anchor that was missing from the first production, and so we decided to put Voltaire into
the play as a narrator, to introduce the characters and to step into the action from time to
time as other characters – our Voltaire became Dr Pangloss, the wicked governor, a
businessman.

44 With Oliver Smith's sets, Jerome Robbins's choreography, and Leonard
Bernstein's symphonic score, *On the Town* (1944) had "a new look and
sound and style of movement" that beckoned Hal Prince "at least nine
times"

"I couldn't envision how the show could work in a conventional proscenium staging," Prince says. "The play was about a journey and I felt we
needed a physical metaphor through which to define Candide's adventures. I
remembered a production I had seen in 1970 in Bryant Park of *Orlando Furioso*
in which the audience followed the action as it moved from one place to
another, and I realized I wanted our production in some way to involve the
audience physically in the staging." Prince instructed his designers, the Lees,
to think of the show as a "carnival": "Hal told us he wanted to be able to stage
scenes 'here and there,' and taking off from his suggestions we worked out a
traveling concept, with the action played out on ramps and booths and a
runway – it was a trick presentation, like a big outdoor fair", Franne Lee
recalls.

When the show moved to Broadway after its limited run at the 180-seat
Chelsea Theatre in the Brooklyn Academy of Music, the design had to be
scaled up in such a way that the audience could still feel involved by being in
the middle of the action as they had in Brooklyn. The sedate Broadway
Theatre was transformed into a stadium with bleacher seating for 800 fans.
Planted amid the seats were ten separate stages connected by ramps and one
larger playing area patterned after the Elizabethan inner stage. The thirteen-
piece orchestra was placed on four separate stages to provide quadrophonic
sound. Making their way through the audience from one "station" to another
in a modern version of medieval street-theatre, the actors were in continual
movement. The kind of fun that the show promised was announced when the
audience first entered the theatre to find the ornate lobby made over into a
circus arena filled with balloons and streamers, with peanuts sold at the
refreshment stand.

In creating this people's theatre on Broadway Prince released the material
from the inhibiting classicism of the Guthrie production. Like Hugh Weeler,
Prince reduced and simplified, while also giving theatrical flight to Voltaire's
satire. A streamlined popular romp, this was a *Candide* happily dislodged
from its "required reading" niche.

"Hal's sideshow idea was to keep it all rough, and all about young kids, like
Judy [Garland] and Mickey [Rooney] putting on a show," Sondheim says.[11]
As he was later to do in *Merrily We Roll Along*, Prince chose raw young actors
to play the leads, partly because of the physical demands of the production.
Cunégonde, Maureen Brennan, was a college junior with no professional
experience; Candide, Mark Baker, had acted in New York but projected an
appealing ingenuousness. "Hal wanted innocence and honesty, and he would
stop us whenever he felt we were being dishonest," Maureen Brennan says.
"He did not want us to comment. The innocence made it funny."

While the actors played virtually on top of the audience, though avoiding
any actual contact (which Prince objects to), the lights were kept on at "a
certain level" so that the audience could see each other and, in effect, remain

45 and 46 Prince's environmental staging of *Candide* (1974), with the
audience surrounding the actors (Mark Baker as Candide, Maureen Brennan
as Cunégonde) and the action played on separate stages connected by
ramps. Production designed by Eugene and Franne Lee (photos courtesy of
Martha Swope © 1987)

aware that they were seeing a show. This strategy — the actors' proximity, the Brechtian house lights — was part of Prince's attempt to correct the sentimentality of the original production. As Maureen Brennan says, "We worked for 'gentle pathos.'"

"The score got short shrift in sheer musicality," Prince admits. "We had only thirteen instruments and some non-singers in the ensemble. Our emphasis was on the book." Songs were dropped, or placed in different settings. In 1956 "Quiet" had been sung by Cunégonde, the Old Lady, and the Governor in the Governor's palace; in Prince's version it was sung on a raft at sea as Candide tries to silence a squabble between the Old Lady and Paquette. To knit music to action and to prevent Bernstein's melodies from stopping the show, Prince and his choreographer Pat Birch embroidered the songs with sight gags and physical business. During "Glitter and Be Gay," the show's most operatic song, Cunégonde snatched jewels worn by her piano accompanist, an action that both prevented the song from becoming a recital and comically expressed the character's greed. As they sang "O Happy We," in which they unknowingly express two very different conceptions of married life, Candide and Cunégonde undressed each other in a frenzy of young lust; the comic action helped to explain why the characters weren't listening to each other:

CANDIDE   Soon, when we feel we can afford it,
             We'll build a modest little farm.

CUNÉGONDE   We'll buy a yacht and live aboard it,
             Rolling in luxury and stylish charm.

"Guthrie's opening number, 'The Best of All Possible Worlds,' was about an idea," Prince says. Having learned from his experience on *A Funny Thing Happened On the Way to the Forum* how crucial a show's first number is Prince asked Sondheim to write lyrics for a new opening number, "Life is Happiness Indeed," which would provide a comic introduction to the characters:

CUNÉGONDE   Life is happiness indeed:
             I have everything I need.
             I am rich and unattached
             And my beauty is unmatched.

MAXIMILIAN   Life is absolute perfection,
             As is true of my complexion.
             Ev'ry time I look and see me,
             I'm reminded life is dreamy.

Sondheim's lyrics freed the show by setting up the figures as comic dupes, unrealistically rosy and fatally lacking in self-awareness.

With musical numbers and episodes trimmed to the bone *Candide* ran an intermissionless one hour and forty-five minutes, an appropriate playing time for a romp. "Voltaire denied he'd ever written *Candide*," Prince noted;

He said it was some schoolboy's prank, and that his name was signed to it. That's the way we conceived it, as a sort of joke, and that's why it's got to be played that way, not taking itself seriously. I wanted audiences to react, as Voltaire's must have, and say, "Oh, that's too much, that's bad taste." Hence, the Grand Inquisitor with dyed-blond hair and lipstick, all those virgins being raped and raped, and the comic Jew.[12]

Following the George Abbott tradition, Prince directed *Candide* as a farce, swiftly paced and studded with inventive stage business. Like Abbott, Prince consciously avoided "art" in order to create a show with popular appeal, which was also an extravaganza of directorial ingenuity prompting the comment that "Hal Prince is the Belasco of recent decades."[13]

Designed as a counter-production to the 1956 original, Prince's first *Candide* diminished Voltaire and Bernstein in order to establish the show's stageworthiness. His second draft, for the City Opera nine years later, restored the majesty of Bernstein's score, with fifty-five instruments and a full chorus, and discovered a broader range of colors in Candide's journey:

In 1973 we dealt with it in an informal way, in which the performers seemed to be improvising, though of course they weren't improvising at all. We gave it a seemingly cynical message which contradicts in the right way the survival instinct in all people.

Candide is very anti-establishment, but nevertheless it's still about surviving, making mistakes, and then getting on with it.[14]

Celebrating this survival instinct, Prince's opera-house version added a heroic dimension that deepened the material without forsaking its humor. At the end of the Broadway *Candide*, a cow died of the pox, confounding yet again the hero's desire to believe the lesson of Dr. Pangloss that this is the best of all possible worlds. At the end of the opera-house production there was no pox; instead the backdrop lifted to reveal a sun-dappled landscape which transmuted Voltairean irony into a redemptive vision of harmony and growth: after catastrophic experience out in the world, the wiser characters retreat to a high-minded isolationism as they set about cultivating an Edenic garden.

47 For his City Opera production of *Candide* (1982), Prince redesigned the show as a street-theatre performance presented on pageant wagons by Dr. Voltaire's band of traveling actors before an on-stage audience. Setting designed by Clarke Dunham; costumes by Judith Dolan (photo courtesy of Martha Swope © 1987)

The challenge of rethinking the play's physical shape for the cavernous New York State Theatre led Prince to replace the journey with a performance framework in which *Candide* is staged by Dr. Voltaire's Traveling Freak Show for an on-stage audience. To accommodate the fluid movement and frequent changes of scene Prince used multiple playing areas – boxes with two levels on either side of the stage, pageant wagons pushed on and off center stage in view of both the on-stage and theatre audiences. As if *Candide* was too kinetic to be contained within the proscenium, action occasionally spilled out into the auditorium, with Candide traveling along the second row of the orchestra as he sang "This Must Be So," and Dr. Pangloss delivering his final homilies from the front box theatre left.

Despite the upscale ambience, Prince retained much of the free-wheeling spirit of his original environmental staging. Pratfalls and sight gags abounded: Dr. Pangloss got entangled in reams of paper as he tried to locate his ultimate words of wisdom; toy ships on a painted sea, plastic rocks to suggest El Dorado, and toy buildings that crumbled during the Lisbon earthquake demonstrated Prince's delight in theatrical sleight of hand. The production was filled with a director's pleasure in demonstrating how theatrical illusion is created, while the gleeful applause of the on-stage spectators at each of the tricks was Prince's comment on the eagerness of audiences to be taken in, to suspend disbelief and give themselves over to the magic of theatrical make-believe.

Directed with swaggering theatricality, Prince's opera-house production substantiated his claim that serious musical theatre and opera share common ground and can have a similar impact on audiences. Like Bernstein's score, by turns passionate and sly, Prince's showmanship filled the huge opera stage, demonstrating finally that *Candide* is a total theatre work which dismantles the boundaries between Broadway and Lincoln Center.

10 The British connection

Like Hal Prince, Andrew Lloyd Weber is a musical-theatre innovator, and it was therefore logical when they joined forces to produce two experimental musicals, *Evita* (London 1978; Broadway 1979) and *The Phantom of the Opera* (London 1986; Broadway 1988).

Although his blatant commercial success has tagged him as a composer who has stooped to conquer, a cool look at Lloyd Webber's canon reveals an often refreshing theatrical imagination. As their titles indicate, *Joseph and the Amazing Technicolour Dreamcoat* (1968, extended 1972) and *Jesus Christ Superstar* (1971) are Bible stories gilded with contemporary references. *Cats* (1981) and *Starlight Express* (1984) are concept extravaganzas with minimal narratives; *Song and Dance* (1982) is a two-part variation on a theme: through a continuous series of linked songs Act I describes the progress and decline of a love affair; with repetitions of a piece by Paganini, the Act II dance drama echoes the characters and setting of the first part, "Tell Me On a Sunday." For his two sturdiest book shows, *Evita* and *Phantom*, Lloyd Webber wanted Prince as director: "*Cabaret* was the best musical I had ever seen on the stage," Lloyd Webber said just before *Evita* opened on Broadway.[1] His subject matter varies, from the trite romantic reversals of *Song and Dance* to the simplistic heroics of *Starlight Express* to the more complex, uneasy celebrations of charismatic figures like Joseph, Jesus, and Evita, yet his shows share a central formal concern in their attempt to create a pop-opera idiom in which song and recitative replace the usual functions of dialogue. "I have always felt that staging continuous music as opposed to a music piece with dialogue is the key to musicals," Lloyd Webber has said. "I want to make musicals a continuous musical event like opera."[2]

Abolishing the difference between a dream world of song and dance and a "real" world of dialogue, his "through-composed" scores have inspired a potent theatricality while also presenting the challenge of maintaining dramatic immediacy entirely through songs. (In their narrative disjointedness and their occasional reliance on narrators to provide frames and transitions, the shows often reveal their origins as high-concept record albums.) While shows like *Cats* and *Starlight Express* set a dangerous example – success = spectacle + volume – judged on their own they have a visual impact that is quintessentially of the theatre; both shows display the childlike delight in theatrical make-believe that is apparent in much of Prince's work.

157

While Lloyd Webber's astonishing box-office record owes much to ingenious state-of-the-art technological displays, ultimately his success rests on his ability to write intoxicating melodies. But although these are published in record albums that precede his shows, and have an appeal independent of theatre, even such hit tunes as "Memories" (from *Cats*) or "Don't Cry for Me Argentina" (from *Evita*) serve important dramatic functions within the contexts of their shows.

Part of Lloyd Webber's success is that he has in fact developed a style that, as Prince says, "many kinds of audiences can be comfortable with." While his innovative practice of incorporating a variety of soft-rock inflections into his scores gives his work a contemporary base, Lloyd Webber is a musical chameleon who quotes from a wide range of sources, from hillbilly to Puccini, from Elvis Presley to Liszt, from French can-can to Mozart, from the Supremes to Paganini. Like Kurt Weill, he blends styles from the concert hall and the cabaret in order to assault the rigid class system that segregates the musical from the operatic and symphonic stages. His pastiche scores, which both satirize and offer affectionate tribute to their sources, have a variety that can sustain a dramatic narrative, which an exclusive dependence on rock would be unlikely to do. If "rock opera" seems a misnomer, or a contradiction in terms — and indeed the musical development in *Evita, Joseph and the Amazing Technicolour Dreamcoat*, and *Jesus Christ Superstar* does not have the complexity of operatic scoring — "opera" nonetheless measures Lloyd Webber's aspirations, as well as setting his work apart from the standard musical which relaxes into dialogue between numbers.

But if the musical signature of a show like *Evita* is not strictly operatic, the demands it makes on singers is. "Vocally it's an opera, you can't treat it as anything else," says Patti LuPone, who originated the title role in New York:

It is *not* a rock musical, and you can't sing the score by being a rock 'n roller. When I first heard the album I thought Lloyd Webber must hate women because he wanted the character to belt so high; the role mixes chest and soprano tones without a crack or break in the voice. I knew how to act the part but it took me twenty weeks of performances to learn how to sing it.

Like Prince, Lloyd Webber clearly believes that musicals can tackle big subjects. *Evita* investigates politicians, *Joseph* and *Jesus Christ Superstar* take on religious icons. In all three pieces the composer and his librettist Tim Rice turn their mythic characters into disturbingly attractive contemporary operators, "superstars" indeed. Glamorous figures with loyal fans, they are presented as high-rolling power brokers susceptible to being corrupted by their own image, a tricky combination that opens the creators' work to charges of vulgarity. But the attempt to musicalize such unlikely subjects is provocative, and their portraits have darker and more ambivalent undercurrents than they are often given credit for.

Joseph, a sixties flower-child and the most innocent of these leaders, is nonetheless motivated more by self-interest than brotherly love. An androgynous rock star with prophetic powers (he interprets the bad dreams of an Elvis Presley pharaoh), he also believes in the Old Testament wisdom of obtaining an eye for an eye as he delays the happy ending by taunting the jealous brothers who sold him into slavery. In the revisionist gospel according to Rice and Lloyd Webber, Jesus is an ambisexual with flowing hair, a chiseled face and body, and a bad conscience, who strikes bargains with God as he questions what crucifixion will do to his image. Seducible and riddled with doubt, this superstar Christ is a latter-day neurotic who is debunked but not dethroned; ultimately the show celebrates his tarnished divinity, although Judas emerges from the shadows to become, both musically and dramatically, the rock opera's true hero.

For their third musical about a leader with star power, a project that demanded a firm narrative arc, Lloyd Webber and Rice turned to Prince. "When they sent me the lyrics for *Evita* I wrote a three-thousand word response about how to transform a group of songs into a dramatic script with tension," Prince recalls;

More than a year later, after the album was number one all over Europe, they came back to me. At this point, taking lyrics from the album, I turned each song into a scene, describing to Lloyd Webber and Rice what I felt the action should be, what the audience should be seeing. I created a script from lyrics by always looking for points of conflict such as Evita's single-mindedness vs Perón's cowardice – he would have quit if she hadn't been pushing, and that kind of pulling is terrific in the theatre. That central conflict together with the Cinderella story of Evita's rise from poverty to power is very seductive. Here and there are a few lines of dialogue: I asked for a monologue in the first act in which we illustrate that Argentina was not like other South American countries because of the large influx of Europeans; and at the end Che makes a short enigmatic speech about the mysterious disappearance of Evita's coffin. But basically *Evita* doesn't break the opera rules. It's a short script – it's like a series of telegrams – in which every moment is well-motivated. My job was to make every word count.

Along with establishing dramatic continuity Prince also insisted on imposing a political perspective, and urged Rice to deepen and complicate his originally admiring portrait. "Of course Eva Perón was mostly evil," Prince says,

but she did some good for her country. She can be explained and I wanted to explain her to a degree where I could partially forgive her. She was born dirt-poor, illegitimate, in a macho-oriented South American country – a far from beautiful woman who transformed herself through diet, dye-pot, persistence and savvy into a glamorous figure. She knew long before others did – this was the forties – that it was better to be Barbara Walters than a movie star.

What I did was make it hard for the audience to make up their minds about Evita . . . I wanted you against your will to think she was glamorous.

48 and 49 Life in the public arena: Evita (Patti LuPone) plays to the crowd, always surrounded by microphones: "Don't Cry for Me Argentina" and just before her death (Bob Gunton as Juan Perón) (*Evita*, 1979) (photos courtesy of Van Williams)

And the way this ambivalence was expressed in performance is well described by Patti LuPone:

Evita was a heinous woman, but you can't develop a character who's one-note. I first had to get the audience on my side – I had to make her appealing – and then I could be tough. I actually made eye contact with the audience: "You'd do the same thing if you were in Evita's shoes," is what I was trying to communicate. I put the screws on the audience. I knew I had them when they laughed in the first act and cried for me in the second act. Ultimately, there was no way I could soft-soap her: she was a ruthless woman – she was *more* ruthless because she was a woman, and in all the photos I looked at I noticed that she *never* smiled with her eyes.

The success of this approach can be indicated by the audience response. "Both pro- and anti-*Peronistas* came back after the show to say I had her exactly right . . . 'You are Evita!', cried the daughter of Evita's embalmer after the opening night. An anti-*Peronista* came backstage and showed me every newspaper on the day of her death and he hated her! That's the kind of power that woman put off."

As both the director's and the star's comments indicate, there is a continuity between the subject matter – Evita's manipulation of her public – and the show's own manipulative methods. Prince's stage management echoes Evita's; Lupone's calculating performance, which alternately lifts and deflates the emotions of the crowd, parallels Evita's. Like the heroine's political theatre, musical theatre is a presentational art in which performers elicit applause. The theatrical references throughout Rice's lyrics – "the actress hasn't learned the lines you'd like to hear," "only an actress would pretend affairs of state are her latest play," – enforce the show's view of politics as a high-stakes entertainment medium. The historical Evita played to the lowest common denominator among her people, milking pathos from her displays of fake humility; and the responses she was able to extract from the mobs she courted and stimulated are very much like the ones the show excites. As well, then, as documenting the power of a driven political figure *Evita* is also about the power of shrewdly manipulated theatrical arts of lighting, design, acting, and particularly music to arouse and to shape – to control – the reactions of an audience. Prince says that, indeed, *Evita* tries to do to its audiences what the Peróns did to Argentina. "It makes them [audiences who see the show as glorifying a tyrant] crazy to feel managed and manipulated by the show, though that is just the point. That's just the way we are managed and manipulated by the media."[3]

While some critics perceived that "to present fascism as show biz is to expose it, not to support it," others pointed to a disturbing moral ambivalence that seemed to reflect the attitudes of the show's creators more than those of the audience: "we are expected to deplore Evita's morals but to adore her circuses."[4] In response to the charge that *Evita* had fallen in love with its subject, Prince, Lloyd Webber, and Rice formed a united front of vigorous denial. "Who in the world would glorify Evita Perón?" Prince asks;

I find Evita herself to be absolutely relevant to contemporary politics, where glamor can mask bad deeds. I wanted the audience to *examine* what they worship. Fifteen years ago I told editors at *Time* that they put villains and felons on their covers, powerful figures who weren't caught. What that show is about is as poisonous now as in Evita's lifetime: how dishonest the news is every night.

"There is no question of us glorifying her," Lloyd Webber said. "It's a kind of cautionary tale. There is no reason why musical theatre should only deal with cozy subjects. It should provoke thought. Eva Perón is a modern myth and we're using theatre to explode the myth. But before you explode it, you've got to explain it." And even Rice commented that "it's insane to say you can't write about someone you don't approve of. Or that we support Eva Perón because we write her story. No country today can claim with confidence that 'it can't happen here.'"[5]

Like other Prince musicals, *Evita* reverses the traditional iconography of the genre by overturning the Cinderella trope, the rags to riches, Horatio Alger myth that has served as a libretto staple from the beginnings of musical comedy and reached its apex in the twenties with such populist shows as *Irene, Sunny,* and *Sally,* that celebrated their plucky heroines' uncomplicated rise from poverty to wealth. *Evita* curdles the Cinderella fantasy the way *Follies,* for instance, darkened the myths that had traditionally fed optimistic, show-must-go-on backstage musicals, making Cinderella not only deter-mined and energetic — a winner — but also demonic. Placing the success-story format in a befouling context, *Evita* is an anti-fairy tale. It is unnerving precisely because we are made to applaud the heroic drive of a reprehensible character, a demagogue, and Patti LuPone played Evita as Lady Macbeth to Bob Gunton's vacillating, weak-willed Perón, though, dangerously, her Evita aroused pity as well as terror.

To counteract the deceptive appeal that both the historical and the theatrical Evita almost magically exert, Prince asked his writers to develop the role of Che as a skeptical commentator who periodically topples the blonde Venus from her musical-comedy throne. Whether or not the character of Che represents "the uneasy conscience of the show's creators,"[6] he is plainly included to prevent the audience from becoming seduced by Evita: "As a mere observer of this tasteless phenomenon, one has / To admire the stage management," Che tells the audience. Che as Brechtian narrator, debunking Evita's self-promotion, provides a distinctly Prince-like frame for the show; like the Emcee in *Cabaret,* Che presents a series of emblematic didactic scenes, which were recognized — and even criticized — as a device that "keeps us permanently outside the action" and that makes the audience "recipients" rather than "participants."[7]

As further insurance against audiences reading the show as a numbing celebration of Evita, Prince directed Mandy Patinkin as Che to be the show's hero, the character the audience feels closest to. "The applause for me was less than for Mandy," Patti LuPone remembers. Patinkin played the part with a messianic heroism laced with disapproval, whereas in London the role was created by a rock star, David Essex, who (according to Larry Fuller, the show's choreographer) was "cool and laid back, menacing in a self-assured way, and with a tremendous amount of gentlemanly charm."

In addition Prince and Fuller found visual translations for Lloyd Webber's musical set-pieces that satirically undercut the characters. "Goodnight and Thank You" demonstrates Evita's ascension through a series of increasingly prominent lovers. "I suggested a door on a revolve as a metaphor for her multiple affairs," says Fuller, "and that each time she emerged from the door she should be dressed in a nicer robe." In "The Art of the Possible," Prince

50 The real Peróns hover over their theatrical counterparts (Bob Gunton
and Patti LuPone) as Che (Mandy Patinkin) looks on with disapproval
(*Evita*) (photo courtesy of Van Williams)

conceived Perón's rise to power as a game of musical rocking chairs among colonels; at the end of the scene, Perón's chair is alone on stage. To dramatize the opposition of both the military and the aristocracy to the upstart Evita, Prince and Fuller created two tight groups who move together in deadly precision. "For the military I wanted a block of identical soldiers performing a close-order drill, like so many automatons," Prince recalls. "The parody military are like wind-up killing machines who smash people like bugs," Fuller says, "while I based the mechanical movement of the aristocrats on mannikins I had seen in Harrod's window."

"We were working from a record album with no real book," says Larry Fuller, who worked closely with Prince throughout the rehearsals. "Hal took those lyrics and made a show, a documentary in revue form. We picked a new image – a new visual metaphor – for each number, and we coudn't repeat or mix the metaphors." While Prince and Fuller devised an image and style of movement for each number, "life in the public arena" was Prince's basic production concept, one which dictated the show's sound and lighting designs. "*Evita* was one of the few times it was legitimate to have voices miked," Fuller says. "Amplification and echoes are thematically justified, an organic part of the show's style. The public-arena idea also influenced the recurrent football-stadium lighting and the spotlights that pinioned the characters." Evita, Perón, and Che often appeared in their own, differently colored spotlights, and a circle of lights on the stage floor ("entirely an outgrowth of *Cabaret*," Prince notes) cast menacing shadows onto the entrapped characters.

The public forum in which Evita constructed her persona also justified Prince's predilection for podiums and platforms. Placed on an elevated podium Evita played to the mob below, while for "Don't Cry for Me Argentina" a revolving balcony contrasted the public and private faces of Evita: on stage she works overtime to promote her sainthood, while off-stage, as the revolving balcony carries her from public view, she gives the finger to Magaldi, her first lover.

"How do you put two hundred thousand people on the stage?" Prince wondered when he first listened to Lloyd Webber's funeral march which opens the show. His solution was to use mixed media as a way of creating an illusion of crowds for the show's moments of spectacle and pageantry: the funeral procession, the Act I finale, "A New Argentina," and Evita's goodwill Rainbow Tour. Startlingly, the show opens in a Buenos Aires theatre where the film is stopped by the announcement that Eva Perón, "the spiritual leader of the nation, has entered immortality." "My image was based on *Citizen Kane*," Prince says;

That film had an enormous influence on the look I worked for in *Evita*: the sense of size which Welles understood so well; the sense of shadow, with much of the action in a kind of fake perspective. And Murnau's *Sunrise* and *The Last Laugh*, which influenced Welles's design for *Citizen Kane*, also had a profound impact: Murnau influenced *Evita* more than Brecht did.

Intermittently the action was counterpointed by still photos and newsreel footage of the historical Peróns projected onto an upstage cyclorama — oversized images that provided an epic frame. Originally Prince conceived the show "like *Cabaret*, as a black box relieved only by footlights and bright white lights instead of blackouts to mark the ends of scenes and to underline transitions in a way I thought would be new and surprising. But we felt something was missing; the stage looked too bare for the crowd scenes. On vacation in Mexico City I saw murals by Sequieros and Rivera in Carlotta and Maximilian's palace and I saw at once the whole of *Evita* as it should look." With monumental murals and placards and flags to fill the stage and photographs and film to extend the sense of space, and with arena lighting and intense amplification, Prince and his design team, Timothy O'Brien and Tazeena Firth, created a simulation of cast-of-thousands pageantry. Out of quite simple means they conjured an illusion of epic amplitude.

Similarly, at the end of the opening-night performance of *The Phantom of the Opera* in London on October 10, 1986, as the exhilarated audience was leaving the theatre, I looked up at the now-empty stage and was startled by its bareness and seemingly small size, which hardly looked capable of having contained the spectacle we had just seen. Like the Phantom himself, Prince's production ("a black box with tricks," as the director calls it) makes use of sleight of hand: now you see it, now you don't. At one point, seated on a chair, the Phantom vanishes in a puff of smoke; Raoul, the Phantom's romantic rival, jumps into water and disappears before our eyes. With ingenuity born of years of practice, Prince sculpts theatrical space and time, from scene to scene transforming the height and depth of the playing area as he divides and rearranges space, creates frames within frames as drapes descend from the flies, reverses perspective, and fuses episodes with fades, dissolves, montage effects, or abrupt cuts. He punctuates the action with *coups de théâtre*: in the prologue a smashed chandelier is magically reassembled and is then dismantled once again for the Act I finale; the Phantom takes Christine, his protegée, to his underground lair on a catwalk that gradually descends from the flies; the Phantom rows Christine on a boat that travels across a misty lake filled with torches that rise up to become ornate candelabras as the lake materializes into the Phantom's gated retreat; from the pediment of the proscenium the Phantom descends over the audience; seen through a scrim, masked revelers dance on the wide sweeping staircase of the opera house.

From time to time, in visual grace-notes, such as a prop elephant turned

51 "The parody military are like wind-up killing machines": choreography
by Larry Fuller (*Evita*) (photo courtesy of Van Williams)

around to reveal a shell in which stagehands are casually playing cards, Prince
lets us in on the fact that we are watching an illusion, a conjuring act. And
across the front of the stage footlights and a prompter's box remind us that
The Phantom of the Opera takes place on a stage, in a world of illusion.

Like *Follies*, *The Phantom of the Opera* is a baroque variation on the backstage
musical – this time the show that must go on is an opera rather than a revue or
a musical comedy. Rather than on 42nd Street or Broadway the story is set on
the stage of the Paris Opera, an intimidating pile of Beaux-Arts magnificence.
Ideally the theatre in which the show is performed should evoke the gilded
splendor of the Paris Opera, and an ornate movie palace (many of which were
in fact modeled on the Paris Opera) would provide an appropriate mirror of
the theatre within the play. To supply exactly that sense of architectural
continuity between stage and theatre Prince and his designer, Maria
Björnson, framed the proscenium of London's Her Majesty's Theatre with
huge gilded figures revealed with a grand flourish when dust-covered

52 "Paraphrasing" Sequieros murals to create an illusion of crowds for the Act I climax, "A New Argentina" (*Evita*) (photo courtesy of Van Williams)

funereal drapes are removed at the end of the prologue (set forty-four years after the story of the Phantom and Christine has already been played out, at an auction on a stage no longer in use), a gesture that returns the moribund theatre to active life.

With its continuous transformations of space and time, Prince's liquid direction, as in *Evita*, supports Lloyd Webber's musical continuity. Although there is more dialogue than in *Evita*, the show creates the impression of having an uninterrupted score. "I wanted to tell the story the same way Stravinsky told *Les Noces*," Prince says,

with the pulse of the story to continue during connective moments. As in *Evita*, I prevented applause from disrupting the continuity, and I used continuous sounds during transitions between scenes . . . We had far less dialogue than when we started out, because I felt the story could be told primarily through images and music: you don't need words. Indeed, the *size* of the way the story is told does not require dialogue.

Except for the entirely spoken prologue, dialogue is embedded in action or sound effects, and never allowed to break scenic and musical momentum.

To serve what he calls Lloyd Webber's "big, soaring melodies," Prince wanted to tell the classic story in a "big, bold manner. I didn't want something subtle or psychologically buried; instead I wanted to stress the rudimentary psychology that is at the core of the material." Working closely with lyricist Charles Hart and co-librettists Richard Stilgoe and Lloyd Webber, Prince trimmed Gaston Leroux's novel down to a scenario that exemplifies what he calls "Abbott shorthand." The original novel's Sherlock Holmes-like narrator systematically demystifies each of the apparently supernatural events, arriving at a logical explanation of each of the Phantom's tricks, whereas the musical's 1905 prologue, using the auction as narrative frame, invests relics of the Phantom's story such as the broken chandelier and a music box with mythic significance.

The show strips the characters of their background: the Phantom's medical history, Christine's attachment to her father, and her childhood relationship with Raoul, are referred to only glancingly. But although the musical does not try for the novel's factual and psychological density, it offers a strong revisionist interpretation of the phantom himself. Prince

got the idea for how I wanted the character to be played while watching a documentary about the physically deformed [*The Skin Horse*] made by the BBC. A quadriplegic propped up in a basket; a beautiful young lady, the victim of thalidomide, no arms, just "buttons" in place of arms and hands, interviewed with her gentleman friend; an old woman so severely handicapped with multiple sclerosis that her words had to be translated like a foreign language on the bottom of the screen – all speak directly to the camera, looking right at you. Then there was a scene from Tod Browning's film, *Freaks*, and a scene from David Lynch's film of *The Elephant Man*. Watching all of this made it clear that there was total conflict within me (and so many of the audience) respecting our perception of physical deformity. We recoil and at the same time our reason tells us that's ridiculous, that we should be ashamed. And then we recoil again. The Phantom has accepted the recoiling mechanism and cannot integrate the fact that Christine, having grown to know him, no longer perceives him that way. It was the quality of the Phantom's common humanity, his *normal* sexual and romantic impulses that get distorted by his physical deformity, that I wanted to emphasize.

Embodying Prince's ideas, Michael Crawford's Phantom is unlike any earlier mad-monster interpretation of the role. Beneath his displays of menace, he's warm-voiced, vulnerable, aching with romantic longings. In both make-up and carriage he has none of the Gothic insignia that defined Lon Chaney's famous performance in the 1925 film. Chaney is ornate and otherworldly. His stately acting is a veritable lexicon of overripe silent-screen telegraphy, a symphony of hunched shoulders, upraised arms, clenched fists, and gripping hands that signify the character's monstrous otherness. The Germanic lighting and the vast sets offer an apt frame for his silent opera, though the film's reluctance to treat the Phantom as anything other than a freak ultimately undermines Chaney's virtuosity. By contrast Michael Crawford plays the Phantom with unexpected realism, as an obsessed lover craving acceptance.

For all his insistence on telling the story quickly, without pause for

53 and 54 Drama and spectacle in *The Phantom of the Opera* (1988): the beast embraces the beauty (Michael Crawford and Sarah Brightman); the Act II opening, a masked ball on the staircase of the Paris Opera (photos courtesy of Clive Barda)

psychological complication, Prince's approach goes deeper than the film's, which plays the material as a straightforward horror story of the beauty and the beast in which there is no suggestion of possible romance between the Phantom and his musical protegée. The show links the two characters in a mystical union that is spiced with mutual sexual interest; one of the strongest moments occurs in Act I when Christine, curious and afraid, caresses the phantom's mask. Her gesture, an acknowledgment of the sexual appeal of physical deformity, has a strong erotic aroma that lingers over the rest of the play and makes possible the climactic action when Christine gently kisses the phantom's unmasked face. As in a fairy tale her generosity breaks the spell in which she has been caught: the phantom releases her and Raoul and then, his dream fulfilled, disappears.

In the film the beauty never overcomes her fear of the beast. In the musical the Phantom is Christine's musical mentor, her surrogate father, and her would-be lover – and her attachment to him rather than to Raoul becomes the story's romantic focus.

It is through his music that the Phantom, also known as the Angel of Music, enchants Christine, and if the show is to work the score must also bewitch us. Since we must be convinced that the music which the Phantom writes and then coaxes out of Christine is glorious, the outpouring of an almost divine inspiration, musicalizing this fable about the power of music is a demonstration of artistic assurance. But in writing the role for his wife Sarah Brightman, Lloyd Webber inevitably invited a host of extra-theatrical specu-lation: Is the show a personal metaphor for how the composer captured his bride by the power of his music? Is Sarah Brightman the Galatea not only to the Phantom but to Lloyd Webber's Pygmalion? As Prince says, "There would have been no show without her, which is why the initial refusal of Actors Equity to allow her to recreate her role in New York was such a grubby and insensitive business. The part was written for her specific talent."

Indeed Sarah Brightman played the role so seamlessly as to erase any sense of separation between her and the character. Her Christine seemed to be heeding the call of a secret voice, drawn unstoppably by the Phantom's music, often moving like a puppet and indeed other characters suggest that the Phantom is in her mind, a figment of her own peculiar imagination. That she both acted and sang the role magnificently – her sparklingly clear amplified lyric soprano soared over the theatre, suggesting the kind of musical splendors the Phantom is supposed to have inspired – and that Lloyd Webber's score is convincing as the work of the show's musical genius, were personal triumphs of a special kind. (Nonetheless, many New York reviewers criticized the score as being saccharine, derivative, and facile.)

As is all too usual for a Lloyd Webber show, the lyrics remain earthbound. The flat lyrics for the young lovers ("Let me be your freedom, / Let daylight dry your tears") are understandable enough, considering that Raoul barely exists as a character, but some of the prosaic statements that issue from the Phantom ("I gave you my music . . . and now, how you've / Repaid me: denied me / And betrayed me") are disappointing. However, the score is his most fully developed and integrated theatre music yet.

Although not aiming for the emotional complexity of grand opera, the intensity of the characters' feelings is of operatic size and the characters express their emotions through almost continuous solos, duets, recitative, and ensembles. At the same time, entwined around the action are fragments of three imaginary operas, "Hannibal," "Il Muto," and the Phantom's "Don Juan Triumphant." Both musically and in the staging the opera bits are presented broadly, as if Lloyd Webber and Prince are signaling us that real opera is not what their show is. "Hannibal" by Chalumeau parodies *Aida*; "Il Muto" (in which Christine plays a trousers role) and "Don Juan Triumphant," in which the Phantom achieves a romantic victory by seducing Christine on stage, attaining through the illusions of art a goal he cannot reach in the real world, have Mozartian echoes; while Lloyd Webber's entire score has melodic reminiscences of Puccini. In their opera quotations both composer and director display their love of the form while also maintaining a wary distance from it.

For Prince the London success of *The Phantom of the Opera* reversed a series of Broadway failures. It also thwarted a possibility his supporters had feared — that with the British musical theatre developing, sometimes almost to the point of parody, the kind of concept musical Prince had helped to pioneer, and with Trevor Nunn adapting many of Prince's original staging ideas, British reviewers might criticize him for failing to keep up with his British imitators. The unofficial and unwarranted rivalry between these two leading musical-theatre directors, like the corollary of Sondheim against Lloyd Webber, revives a long-dormant contest between American and British approaches to the genre. Until the twenties British imports had a great influence on the evolving American musical theatre. But for the last fifty years, except for an occasional composer and performer like Noël Coward or a show like Lionel Bart's *Oliver!*, American musicals dominated the London stage — until Lloyd Webber and his collaborators, director Trevor Nunn, designer John Napier, choreographers Arlene Phillips and Gillian Lynne, formed a theatrical team which in many ways resembles the Prince–Sondheim *entente* of the seventies. Like the Prince–Sondheim shows, the Nunn–Lloyd Webber musicals have been notable for their combustible theatricality, their innovative designs, their explorations of new ways of using music to tell stories, establish atmosphere, and depict characters, and their ensemble rather than star-oriented focus.

When Nunn directs a "book" show like *Les Misérables*, there is a clear similarity to Prince's work in his fluid staging and strong characterization. However, "concept" shows like *Cats* and *Starlight Express* (and their inferior imitators like *Chess* and *Time*) are ultimately quite different from Prince's original concept musicals. Where Prince minimizes dance, and insists on subordinating musical performance to dramatic and narrative context, Nunn's work is highly choreographed and he permits his actors to "sell" numbers in a concert-hall style, with performance energy often directed more to the audience than to the action on the stage. Where the unusual venues in Prince musicals have symbolic implications, Nunn's environments exist primarily as showcases for twinkling lights, amplified wrap-around sound effects, turntables and catwalks that lift and lower and blink and spin like rockets. *Cats* and *Starlight Express* are entertaining, high-tech vaudeville that do not have the kind of thematic thrust and challenge that Prince demands. Indeed, when Lloyd Webber showed him the "book" for *Cats*, Prince asked if it was some kind of elaborate British political metaphor that, as an American, he could not understand. (But no, *Cats* is really – and only – about cats.)

Both the super-revue format of a show like *Cats* and the musical metaphors of shows like *Company* and *Follies* have demonstrated their validity, and have in fact helped to make the concept musical an inviting and open-ended form. Similarly, and happily, the genre is large enough to accommodate the gifts of diverse directors like Nunn and Prince and diverse composers like Lloyd Webber and Sondheim. If, nonetheless, Prince directing a Lloyd Webber show in London was something of a test, it was one he easily passed: his production radiated an invigorating theatrical imagination, and with his spectacularly well-crafted work Prince was back where he has always wanted to be, at the heart of the commercial theatre that he has served for forty years.

Theatrical chronology

1954   Co-produces *The Pajama Game*
1955   Co-produces *Damn Yankees*
1957   Co-produces *New Girl in Town*
      Co-produces *West Side Story*
1959   Co-produces *Fiorello!*
1960   Co-produces *Tenderloin*
1962   Directs *A Family Affair*
      Produces *A Funny Thing Happened On the Way to the Forum*
1963   Produces and directs *She Loves Me*
1964   Produces *Fiddler on the Roof*
1965   Directs *Baker Street*
      Produces *Flora, the Red Menace*
1966   Produces and directs *It's a Bird . . . It's a Plane . . . It's Superman*
      Produces and directs *Cabaret*
1968   Produces and directs *Zorbá*
1970   Produces and directs *Company*
1971   Produces and co-directs *Follies*
1973   Produces and directs *A Little Night Music*
      Directs *Candide* off Broadway
1974   Co-produces and directs *Candide* on Broadway
1976   Produces and directs *Pacific Overtures*
      Directs *Ashmedai* for the New York City Opera
1978   Directs *On the Twentieth Century*
      Directs *Evita* in London
      Directs *Girl of the Golden West* for the Chicago Lyric Opera
1979   Directs *Sweeney Todd*
      Directs *Evita* on Broadway
1980   Directs *Silverlake* for the New York City Opera
1981   Co-produces and directs *Merrily We Roll Along*
      Directs *Willie Stark* for the Houston Grand Opera
1982   Co-produces and directs *A Doll's Life*
      Directs *Madame Butterfly* for the Chicago Lyric Opera
      Directs *Candide* for the New York City Opera
1983   Directs *Turandot* for the Vienna State Opera
1984   Directs *Sweeney Todd* for the New York City Opera

1985 Co-produces and directs *Grind*
1986 Directs *Phantom of the Opera* in London
      Directs *Roza* for the Baltimore Center Stage
1987 Directs a revival of *Cabaret* for a national tour; opens on Broadway in
      October
      Directs *Roza* for the Mark Taper Forum, Los Angeles; production
      opens on Broadway in October
1988 Directs *Phantom of the Opera* on Broadway

In progress: *Don Giovanni* for the New York City Opera (1989); a production
of *Faust* for the Metropolitan Opera (1990); a musical of *Kiss of the Spider
Woman*.

Notes

1 Overture

1. Unless specifically attributed, all quoted material throughout my text is drawn from personal interviews which I conducted between March 1986 and October 1987.
2. Stephen Sondheim notes that two years earlier *Allegro* also had no breaks between scenes. "I was an apprentice on that show and I remember that at Oscar Hammerstein's suggestion Jo Mielziner devised a serpentine curtain which allowed for continuous action; Oscar then suggested the curtain to Josh Logan for *South Pacific*."
3. Significantly, most of the good film musicals have been based on original material: most of the Astaire–Rogers series, the Busby Berkeley production numbers designed for the camera, the work of directors like Rouben Mamoulian, Vincente Minnelli, Gene Kelly, and Stanley Donen with an intuitive grasp of film form. In contrast, Hollywood's track record adapting Broadway musicals has been dismal. Throughout the thirties and forties it was standard practice for studios to dismantle the Broadway properties they had paid a lot of money for; both librettos and scores were treated cavalierly. (For a complete, dispiriting record of how Hollywood regularly mangled the Broadway scores of Rodgers and Hart, Cole Porter, and the Gershwins by interpolating the hackwork of composers and lyricists employed by the studios, see Roy Hemming, *The Melody Lingers On* [New York, 1986].) To me, the most senseless of all Hollywood decimations was the job that was done on *On the Town* (1949) which retains only three songs and some dance music from Leonard Bernstein's exhilarating score; Roger Edens's interpolations make no attempt to simulate Bernstein's driving percussive rhythms or Comden and Green's smart lyrics. A second, lesser, and opposite fault in translating Broadway hits to film has been to treat the original as sacred text, an embalming approach that kills the spontaneity and immediacy on which all musicals depend. The adaptation that is both faithful to its source as well as lively – *The Pajama Game* and *West Side Story* are two examples – is rare.

   For performers as well as properties, success on Broadway has seldom translated into success in films. For the examples of Fred Astaire or Barbra Streisand who registered in both mediums there are the more plentiful cases of Marilyn Miller, Fanny Brice, Ethel Merman, Mary Martin or Gwen Verdon who did not project on the screen the kind of magnetism that had guaranteed their success on stage. (In Merman's case, the close-up camera betrayed absolutely dead eyes.) The failures point up the difference in performance demands between the two media – the naturalism of film acting against the bravura overstatement required of the musical-theatre star.
4. Fred Astaire, *Steps in Time* (New York, 1959), p. 127.
5. Sondheim made these comments in an interview conducted at Lincoln Center on June 2, 1975, and placed on file in the videotape collection of the Library of Performing Arts. Further quotations from this interview will be identified below as from "the Lincoln Center interview."

2 The Abbott touch

1. Abbott made his comment at a symposium, "Classic Broadway," held in honor of his one-hundredth birthday, in Cleveland, Ohio, May 28–30, 1987, and sponsored by the Great Lakes Theatre Festival (Gerald Freedman, Artistic Director).

2. At the "Classic Broadway" symposium.
3. Ibid.
4. After working with the Abbott–Prince–Griffith team on *The Pajama Game*, novelist Richard Bissell wrote a satire of the Broadway "game" called *Say, Darling* (Boston, 1957) in which Prince appears, thinly disguised, as Sam Snow, anxious young producer. George Abbott is Richard Hackett, a showman with a golden touch; the "property" is *The Girl from Indiana*, a musical comedy about a rural lass who falls for a city-slicker. Bissell casts himself as a country boy, a character out of George Ade or Ring Lardner, who writes in a homespun style and who is open-mouthed at the hectic pace and the compulsions of the Broadway crowd who improbably turn his play into a New York smash. As in most satire, Bissell treats his subject with a mixture of affection and animosity; his stand-in is both impressed by and disapproving of the canny commercial instincts of the theatrical pack who write and rewrite his show. Tall and good-looking, a celebrated womanizer who speaks in terse sentences and who maintains his confidence that the show can be made to work, Richard Hackett is clearly the boss; his colleagues treat him like a deity – he's a theatrical alchemist who converts dross into Broadway gold. Sam Snow is an unfriendly picture of the young Hal Prince; quite unlike the real Hal Prince, Sam Snow is always on the town, a hard-drinking, woman-chasing habitué of "in" spots. More true to life is Snow's collegiate eagerness, his volubility, his jittery nerves, his desire for success, his interest in "literate" scripts and literary ideas.
5. *Time*, May 23, 1954.
6. George Abbott and Richard Bissell, *The Pajama Game* (London, 1954), p. 5.
7. Prince says "it's worth knowing that Gwen Verdon called me and asked to be considered for the title role. George disapproved on the grounds that she would want to dance in the show. When I repeated that to her, she agreed to keep it an acting and singing role. When the show didn't live up to our expectations in Boston in its pre-Broadway run, she 'fudged.' In fact, she took sick until we agreed to let Bobby Fosse choreograph a major whorehouse ballet for her. In the meantime the show lost momentum. I remember it took three understudies to cover her one role."
8. Smith, "Classic Broadway" symposium.

3 On the job

1. Although Prince expected some negative critical response, he was surprised by the intensity of some of the notices. "I had felt all along that the show was wrong for Broadway, but still I am a big boy and I allowed *Roza* to come in. I felt the creators deserved to have their shot, and I am comfortable and relieved that we did it here, despite the reaction. I got some wonderful responses from my peers – I especially appreciated a letter from George Abbott which concluded, 'When I was young and in the midst of some youthful tribulation my mother said "ten years from now it won't make any difference." I pass it on to you. As always, George.'"
2. Sondheim says that his problems with Gingold grew out of the fact that "she rewrote the lyric for 'Liaisons' and thought that was swell."

4 Musical metaphors

1. Although *Cabaret* treats Isherwood's material with respect, and gives it much greater impact than van Druten's play, Prince heard that the author "was not pleased. I'm very cautious and solicitous about writers, and when we started I wrote to Isherwood telling him that we would honor his perspective although we would not adapt directly. 'This is a musical,' I wrote to him, 'and that means a different structure and form than a play.' I heard he resented what we had done, but I don't know if he ever actually saw our work. I do

know that he earned more money from *Cabaret* than from anything else. Years after *Cabaret* opened, Isherwood and I both happened to be at the Polo Lounge in the Beverly Hills Hotel; Isherwood, who was there with his friend Don Bachardy, left the restaurant because I was there, but I'm tempted to think it was at Bachardy's initiation."

2. After a seven-month national tour, *Cabaret* opened on Broadway on October 22, 1987, to generally positive notices and good if not capacity business. "A few days after the reviews came out I told the cast that they were in a hit, despite the bad notice we got from Frank Rich in the *Times*; the only reason we were able to survive that review was because the show was a revival of a show that audiences were familiar with and had good feelings about: if it had been a new musical, Rich's review would have closed us on Saturday night," Prince says.

3. Joseph Stein and Fred Ebb, *Zorbá* (New York, 1969), p. 3.

5 A little Sondheim music (I)

1. Sondheim, the Lincoln Center interview.
2. "I'm an eclectic, and there's no point in trying to conceal this," Sondheim says, "and I openly acknowledge my indebtedness to composers like Ravel, Rachmaninoff, Gershwin."
3. Prince, "Classic Broadway" symposium.

6 A little Sondheim music (II)

1. Prince, quoted in an interview with Richard Townsend, *Daily News*, June 20, 1976.
2. Sondheim, quoted in Craig Zadan, *Sondheim & Co.* (New York, 1974), p. 140.
3. April 29, 1970.
4. Alan Bunce, *The Christian Science Monitor*, May 11, 1970.
5. Quoted in Zadan, p. 131.
6. In *The New York Times*, May 3, 1970.
7. In *The Village Voice*, May 7, 1970.
8. Quoted in Zadan, p. 131.
9. *The Village Voice*, May 7, 1970.
10. Quoted in Zadan, p. 174.
11. Prince, the Lincoln Center interview.
12. Set in 1971, the thirtieth reunion commemorates the last performance of "Weismann's" [Ziegfeld's] Follies, a historical inaccuracy since the Follies was no longer in existence in 1941: Ziegfeld produced his last extravaganza in 1933.
13. Surprisingly, since the song seems an ideal fit for a neurotic like Sally, "Losing My Mind" was intended originally for both Phyllis and Sally. Collins remembers that "Hal came in the day before we went to Boston to say, 'I want Dorothy Collins's low, bluesy sound for "Losing My Mind," and I want no discussion,'" though according to Sondheim the suggestion came from Alexis Smith.
14. James Goldman and Stephen Sondheim, *Follies* (New York, 1971), p. 108.
15. *Follies* ran for over a year but nonetheless was a financial failure. Over the years it has developed a reputation as a daring musical whose high cost and uncertain box-office appeal would prohibit revival, but *Follies* has had two resurrections, both jubilantly received: an all-star concert at Lincoln Center in September 1985 and the London premiere in July 1987. "The concert was thrilling, as well as a vindication: look at the reviews of the original! – but it wasn't the show, it was like doing soliloquies from *Hamlet*," Sondheim

says. For the London production Sondheim wrote four new songs to replace four songs from the original. "James Goldman wanted to redo it, the original embarrassed him. He has made it more naturalistic, the tone is lighter and less arch, less pretentious – exactly the qualities Hal and I loved. But it's a huge hit."

7 A little Sondheim music (III)

1. Prince, *Contradictions* (New York, 1974), p. 183.
2. Prince disputes the popular criticism that many of his shows are both non-plot and non-linear. "*Cats* has no plot, but *Company* and *Follies* and *Pacific Overtures* have stories and they are primarily linear as well, though their structure is unusual, and I think that's what throws people off."
3. Sondheim, the Lincoln Center interview.
4. Jack Kroll, *Newsweek*, January 26, 1976.
5. Quoted in an interview with Clive Hirschhorn, *The New York Times*, January 4, 1976.
6. Quoted in *Time*, January 26, 1976.
7. Prince says he chose Mako as the narrator because of his harsh voice. "He snapped out the lines in a guttural declamatory style that was true to the tradition of the Kabuki storyteller: it is not a pretty sound to our ears."
8. T. E. Kalem, *Time*, January 26, 1976.
9. In *The New York Post*, January 17, 1976.
10. Ibid.
11. Quoted by Mel Gussow, *The New York Times*, February 1, 1979.
12. Jack Kroll, *Newsweek*, March 12, 1979.
13. Quoted by Mel Gussow, *The New York Times*, February 1, 1979.
14. George Abbott, who knows good direction when he sees it, wrote Prince (June 18, 1979) that his direction of *Sweeney Todd* was "most inventive and indeed it was hard to see how it could have been effective without all of those ingenious details. It is the kind of show that stays with you. I mean the picture of the royster-doister crowd eating the meat or the sudden vision of the lunatic asylum. I liked Sondheim's music the best of anything he's ever done. Not only was it 'high brow' but it seemed to my ear it was more melodious than usual – some very lovely melodies."
15. Betsy Joslyn, a member of the ensemble in *Sweeney Todd*, says that "Hal chose different physical types for the chorus. He told each of us to find a life for our character. Hal and Larry Fuller staged us viewing the action, commenting and watching. We were treated like a separate character, and kept apart from the book rehearsals. Paul Gemignani, who really directed the chorus, approaches music from an acting standpoint. He's able to give you the one word which will make the drama in the song clear to you. Sondheim wants all the notes in a song to be there, and Paul is able to help everybody to do that through the drama of what's going on in the song."
16. Prince in a letter to George Abbott, June 22, 1980.

8 A few follies

1. With James Lapine directing and actors in their thirties playing the roles, a revised *Merrily We Roll Along* was staged in La Jolla, California in 1984. "It was five thousand times better than on Broadway," Sondheim says.
2. Quoted by Judy Klemesrud, *The New York Times*, November 15, 1981.
3. John Corry, *The New York Times*, September 3, 1981.
4. T. E. Kalem, *Time*, May 9, 1985.
5. Interview with Steven Watson, *Newsday*, April 7, 1985.

9 Nights at the opera

1. June 9, 1982.
2. In a letter to June Havoc, January 20, 1983.
3. Quoted by Glenna Syse, *The Chicago Sun–Times*, September 17, 1978.
4. Prince developed *Willie Stark* with composer Carlisle Floyd exactly as if it were a new musical intended for Broadway, and indeed before the disappointing reviews and a score Prince felt was too "difficult" for Broadway he had hoped that the piece would have been the first opera since *Porgy and Bess* to open on a commercial basis. 'I worked with the composer for two years on *Willie Stark*; I cast it as I would a musical, unprecedented in opera. We rehearsed it for six weeks in Houston, during which time I would say to the composer, "This section goes on too long.' He said he wanted to keep it, and I said I would stage it but it would go out if it didn't work. Donal Henahan savaged us at the first public performance: ['*Willie Stark* has retold Mr. Warren's many-leveled tale in a one-dimensional Broadway musical style . . . a remarkably thin score, a parody of Britten and Menotti . . . strident, prosaic recitative . . . only half a dozen moments when the actors leave off declaiming and attempt anything even vaguely lyrical' (*The New York Times*, April 27, 1981).] We cut it, then went to Washington, where it improved. I continued to work on it, and when we filmed it for P.B.S. I cut forty-five minutes. The show was now the way I wanted it. The *Times* now gave it a rave, the result of our having worked on it for five weeks. When *Madame Butterfly* premiered at La Scala, it was savaged, and Puccini pulled it."
5. March 24, 1982.
6. In *The Record*, March 21, 1980. Although *Silverlake* was impure Weill – "the German specialists were up in arms," Hugh Wheeler reported – Prince's adaptation pleased Weill's widow, Lotte Lenya, who wrote: "I cannot thank you enough to have brought this work so imaginatively to life." (Letter to Prince, November 4, 1980.)
7. Frank Rich, *The New York Times*, April 19, 1976.
8. David Hamilton, *The Nation*, May 2, 1976.
9. In *The New York Herald Tribune*, December 3, 1956.
10. Sondheim, the Lincoln Center interview.
11. Ibid.
12. Quoted in *People*, July 22, 1974.
13. Albert Bermel, *The New Leader*, June 10, 1974.
14. Quoted by Bill Zakariasen, *The New York Daily News*, October 12, 1982.

10 The British connection

1. In an interview with Michael Owen, *The New York Times*, September 23, 1979.
2. Ibid.
3. Quoted by Mel Gussow, *The New York Times*, January 20, 1980.
4. Julius Novick, *The Village Voice*, October 18, 1979; Clive Barnes, *The New York Post*, October 8, 1979.
5. Quoted by Mel Gussow, *The New York Times*, January 20, 1980.
6. Jack Kroll, in *Newsweek*, October 8, 1979.
7. Walter Kerr, *The New York Times*, January 26, 1979. Prince objects to the frequent criticism the show received for placing Che and Evita, who never met, within the same frame: "Che was exiled from Argentina during the Perón regime, but his political connection to Perónism couldn't have been stronger. That we were attacked for linking Che and Evita together was typical critical snobbery toward musicals: nobody chastised Tom Stoppard in *Travesties* for putting together historical and literary figures who had never actually met."

Select bibliography

Abbott, George. *"Mister Abbott."* New York, 1963
  New Girl in Town. New York, 1958
Abbott, George, Douglass Wallop and Jerry Ross. *Damn Yankees.* New York, 1956
Abbott, George, Richard Bissell and Jerry Ross. *The Pajama Game.* London, 1954
Astaire, Fred. *Steps in Time.* New York, 1959
Aylesworth, Thomas G. *Broadway to Hollywood. Musicals from Stage to Screen.* New York, 1985
Bissell, Richard. *Say, Darling.* Boston, 1957
Bond, C. G. *Sweeney Todd. The Demon Barber of Fleet Street.* London, 1984
Bordman, Gerald. *American Musical Comedy. From Adonis to Dreamgirls.* New York, 1982
  American Musical Revue. From The Passing Show to Sugar Babies. New York, 1985
  Jerome Kern. His Life and Music. New York, 1980
Burton, Brian J. *Sweeney Todd the Barber.* London, 1984
Comden, Betty, and Adolph Green. *A Doll's Life.* New York, 1983
Davis, Sheila. *The Craft of Lyric Writing.* Cincinnati, 1985
Dietz, Howard. *Dancing in the Dark.* New York, 1974
Engel, Lehman. *The American Musical Theatre.* New York, 1975
  The Making of a Musical. Creating Songs for the Stage. New York, 1986
  Their Words Are Music. The Great Theatre Lyricists and Their Lyrics. New York, 1975
  Words with Music. The Broadway Musical Libretto. New York, 1981
Ewen, David. *Composers for the American Musical Theatre.* New York, 1968
Feuer, Jane. *The Hollywood Musical.* Bloomington, 1982
Fordin, Hugh. *Getting to Know Him. A Biography of Oscar Hammerstein II.* New York, 1977
Gershwin, Ira. *Lyrics on Several Occasions.* New York, 1973
Green, Stanley. *The World of Musical Comedy.* Fourth edition. New York, 1984
Guernsey, Otis L., Jr., editor. *Broadway Song and Story.* New York, 1985
Hammerstein, Oscar, II. *Lyrics.* Milwaukee, 1985
Hart, Dorothy, and Robert Kimball, editors. *The Complete Lyrics of Lorenz Hart.* New York, 1986
Hart, Moss and Ira Gershwin. *Lady in the Dark.* New York, 1941
Hellman, Lillian. *Candide.* New York, 1970
Hemming, Roy. *The Melody Lingers On. The Great Songwriters and Their Movie Musicals.* New York, 1986
Hibbert, Christopher. *Gilbert and Sullivan and Their Victorian World.* New York, 1976
Hunt, Gordon. *How to Audition.* New York, 1977
Isherwood, Christopher. *Berlin Stories.* New York, 1954
Jarman, Douglas. *Kurt Weill. An Illustrated Biography.* Bloomington, 1982
Kazantzakis, Nikos. *Zorbá the Greek.* New York, 1952
Kerman, Joseph. *Opera as Drama.* New York, 1956
Kimball, Robert, editor. *The Complete Lyrics of Cole Porter.* New York, 1983
Kimball, Robert, and Alfred Simon. *The Gershwins.* New York, 1973
Kislan, Richard. *Hoofing on Broadway.* New York, 1987
Kowalke, Kim H. *Kurt Weill in Europe.* Ann Arbor, 1979
Kreuger, Miles. *Show Boat. The Story of a Classic American Musical.* New York, 1974
Laurents, Arthur, and Stephen Sondheim. *Anyone Can Whistle.* New York, 1976

Lerner, Alan Jay. *The Musical Theatre. A Celebration*. New York, 1986
Leroux, Gaston. *The Phantom of the Opera*. London, 1985
Lindenberger, Herbert. *Opera. The Extravagant Art*. Ithaca, 1984
Logan, Joshua. *Josh*. New York, 1976
Mast, Gerald. *Can't Help Singin'. The American Musical on Stage and Screen*. Woodstock, 1987
Masteroff, Joe, and Sheldon Harnick. *She Loves Me*. New York, 1963
McCabe, John. *George M. Cohan. The Man Who Owned Broadway*. New York, 1973
McKnight, Gerald. *Andrew Lloyd Webber*. New York, 1984
Merman, Ethel, with George Eells. *Merman*. New York, 1978
Mordden, Ethan. *Broadway Babies. The People Who Made the American Musical*. New York, 1983
   The Splendid Art of Opera. New York, 1980
Morley, Sheridan. *Spread a Little Happiness. The First Hundred Years of the British Musical*. New York, 1987
Nolan, Frederick. *The Sound of Their Music. The Story of Rodgers and Hammerstein*. New York, 1978
O'Hara, John and Lorenz Hart. *Pal Joey*. New York, 1983
Orrey, Leslie. *A Concise History of Opera*. New York, 1972
Osborne, Charles. *The Complete Operas of Puccini*. New York, 1982
Peyser, Joan. *Bernstein. A Biography*. New York, 1987
Prince, Harold. *Contradictions*. New York, 1974
Rice, Tim. *Evita. The Legend of Eva Perón (1919–1952)*. New York, 1979
Richards, Stanley, editor. *Ten Great Musicals of the American Theatre*. (Includes *Of Thee I Sing*; *Porgy and Bess*; *One Touch of Venus*; *West Side Story*; *Gypsy*; *Fiddler On the Roof*; and *Company*.) Radnor, Pennsylvania, 1973
   Great Musicals of the American Theatre, volume 2. (Includes *A Little Night Music*; *Cabaret*; *Fiorello!*; *Lady in the Dark*; *Lost in the Stars*; and *Wonderful Town*.) Radnor, 1976
Rodgers, Richard. *Musical Stages*. New York, 1975
Rodgers, Richard, and Oscar Hammerstein II. *Six Plays*. (Includes *Oklahoma!*; *Carousel*; *Allegro*; *The King and I*; *South Pacific*, and *Flower Drum Song*.) New York, 1959
Rosser, Austin. *Sweeney Todd. The Demon Barber of Fleet Street*. London, 1971
Sanders, Ronald. *The Days Grow Short. The Life and Music of Kurt Weill*. New York, 1980
Schwartz, Charles. *Cole Porter*. New York, 1977
   Gershwin. His Life and Music. Indianapolis, 1973
Shevelove, Burt, and Stephen Sondheim. *The Frogs*. New York, 1975
Shevelove, Burt, Larry Gelbart, and Stephen Sondheim. *A Funny Thing Happened On the Way to the Forum*. New York, 1975
Silver, Fred. *Auditioning for the Musical Theatre*. New York, 1985
Smith, Cecil. *Musical Comedy in America*. New York, 1950; revised, 1981, with additions by Glenn Litton
Stein, Joseph, and Fred Ebb. *Zorbá*. New York, 1969
Traubner, Richard. *Operetta. A Theatrical History*. New York, 1983
Waters, Edward N. *Victor Herbert. A Life in Music*. New York, 1978
Weidman, Jerome, and George Abbott. *Fiorello!* New York, 1960
Weidman, John, Hugh Wheeler, and Stephen Sondheim. *Pacific Overtures*. New York, 1977
Wheeler, Hugh, and Stephen Sondheim. *Sweeney Todd. The Demon Barber of Fleet Street*. New York, 1979
Wheeler, Hugh, and Richard Wilbur, John LaTouche, and Stephen Sondheim. *Candide*. New York, 1976
Wilder, Alec. *American Popular Song. The Great Innovators 1900–1950*. New York, 1972
Wilk, Max. *They're Playing Our Song*. New York, 1986
Wodehouse, P. G., and Guy Bolton, *Bring On the Girls!* New York, 1984
Zadan, Craig. *Sondheim & Co*. New York, 1974; revised, 1986

Index

Abbott, George, 2, 22–27; and *Company*, 87; directing, 24–25; lighting, 91; *On the Town*, 149; *On Your Toes*, 8, 19; and Prince, 3–4, 22, 26–27, 38–39; Prince's productions for, 28–34; and Robbins, 35–37; and *Sweeney Todd*, 179n. (14); his "touch," 22–24; and *West Side Story*, 77

Adler, Richard, 30–32

Allegro, 20–21

Allen, Woody, 86

Anderson, John Murray, 1

Anderson, Maxwell, 14

Anouilh, Jean, 106

Anyone Can Whistle, 75, 79, 82–84

Anything Goes, 8–9

Aronson, Boris, 40, 59, 91, 101–102, 108, 111, 114, 116

Ashmedai, 3, 141–142, 145, 147–148

Astaire, Adele, 2, 7

Astaire, Fred, 2, 7

Baker, George Pierce, 22–23

Baker, Mark, 151–153

Baker Street, 3

Balanchine, George, 2, 19

Baxley, Barbara, 56–58

Bécaud, Gilbert, 50–52

Belasco, David, 4, 24, 25, 142

Bennett, Michael, 2, 90–91, 101, 104–105

Berenson, Marisa, 60

Bergman, Ingmar, 106

Bernardi, Herschel, 70

Bernstein, Leonard, 14, 15, 74, 76–77, 147–150, 154

Billington, Ken, 51, 121, 139, 145

Birch, Patricia, 51, 108, 115, 118, 153

Bissell, Richard, 28, 177n. (4)

Björnson, Maria, 167

Black Crook, The, 9

Bolton, Guy, 10

Bond, Christopher, 74, 118, 124–125, 127

Brando, Marlon, 4

Braudy, Susan, 58

Brecht, Bertolt, 14–17

Brennan, Maureen, 55, 57, 151–153

Brightman, Sarah, 170–171

Broadway, 26–27

Broadway, 4, 4–6

Brown, Georgia, 51

Burns, David, 81

Cabaret, 1, 3, 4, 26, 40–49, 59–68, 178n.

Cacoyannis, Michael, 69

Candide, 3, 4, 147–156

Cantor, Eddie, 7

Cariou, Len, 56, 107, 121, 124, 126, 128

Carousel, 19–20

Carradine, John, 81

Cats, 157, 173

Champion, Gower, 2

Chaney, Lon, 169

Chapman, David, 40

Chicago Lyric Opera, 3, 142

Chryst, Gary, 146

Church, Sandra, 79

Clooney, Rosemary, 76

Close, Glenn, 56

Coca, Imogene, 39

Cohan, George M., 9

Coleman, Cy, 38

Collins, Dorothy, 55–58, 94–95, 98–99, 101, 103–104

Comden, Betty, 38–39, 136, 149

Company, xii, 3, 71, 72, 85–92

Convy, Bert, 66

Crawford, Michael, 169–170

Crouse, Timothy, 9

Damn Yankees, 3, 28–29, 32

Daniele, Graciela, 97

de Carlo, Yvonne, 103–104

de Mille, Agnes, 2, 18, 19

Desert Song, The, 6

directors of musicals, 1–2, 25

Do I Hear a Waltz?, 74, 76

Dolan, Judith, 155

Doll's Life, A, 3, 131, 135–137

d'Orsay, Fifi, 103

Dunham, Clarke, 139, 155
Dunning, Philip, 22

Ebb, Fred, 59–60, 69–70
Edelman, Gregg, 43, 50
Edwardes, George, 8
Elmore, Steve, 92
English National Opera, 147
Essex, David, 163
Etting, Ruth, 7
Evita, 3, 4, 39, 157–167, 181n.

Family Affair, A, 3
Fellini, Federico, 95
Ferber, Edna, 10
Fiddler On the Roof, 3, 34–36
Field, Ron, 67, 133
film, musicals on, 5, 176n. (3)
Fiorello!, 3, 29–30, 32
Firth, Tazeena, 137, 166
Fitzhugh, Ellen, 138
Flora, the Red Menace, 29–31
Floyd, Carlisle, 145
Follies, xii, 3, 4, 72, 85, 93–105, 178n. (15)
Fosse, Bob, 2, 32, 66, 68
Fowler, Beth, 107
Fox, Carol, 141
Friml, Rudolf, 6
Fuller, Larry: Evita, 163, 165, 167; Merrily We
    Roll Along, 132–133; On the Twentieth
    Century, 39; on Prince, 57–8; Silverlake, 142,
    145; Sweeney Todd, 120, 123, 125, 179n. (15)
Funny Thing Happened On the Way to the Forum,
    A, 3, 29, 37, 74–75, 79–83
Furth, George, 72 86, 89, 132

Garland, Judy, 30
Gary, Romain, 50–51
Gaxton, William, 12
Gelbart, Larry, 79
Gemignani, Paul, 112, 179n. (15)
Gershwin, George, 2, 11–14
Gershwin, Ira, 2, 11–13, 14, 17
Gilbert, W.S., 6
Gilford, Jack, 81
Gingold, Hermione, 56, 107
Girl of the Golden West, 3, 141–144
Glass, Joanna, 131
Goldman, James, 72, 93, 95
Gottfried, Martin, 113, 116
Green, Adolph, 38–39, 136, 149

Green, Paul, 14
Grey, Joel, 45, 48, 60, 62–4, 66, 145–146
Griffin, Victor, 97
Griffith, Robert, 3, 28–29
Grind, 3, 131, 136–140
Grossman, Larry, 136, 139
Gunton, Bob, 160, 163–164
Gussow, Mel, 58
Guthrie, Tyrone, 147–149
Gypsy, 75, 76, 78–79

H.M.S. Pinafore, 6
Hammerstein, Oscar, 10, 18, 19–21, 74
Happy End, 14–15
Hart, Charles, 169
Hart, Lorenz, 18–19, 74, 80, 131–132
Hart, Moss, 14, 17
Havoc, June, 25, 56–58
Haworth, Jill, 68
Hecht, Ben, 38
Hellmann, Lillian, 147–149
Hepburn, Katharine, 141
Herbert, Victor, 6
Herrmann, Bernard, 123
Holliday, Billie, 148
Houston Grand Opera, 3, 142
Howland, Beth, 92
Hughes, Langston, 14

Isherwood, Christopher, 59, 65–66
It's a Bird . . It's a Plane . . It's Superman, 3, 36

Jennings, Ken, 126
Jesus Christ Superstar, 157–159
Johnny Johnson, 14, 17
Joseph and the Amazing Technicolour Dreamcoat,
    157–159
Joslyn, Betsy, 55, 58, 136, 179n. (15)

Kahn, Madeline, 55
Kaiser, Georg, 144
Kalfin, Robert, 149
Kander, John, 59–60, 69–70
Kanin, Fay, 138
Karnilova, Maria, 70
Kaufman, George, S., 4, 11–13, 23, 26, 131–132
Kazan, Elia, 4, 56
Kazantzakis, Nikos, 69–70
Kelly, George, 25
Kern, Jerome, 2, 10–11
Kerr, Walter, 88, 149

Klein, Sally, 134
Klotz, Florence, 139
Klugman, Jack, 79
Knickerbocker Holiday, 14, 17
Kopit, Arthur, 131

Lady, Be Good!, 7
Lady in the Dark, 14, 17
Lahr, John, 88, 90
Lang, Barbara, 107
Lansbury, Angela, 51, 82, 121, 124–125
Lapine, James, 135
Laurents, Arthur, 75, 77, 79, 83
Lawrence, Gertrude, 2
Leave it to Jane, 10
Lee, Eugene, 57, 120–121, 124, 143, 145, 152
Lee, Franne, 57, 121, 142–143, 145–146, 152
Lehár, Franz, 6
Leibnitz, G.W. von, 148
Lenya, Lotte, 59–60, 67
Lerner, Alan Jay, 14
Leroux, Gaston, 169
Let 'Em Eat Cake, 13
librettos, musicals, 8–9
Little Johnny Jones, 9
Little Night Music, A, 3, 72–73, 106–109
Lloyd Webber, Andrew, 157–173
Loesser, Frank, 23
Logan, Joshua, 2
Lost in the Stars, 17–18
Louise, Merle, 126
Love Life, 14, 17–18
LuPone, Patti, 56, 158, 160–164
Lutgenhorst, Manuel, 145
Lyng, Nora Mae, 49
Lynne, Gillian, 61, 172

MacArthur, Charles, 38
McCarty, Mary, 103–104
McMartin, John, 94, 100, 102–103
Madame Butterfly, 3, 142–144
Mako, 114, 116, 119
Mamoulian, Rouben, 2
Martin, Hugh, 28
Martin, John J., 104
Martin, Mary, 18
Masteroff, Joe, 57–58, 59–61, 66–68
Merlin, Joanna, 35, 54–55, 57–58
Merman, Ethel, 78–79
Merrill, Bob, 33–34
Merrily We Roll Along, 3, 71, 72, 85, 131–135

Merry Widow, The, 6
Milholland, Bruce, 38
Miller, Marilyn, 2
Minnelli, Liza, 30–31, 67
Misita, Michael, 97
Mitchell, Julian, 1
Mitchell, Ruth, 26, 45, 48–49
Montgomery, David, 6
Moran, Lois, 12
More, Julian, 50–51, 54
Morrison, Ann, 57–58, 132, 134
Morrison, Hobe, 88
Mostel, Zero, 81
musical comedies, 7–9
musicals, 4–21; directors, 1–2, 25; on film, 5,
    176n. (3); history, 9–11; librettos, 8–9
Musser, Tharon, 102, 108

Napier, John, 172
Nash, Ogden, 18
Nassif, Robert, 26
Neher, Caspar, 16
Nelson, Gene, 103–104
New Girl in Town, 3, 28–29, 33–34
New Moon, The, 6
New York City Opera, 3, 141–142, 147
No, No, Nanette, 8
Nunn, Trevor, 172–173

O'Brien, Timothy, 137, 166
Of Thee I Sing, 11–13
O'Hara, John, 19
Oklahoma!, 19–20
Okun, Alexander, 51–52
On the Town, 148–150
On the Twentieth Century, 3, 38–39
On Your Toes, 8, 19
One Touch of Venus, 18
O'Neill, Eugene, 23, 33
operetta, 6–7

Pacific Overtures, xii, 3, 4, 109–119, 147
Pajama Game, The, 3, 28–29, 30–32
Papp, Joe, 140
Pastor, Tony, 7
Patinkin, Mandy, 163–164
Paton, Alan, 14
Perón, Eva, 159–160, 162
Phantom of the Opera, The, 3, 4, 157, 166–172
Phillips, Arlene, 172
Porgy and Bess, 13–14, 72

Porter, Cole, 7–8
Price, Lonny, 57, 132–134
producers of musicals, 28, 177n. (4)
Puccini, Giacomo, 142–144

Quinn, Anthony, 69

Ralston, Teri, 107
Rayson, Benjamin, 107
Red Mill, The, 6
Reed, Alyson, 43–44, 46–47, 49
Resnik, Regina, 43–47
Rice, Elmer, 14
Rice, Sarah, 122
Rice, Tim, 158–159, 162
Riskind, Morrie, 11–12
Ritter, Thelma, 34
Robbins, Jerome, 2, 15, 35–37, 43, 77, 149
Rodgers, Richard, 10, 18–21, 74, 76, 80
Rolph, Marti, 94
Romberg, Sigmund, 6
Rosato, Mary-Lou, 48
Ross, Jerry, 30–32
Roza, 3, 50–54
Rudel, Julius, 141

She Loves Me, 3, 34
Shevelove, Burt, 74, 79–80
Short, Hassard, 2
Show Boat, 10–11
Shutta, Ethel, 96, 103
Signoret, Simone, 50
Sills, Beverly, 141, 143, 147
Silverlake, 3, 142, 144–146
Smith, Alexis, 102–104
Smith, Oliver, 26, 35, 77, 150
Sondheim, Stephen, 71–78; Anyone Can Whistle,
    75, 82–84; on Brecht and Weill, 15, 17–18;
    Company, 85–92; on directing, 25, 27; Do I
    Hear a Waltz?, 74, 76; Follies, 93–105; A
    Funny Thing Happened on the Way to the
    Forum, 79–83; Gypsy, 74–75, 78–79;
    influences on, 72–75; A Little Night Music,
    106–109; Merrily We Roll Along, 131,
    133–135; on musicals, 10, 13–21 passim;
    Pacific Overtures, 109–119; on Porgy and Bess,
    13; on Prince xiii–xiv; productions with
    Prince, 3, 71–73, 79–83, 85–105, 106–130;
    on Robbins, 37; on Rodgers and
    Hammerstein, 20–1, 74, 176n. (2); songs and
    lyrics, 76–78; Sunday in the Park with George,

135; Sweeney Todd, 74, 118–130; West Side
    Story, 35, 74–78
Song and Dance, 157
South Pacific, 2, 20
Staller, David, 43–44
Starlight Express, 157, 173
Stewart, Michael, 8, 71–72
Stilgoe, Richard, 169
Stone, Fred, 6
Street Scene, 14, 17–18
Stritch, Elaine, 90
Student Prince, The, 6
Styne, Jule, 74, 76
Sullivan, Sir Arthur, 6
Sunday in the Park with George, 135
Sweeney Todd, 3, 4, 74, 76, 118–130, 147,
    xiii, 179nn. (14&15)

Tal, Josef, 141, 145
Taylor, Elizabeth, 107–109
Tenderloin, 29
Threepenny Opera, The, 14–16
Throckmorton, Cleon, 16
Tune, Tommy, 2
Tunick, Jonathan, 91
Turandot, 3, 142, 144
Turner, Jayne, 97

Ure, Mary, 55

van Druten, John, 59
Varrone, Gene, 107
vaudeville, 7
Verdon, Gwen, 33–34
Vereen, Ben, 55, 138–139
Vienna State Opera, 3, 142
Voltaire, 148–154

Walker, Bonnie, 48
Walker, Gerald, 58
Warner, Keith, 147
Warren, Robert Penn, 145
Webber, Andrew Lloyd, see Lloyd Webber,
    Andrew
Weidman, John, 9, 109, 111–112, 115
Weill, Kurt, 14–18, 144–145
Welles, Orson, 165–166
Werfel, Franz, 14
West Side Story, 3, 26, 29, 34–37, 76–78
Wheeler, Hugh, 57, 72–73, 118, 126, 144,
    149–150

Whoopee!, 7
Williams, John, 123
Willie Stark, 3, 142, 145, 180n. (4)
Winters, Shelley, 60
Wodehouse, P.G., 10
Wonderful Town, 148–149
Wynne, Peter, 145

Zeffirelli, Franco, 143
Ziegfeld, Florenz, 1, 4, 7, 11, 98
Zipprodt, Patricia, 40
Zorbá, 3, 69–70